THE

# CASE STUDY
# HANDBOOK

# THE
# CASE STUDY
# HANDBOOK

## How to Read, Discuss, and
## Write Persuasively About Cases

## William Ellet

Harvard Business School Press
*Boston, Massachusetts*

Library of Congress Cataloging-in-Publication Data
Ellet, William.
     The case study handbook: how to read, discuss, and write persuasively about cases / William Ellet.
        p.   cm.
     ISBN-13: 978-1-4221-0158-2 (hardcover: alk. paper)
     1. Management—Case studies—Study and teaching.  I. Title.
     HD30.4.E435 2007
     658—dc22

                                                              2006034445

The paper used in this publication meets the requirements of the American National Standard for Permanence of Paper for Publications and Documents in Libraries and Archives Z39.48-1992.

# CONTENTS

### PART I

## ANALYSIS

### PART II

## DISCUSSION

## PART III

# WRITING

## PART IV

# CASES FOR ANALYSIS AND WRITING

# INTRODUCTION

*The Case Study Handbook* has emerged from sixteen years of work with business school students. The impetus for it was a void in the guidance I could give them about case essays.

When I first worked with MBA students, I confined myself to conventional writing advice—coherent paragraphs; active voice; essays with a discernible beginning, middle, and end. The advice had an impact, but not as much as I hoped. Eventually, I realized that in case examinations, students often didn't know how to recognize the need for an argument or were unclear about how to write one. (This lack of knowledge isn't the fault of students; it's the fault of the writing instruction they have received.) I immediately placed argument at the forefront of my instruction. I experimented with thesis statements derived from an enthymeme. I tried Stephen Toulmin's syllogistic approach to the structure of an argument. In the end, I kept it simple: conclusion, reasons, and evidence.

Understanding when an argument is needed and how to construct one helped many of the writers. Nevertheless, I remained concerned about the trouble students had with case-based essays. Their writing was often characterized by fuzzy points of view, disjointed discussions of issues, and uneven use of evidence. It took me a long time to realize that these essays were unwittingly mirroring the cases the writers were supposed to be interpreting. Argument therapy was an incomplete solution to this problem. The students needed more, and I didn't have more to offer.

I knew that if there was a solution, it was in the cases themselves—but my jurisdiction was writing. Reluctantly, I sat in on case discussions and read many case exams. I read cases that students were writing about and compared them to the essays written about them. Some students intuitively knew how to respond to questions like these: What is the best decision? Why is this organization performing badly? I marveled at their clarity of purpose, despite the pressure of an exam, the challenge of a case, and the lack of information about the reader's expectations. I learned from the successful essays and those that fell short.

Gradually, the ideas in this book took shape, and I tried them out with MBA students to see if I could finally offer advice that spoke to all their needs.

The ideas weren't confined to writing. I found myself reverse-engineering a method that could be used for analyzing a case. I have been using the ideas detailed in this book for five years, and the results have been consistently positive in class discussion and case-based exams—not as judged by me but by the grades of MBA instructors who know nothing of the method and have no reason to know. I have been especially happy about the students who have been able to lift themselves out of academic trouble.

I make statements in this book that could be construed as a theory of cases. Readers, especially business academics, need to understand what this book is not. It has no theoretical ambitions. It is not a rhetoric or generative theory of cases or a taxonomy with exclusive categories. It does not break new ground on argumentation. It describes a pragmatic method grounded in observations about situations that frequently occur in cases and in students' responses to them. Strictly speaking, this book isn't about the case method because such situations also occur in the real world—not surprising, given that cases mirror the real world. The method doesn't account for every situation encountered in cases or every combination of situations. It simply takes advantage of the fact that many cases *do* involve certain well-defined situations.

Each of these situations has its own logic, and an awareness of it can help students read cases more efficiently, discuss them more effectively, and write about them more cogently. The links between analysis, discussion, and writing are a primary advantage of the method, However, it is *not* a substitute for the theories, frameworks, processes, and quantitative methods taught in business courses. In fact, it is intended to complement and facilitate their use. The method shouldn't detract or distract from them but accelerate recourse to them and focus their application.

The essays and essay excerpts in the book are based on the writing of MBA students. I have disguised the writing to protect the privacy of the authors. Because the original essays were examinations written under time pressure, I have also edited them so that they are better examples of the points made in the book. However, I restrained the editing to avoid the appearance of "ideal" examples. Only a single example of bad writing is used; it is a contrast to a good example on the same case. I think examples of bad writing tend to reinforce bad writing.

All of the cases in the book are from Harvard Business School. To avoid causing problems for instructors, the cases have been carefully researched to ensure that they are no longer being ordered for classroom use anywhere in the world. I use these inactive cases to demonstrate the method put forward in the book. I stress to the reader that my interpretations are no more definitive than anyone else's, and in those interpretations I include open questions and other ways to look at the case. In other words, I do everything I can to discourage the notion of a "right answer" to a case. Some short excerpts from cases that are still taught have been carefully disguised to prevent a student from gaining an unfair advantage—although it's hard to imagine that the brief quotations could provide any even if they weren't disguised.

*The Case Study Handbook* hasn't been written with the pretension of being indispensable. On their own, business students develop approaches to cases that work and smoothly adapt to writing case-based essays. Nonetheless, too many students don't arrive at a reliable approach to cases, and that hinders their learning. The same can be said about writing—too many students struggle with it in business school. With the long-term growth in MBA enrollments and the widespread use of cases, the worldwide pool of students who will encounter the case method continues to expand.

This book is intended for all case method students, current and prospective. My hope is that the benefits will extend even more widely. Everyone gains if learners are better prepared for classroom discussion and written arguments—the student, peers, professors, and future employers.

CHAPTER 1

# PERSUASION, ARGUMENT, AND THE CASE METHOD

Each year, entering business school students encounter an approach to teaching and learning new to many of them: the case method. By *case*, I mean the substantial studies from business schools or corporations, not the slender vignettes included in many business textbooks. For novices, the first encounter can be perplexing. A case appears to be a straightforward narrative, but when these students finish reading them, they wonder what point the case is trying to make. A case study of a restaurant chain ends with the president turning over in his mind basic questions about the business. He gives no answers and the case doesn't either. In another case study, a young MBA has accidentally learned of alleged office behavior that could have serious consequences for the individuals involved, including him. At the conclusion of the case, he has a literal and figurative headache—and nothing explicit is mentioned about what he should do.

In classroom discussions of cases like these, instructors use the Socratic method, in which students carry the discussion through answers to a stream of questions. Students can feel vulnerable, and the classroom atmosphere can be strained and edgy, particularly in the first months. Written case-based examinations pose another challenge. In class, the entire group, including the instructor, works collaboratively on a case. Depending on the size of the class, each student is likely to contribute only a small number of comments to the discussion. On exams, students are on their own. They not only have to analyze the case in response to one or more questions but also write an essay that satisfies and persuades an expert reader—all in a limited time.

In class and on exams, case method students are asked questions like these:

- Is the change effort described in the case worthwhile? If it is, why has it failed? How can it be successfully implemented?

- How attractive is the industry described in the case? Are some segments more attractive than others? Why? Identify, analyze, and evaluate the strategy of the company featured in the case.

- Thinking from the perspective of current European Union members, do you agree with their decision to enlarge the EU by ten new members? What are the pros and cons? What is the impact on the world economy?

## SKILLS FOR STUDYING CASES

From time to time, MBA students have told me they feel there is a secret to the case method that some people get and some don't. If you get it, you do well; if you don't, you scrape by as best you can, always fearful that you will be exposed.

The case method requires a lot from the student. At the same time, it isn't a secret society in which a few fortunate individuals get it and thus outperform their peers. Case method students need two distinct sets of skills. First, they need to be able to analyze a case, to give it meaning in relation to its key issues or questions that have been asked about it. The goal is to come to conclusions congruent with the reality of the case, taking into account its gaps and uncertainties. Second, students have to be able to communicate their thinking effectively.

This book provides a method of organizing and directing case study and guidance on how to communicate the results. The method should help you use the business concepts that are already part of your working knowledge or are taught in business courses—concepts such as:

- Expectancy Theory (Victor Vroom)

- 5 Cs analysis of marketing situations[1]

- 5 Ps Model of Leadership (Mildred Golden Pryor, J. Christopher White, and Leslie A. Toombs)

- Macroeconomics

- Value Chain (Michael Porter)

The combination of a method to organize thinking about a case and business concepts will help you come to conclusions and explain why you think they're valid. In education and in business, your conclusions have little meaning unless they're shared with others. The case method is about stating and comparing opinions and learning from the differences and similarities. In an academic program, communicating conclusions about a case occurs orally, in study groups and class discussions, or in formal presentations. It also occurs in writing, in class assignments, research projects, and examinations. Each type of communication has its own needs and requirements. In class, you have to meld your insights with the overall discussion.

The role of each individual is to advance the discussion and contribute to the collective understanding of the case. Individual or group presentations usually aim at persuading the audience. A case-based essay also aims at persuasion. This book is divided into three separate skills: case analysis (part I), discussion (part II), and writing about cases (part III).

## RECEIVING KNOWLEDGE VERSUS MAKING IT

Many entering business school students have been educated in a lecture system. A lecture is an efficient way for an expert to deliver content to many individuals at once. In combination with textbooks, which are lectures in print, this learning model can deliver volumes of content in a short time.

The lecture model is good at transferring information. Like any learning model, it has limitations. One of the most important is that it doesn't encourage listeners to think about the content and apply it. Lectures on organizational development or macroeconomics aren't truly meaningful until the learner can apply the content to issues to better understand organizations or countries. Concepts that are meant to be applied require practice opportunities. The lecture method generally doesn't afford students the chance for rigorous practice, and learners tend to be graded on recall of facts.

When students enter a case-based program, they understandably assume that regurgitation of case facts is a central task. They are surprised when their professors not only expect them to know the facts but to use them to support an opinion about an issue the case raises. It doesn't help that incoming business school students often aren't told what the case method asks of them. A sink-or-swim mentality seems common in professional education, at least in the United States. In the lecture method, learners *receive* knowledge from an expert. In the case method, learners *make* the knowledge with the assistance of an expert. This fundamental shift causes many new case method students to be confused and uncertain about how they should go about learning.

## WRITING AND PERSUASION

A graduate once summed up his feelings about writing instruction in an MBA program: "I didn't go to business school to learn how to write!"

Fair enough. But many business school students don't think they have strong writing skills and aren't sure how to write an argument. Graduates of undergraduate programs often have had little practice in writing after a required freshman composition course and very little meaningful feedback on what they do write. Individuals with degrees and backgrounds in science and technology may have done no significant writing since high school. Yet, quality MBA programs—classroom based and online—require students to write, and the dearth of prior instruction and practice can be a liability. It can also reduce graduates' career effectiveness. The title of a much discussed *New York Times* article captures the state of writing in the United States: "What Corporate America Cannot Build: A Sentence."[2]

The ability to think clearly and communicate convincingly has always been an important skill for managers and leaders. It is now arguably more important. Rapid globalization, the increase in geographically dispersed work groups, and the Internet put a new premium on text communication. The *New York Times* article just cited illustrates the daily chaos that badly written e-mails cause in companies. In the "knowledge economy," employees are expected to think and act on their own. These skilled and intelligent individuals expect management to explain and persuade, not issue orders. With employees distributed around the world, the most practical way of reaching them is writing. Well-written documents can be a hidden source of competitive advantage.

Persuasion is the art of convincing an audience, listeners or readers, to believe, think, or act as the speaker or writer wants them to. The art has a long history, going back more than two thousand years in the West. It is still as vital today as it was in its ancient forms. Argument and persuasion are necessary to resolve controversy—to assist people with very different views of the same thing to find common ground. That function has particular importance in business, with its emphasis on action. Differences of opinion need to be negotiated so that a company can take intelligent action.

Cases have multiple meanings and thus are always controversial. In a class of forty students, there are likely to be forty different views of a case. To persuade classmates and professors in a case method setting, writers must deal with two obstacles: the shared text (the case) and the critical outlook or attitude of the audience. The audience knows the text and the facts so writers can't afford to make factual mistakes. In addition, because the audience members are familiar with the case and will have their own opinions about it, writers must meet a high standard of proof.

On the other hand, the audience's knowledge of the case is an asset. It relieves writers of having to describe the case situation, define the terms used in it, and other tasks speakers and writers often have to perform when the audience isn't intimately familiar with the topic. Also, most professors are less interested in the position writers take on a case than in how well they can prove it.

There are many ways to persuade an audience—emotional appeals; tricks of logic; appeals to authority; or reasoning and evidence. In an academic or business setting, the best way to persuade is through argument. Academic work is founded on rational, logical thinking and discourse, and argument is essential to both. For business students, learning to analyze a situation accurately and persuade through rational argument has great importance. Managers and executives need to be able to think logically about the businesses they are trying to run, the people they are trying to lead, and the goals they are trying to achieve. Thinking chronically clouded by emotion, lapses in reason, or an unwillingness to look hard at the facts generally leads to trouble for both managers and their organizations.

Broadly speaking, an argument is a series of logically related statements. The fundamental relationship, the one that matters most, is between the statement of a conclusion and the evidence for it. You make a conclusion about a case—the president of the country is right to default on its foreign debt—and readers nod their heads and say, "Fine, but what can you say to prove it?"[3] For the audience to take your conclusion seriously, you need to show them why they should.

Here's an illustration of the conclusion-evidence relationship:

*What? (conclusion)*  *[because]*  *Why? (evidence)*
The president is right to default on the country's foreign debt.  Full payment of the debt will destabilize the country.

The statement "Full payment of the debt will destabilize the country" won't persuade anyone on its own. The audience needs to see the evidence proving that full payment will destabilize the nation.

*What? (conclusion)*  *[because]*  *Why? (reason)*
The president is right to default on the country's foreign debt.  Full payment of the debt will destabilize the country.

*Evidence*
1. Debt payments will take money out of the country that is badly needed to support the economy and meet social needs such as education and healthcare.
   Evidence includes historical narrative showing that past economic downturns have impoverished the population and created political conflict that worsened the economic situation.
2. National finances are depleted.
   Evidence includes data and calculations showing that poor management of the economy has resulted in deficit spending and spotty tax collection.
3. The national economy is just beginning to recover.
   Evidence includes data and calculations showing that GDP has increased by 3 percent and 5 percent

the last two years, respectively; inflation has declined 5 percent in a year; but unemployment has risen sharply.

4. The standard of living and other indicators of social well-being are improving, but a downturn in the economy will reverse the gains.

   Evidence includes data showing that per capita income has risen slightly (2 percent). Major crime is down 6 percent and the decline coincides with improved economy.

5. A political crisis has just been resolved, but if the economy declines, there is potential for more.

   Evidence includes recent political history of political turmoil that has prevented the government from taking the difficult steps necessary for economic growth.

The argument began with a conclusion and a statement summarizing the proof. Arrayed under the statement are other, more detailed, statements. Each needs to be accompanied by further evidence that corroborates it. (In order to keep the outline uncluttered, most of this detailed evidence has not been included.) Note that the evidence is not only specific but is also derived from different sources including economic statistics and political history. Generally, the broader the range of evidence that aligns with a conclusion, the more convincing the argument is.

Keep this simple model of argument in mind, especially in the chapters on case-based writing. Cases constantly invite immersion in the details of fact and data. You want that detail—but you also want a structure that manages the detail and links it to a conclusion.

### NOTES

1. See Robert J. Dolan, "Note on Marketing Strategy," Note 9-598-061 (Boston: Harvard Business School Publishing, 1997).

2. Sam Dillon, "What Corporate America Cannot Build: A Sentence," *New York Times,* December 7, 2004.

3. Paraphrase of Stephen Toulmin, *The Uses of Argument* (Cambridge: Cambridge University Press, 1958), 13.

# CHAPTER 2

# WHAT *IS* A CASE?

In a case method classroom, both the instructor and student must be active in different ways. Each is dependent on the other to bring about teaching and learning. Instructors are experts, but they rarely deliver their expertise directly. The art of a case method instructor is to ask the right question at the right time, provide feedback on answers, and sustain a discussion that opens up meanings of the case.

To illustrate the pattern of question and response, here is a portion of a simulated case discussion of the Harvard Business School case "Malaysia in the 1990s (A)":

*Instructor:* What do you think the prime minister should do? What should he say at the United Nations?

*Student A:* He shouldn't give in to the environmentalists. The country should be free to do what it wants inside its borders. That's nobody else's business. The environmentalists should worry about problems in their own countries.

*Instructor:* So he should go it alone, then? Say you were interested in putting your money into the country. Which would you prefer: a government open to discussion and negotiation about issues, or one that takes a hard line with outsiders?

*Student A:* I guess I would want the government to be willing to talk. But I don't think this is an issue that needs to be discussed.

*Instructor:* You said you think environmental groups should only concern themselves with issues in their home countries?

*Student A:* Yes.

*Instructor:* Does Malaysia have a strong environmental movement?

*Student A:* I . . . I don't know. The case doesn't say.

*Instructor:* Let's assume it doesn't. Does an environmental point of view have any utility for a developing nation? Are there any results that could damage the country's development, or is it just a matter of saving, say, a species of frog that Western scientists have not yet had a chance to study?

*Student A:* I think the country can't afford to have Western standards for environmental protection.

*Student B:* The case does mention some negative consequences for Malaysia, things like erosion, floods, and some types of plants that might be destroyed which could be developed for medicines.

*Instructor:* OK. Can deforestation hurt the country's long-term development?

*Student C:* It could. Harvesting trees at a rate that isn't sustainable means the timber harvest will get smaller and smaller. Eventually, the industry and the revenue from it will disappear.

*Instructor:* Is this a big problem, a small problem, or something in between?

*Student C:* I think it's mostly in one area.

*Instructor:* Is there anything in the case that tells us the scope of the problem? Has anyone got numbers that help define it?

*Student C:* I don't have specific numbers. I know timber is going down as a percentage of exports . . .

Students provide most of the content of a case discussion. They are indispensable to the creation of knowledge. In fact, if they don't come to class well prepared, the case method will fail because the people responsible for making meaning from the case are not equipped to do it. In a lecture-, or expert-based, teaching method, facts tend to be configured in a way that yields a single interpretation, the "truth." Case discussions are replete with facts and information, but they aren't shaped into a single truth.

The logic of the method sounds fine, even inspirational. The reality of the experience can be baffling. Case method instructors usually don't provide a packaged summation or give a personal opinion of students' conclusions and plans for action. They may teach concepts for analyzing cases studied in the class. What they don't do is announce definitive conclusions or right answers, although they may discriminate between more and less plausible solutions. Students enter and leave the classroom responsible for the outcomes of the discussion.

For students, this can be a monumental shift in the educational experience, from the comfort of authority and the officially sanctioned truth to the hard work of personal responsibility and the unease of ambiguity and multiple meanings.

## WHAT A CASE IS, WHAT IT DOES,
## WHAT IT DOESN'T DO

A business case imitates or simulates a real situation. Cases are verbal representations of reality that put the reader in the role of a participant in the situation. The unit of analysis in cases varies enormously, from a single individual or organization to an entire nation or the world. Cases can range from one page to fifty or more. But they all have a common purpose: to represent reality, to convey a situation with all its cross currents and rough edges—including irrelevancies, sideshows, misconceptions, and little information or an overwhelming amount of it.

Most educational texts represent the real as logical and coherent. But real business situations are fluid and inevitably involve uncertainty; they don't present selected and sorted information. Cases don't either. Real situations consist of some clarity, too much or too little information, and lots of contingency—and so do cases. They provide business students with the equivalent of laboratories used for educating scientists and doctors. To fulfill its role, a case must have certain characteristics. As an analog of reality, a substitute for the direct experience of a business situation, a case must have these three characteristics:

- A significant business issue or issues

- Sufficient information on which to base conclusions

- No stated conclusions

A case without a significant issue has no educational value. You can therefore assume that every case deals with something important (e.g., a pricing dilemma, debt-equity trade-offs, a major problem in a plant). A case must have an adequate fact base to make possible reasonable conclusions, but it doesn't state any conclusions.

Many cases have these complicating properties:

- Information that includes "noise"—irrelevancies, dead ends, and false, biased, or limited testimony by characters in the case

- Unstated information that must be inferred from the information that is stated

- A nonlinear structure in which related evidence is scattered throughout the text and is often disguised or left to inference

A well-written case *must* have these characteristics in order to simulate reality. As a reader of cases, therefore, you must be able to:

- Construct conclusions from the information in the text

- Filter out irrelevant or low-value portions of the text

- Furnish missing information through inferences

- Associate evidence from different parts of the case and integrate it into a conclusion

Cases may put statements that sound conclusive in the mouths of case characters, but every case character is subject to skepticism based on his or her self-interest and limited point of view. Many cases have elaborate padding in the text and exhibits that serve as noise to distract the reader and make it harder to distinguish useful information. Noise is a characteristic of real situations. Today, we are awash in information, much of it of little value. Cases provide a hard but invaluable education in filtering information according to its relevance and value. Some of the best cases, however, use the opposite strategy. They offer what seems to be a hopelessly inadequate fact base. They mimic situations in which information is scarce, placing a premium on the reader's ability to make inferences. Every case, whether it has a large amount of information or very little, requires the reader to make inferences. This can be the most difficult transition from textbooks and lectures. If memorization is the primary skill of the lecture model, inference is the primary skill of the case model.

Cases look like they have a linear structure. They can have an introduction and a conclusion, a sequence of headings and subheadings, and a series of exhibits that look like those in textbooks. The introduction and conclusion can provide invaluable information, as we shall see, but they don't always. Headings and subheadings seem to divide the case into sections with the logic of a textbook or a *Wall Street Journal* article. Business cases imitate the structure of linear documents such as textbooks, but they are nonlinear, meaning the content is not presented in the most logical way. Along with inferential information, this characteristic is probably the greatest challenge for readers. Inexperienced students read cases assuming that the text has a logical order. They are puzzled when the content follows an organization that isn't completely illogical but is still confusing. They can then steel themselves to try harder, to spend more time on cases, to take better notes. Instead, they should question whether the way they read matches the nature of the text.

## TAMING AN INDETERMINATE TEXT

Cases require active readers. The texts most of us regularly read encourage us to be passive readers. The journalism of newspapers, magazines, television, and the Internet, whether reporting or opinion, tells the reader what it means. If it doesn't, it has failed. A newspaper article, for example, states its subject clearly, often in the first paragraph, and carefully declares its main points, which are usually explained and amplified through specific examples. For instance, a recent front-page article in a U.S. newspaper began with an anecdote about a doctor who discovered that a pharmaceutical company representative knew a great deal about which drugs he was prescribing. Here is the third paragraph of the story:

> *Drug makers, in a level of detail unknown to many physicians, are spending millions of dollars to develop secret reports about individual doctors and their patients, according to consultants to the drug companies.*[1]

The paragraph succinctly states the overall point of the story. The balance of the text provides examples of the data collection and explores the reasons why the companies want to collect it.

In a textbook, an expert delivers the truth, as he or she sees it, to readers. A history text on ancient Rome asks this "fundamental question" on page 1:

> *How was it possible, on Italian soil and on the basis of a league presided over by one of its members, to create a single power with a strong army and a rich treasury, whereas Greece, in spite of her creative genius, never succeeded in any of her attempts to secure the same result? In other words: why did Rome, just such a city-state as Athens or Sparta, succeed in solving the puzzle which had baffled both Athens and Sparta and even the Greek monarchies founded upon military strength by the successors of Alexander?*[2]

The rest of the text—more than three hundred pages—seeks to answer this question.

The Harvard Business School case "Malaysia in the 1990s (A)" begins with the prime minister of the country, Mahathir bin Mohamad, about to address the United Nations General Assembly and have meetings with potential investors. Western environmentalists have been criticizing his country for deforestation. The prime minister must consider his country's development strategy in relation to internal and external interests. At the end of the case, he is left wondering whether he should accept his speechwriters' confrontational statements dismissing the environmentalists and their criticism. The rest of the case doesn't report only those facts relevant to the controversy or offer the views and reasoning of all the parties to the dispute and evaluate which one has the most legitimate position. Compared with a news story or textbook, the case's opening and closing sections seem to have little to do with the text in between.

## THREE WAYS TO READ

There are at least three possible approaches to reading a case:

- Receive it.

- Find it.

- Make it.

The first approach, "Receive it," fits a text that states both a subject and its significance, as a news story or an online product review does. The second, "Find it," is adapted to a text that has keys or clues that the reader recognizes and puts together for a solution. A mystery novel is a good example. (So, oddly enough, are highly quantitative cases, which give clues that help identify the correct formulas or equations that will fill a need stated or implied in a case.) The final approach, "Make it," is appropriate for cases.

In "Malaysia," the beginning and end of the case are clear enough. We can assume that the criticism of Western environmental groups has some basis—which is not say it is true as stated—and it could complicate the government's development strategy. But when we read the case, the information varies considerably in its apparent relevance to the issue raised at the beginning. A reading of the case induces an uneasy feeling that although the content bears on the issue, how it does is unclear. Indeed, the most basic matters of fact are not clearly stated or are stated in multiple ways. If this were a news story, the editor would send it back to the reporter for a complete rewrite.

By design, a case doesn't tell you what it means. On first reading, it can seem to be a whole that is less than the sum of its parts. Therefore, you can't sit back and let the text do the work. You have to read a case actively and construct your own meaning.

### NOTES

1. Liz Kowalczyk, "Drug Companies' Secret Reports Outrage Doctors," *Boston Globe*, May 25, 2003, section A.

2. Michael Ivanovich Rostovtzeff, *Rome* (New York: Oxford University Press, 1960), 1.

PART I

# ANALYSIS

# CHAPTER 3

# HOW TO ANALYZE A CASE

A case is a text that refuses to explain itself. How do you construct a meaning for it?

Start by recognizing some contextual factors that help limit and narrow the analysis. Cases are usually studied in a course. A marketing case requires you to think as a marketer, not a strategist or manufacturing manager. Courses are often divided into different modules or themes defined by certain types of situations and, often, concepts, theories, and practices appropriate for these situations. You can expect to encounter the themes in the cases that are part of the modules and opportunities to put to work the analytical tools and best practices you have learned. Past case discussions provide a foundation for thinking about a new case, and study questions can call attention to important issues. You should make use of all these contextual factors, but they don't amount to a method for analyzing a case.

## STARTING POINT FOR UNDERSTANDING

The case method is *heuristic*—a term for self-guided learning that employs analysis to help draw conclusions about a situation. *Analysis* is derived from a Greek word meaning, "a dissolving." In English, analysis has two closely related definitions: to break something up into its constituent parts; and to study the relationships of the parts to the whole. To analyze a case, you therefore need ways of identifying and understanding important aspects of a situation and what they mean in relation to the overall situation.

Each business discipline has its own theories, frameworks, processes and practices, and quantitative tools. All of them are adapted to help understand specific types of situations. Michael Porter's concepts are productive when investigating competitive advantage—but they aren't very helpful for deciding whether to launch a product at a particular price or choosing the best method to finance the growth of a business. Porter's five forces can describe and explain the industry context in which a firm operates.[1]

No one would expect Porter's framework to guide a product launch decision. Specialized methods are fruitful because they're tailored to fit well-defined purposes. They're often complex, though, and hard to apply, especially for people who are just learning how to use them.

This book teaches an approach to cases that complements business concepts and theories. Its purpose is to provide a starting point for analysis that aids the use of theories and frameworks and quantitative formulas, all of which are indispensable for reaching conclusions about a case and building an argument for those conclusions. The case situation approach identifies features of a case that can be helpful to its analysis and encourages active reading.

## THINKING, NOT READING, IS KEY

Students new to the case method usually believe the most reliable way to understand a case is to read it from start to finish and then reread it as many times as necessary. (That's why many business school students think speed-reading courses can help them.) They rush into a case, highlighter in hand, reading as if the case were a textbook chapter. For case analysis you need to know when to read fast and when to read slowly. You should also spend more time thinking about a case than reading it.

When you begin work on a new case, you don't know what to look for. That is the major dilemma that confronts everyone who reads a case. In an active approach to a case, you start thinking *before* you read the case. And as you start reading it, you ask questions about the content. Then you seek answers in the case itself. As you find partial or full answers, you think about how they relate to each other and to the big picture of the case. You don't make knowledge by reading. Reading is never the primary resource of case analysis. Reading is simply an instrument directed by the thought process that makes meaning from the text.

## TYPES OF CASE SITUATIONS

Four types of situations occur repeatedly in cases:

- Problems
- Decisions
- Evaluations
- Rules

People sometimes react indignantly to this classification. They insist that there are a multitude of situations portrayed in cases, and it's misleading to say they're reducible to four. The four are not the *only* situations found in cases, but many case situations *do* belong in one of the four categories, and when they do, an awareness of which one can help organize analysis. This approach isn't the only correct way—it is one way. Try it and see if it helps.

Feel free to integrate pieces of it with your own way of dealing with cases. The greatest value of the case situation approach may be that it causes you to think about how you think about case studies.

## Problems

The word *problem* has many meanings. The meaning can be vague, referring to something that's difficult or troubling. The definition of *problem* as a case situation, however, is quite specific. It is a situation in which (1) there is a significant outcome or performance, and (2) there is no explicit explanation of the outcome or performance. To put it simply, a problem is a situation in which something important has happened, but we don't know why it did.

Cases provide many examples of problems defined this way. In one, a well-trained, well-intentioned manager has tried to introduce a worthwhile change in the sales strategy of an organization—a change supported by a detailed, data-driven analysis everyone admits is a breakthrough—and has failed to get any of the sales staff to go along. In another, an accounting manager of a manufacturer notices that two good retail customers suddenly have accounts payable that are large and overdue enough to be worrisome. He has no idea why the two firms would fall so far behind in their payments.

Both of these cases describe situations that involve negative outcomes. The causes of these sorts of outcomes are important to know for a practical reason: the knowledge can help improve the situation. The change effort may be self-destructive because it has weaknesses that are not apparent, or the manager may be good at many things but is a poor change agent. The manufacturer's retail customers may have large accounts payable because they have sloppy internal controls—or they may both be on the verge of bankruptcy. These possibilities illustrate why accurate causal analysis is vital. A conceptually flawed change is addressed very differently from an individual who isn't well suited to lead change. If both situations exist, the corrective action is that much more complex. Retail operations that need to clean up their accounting processes might require the manufacturer to engage in negotiations over a period of time, but two firms with bad debts that might go bankrupt require the supplier's immediate attention.

Success can also be a problem in the special meaning used here. Take the case of a company that specializes in outdoor advertising. It operates in three different market segments, but the case doesn't tell you which is the most profitable, much less why. Another case describes the development of a country over a period of thirty years or so; after severe political and social upheaval, the country slowly recovers and exceeds the performance of most countries in the region. But the case doesn't state how much more successful the country has been relative to its neighbors, and while it provides a great deal of data, both economic and demographic, it doesn't enumerate the reasons for the country's revival.

Problem analysis begins with a definition of the problem. That seems obvious, yet many cases don't state a problem. So first, you need to realize a problem exists and then define it for yourself. Next, you work out an explanation of the problem by linking the outcome or performance to its root causes—this is the main work of problem analysis. To carry it out, you'll need relevant tools, the specialized methods of business disciplines such as organizational behavior or operations management.

## Decisions

Many cases are organized around an explicit decision. The second paragraph of "General Motors: Packard Electric Division" (reproduced in this book) begins with this sentence: "The Product, Process, and Reliability (PPR) committee, which had the final responsibility for the new product development process, had asked [David] Schramm for his analysis and recommendation as to whether Packard Electric should commit to the RIM grommet for a 1992 model year car." Like many cases, this one complicates that decision immediately: Schramm must make up his mind within a week, and the product development people and manufacturing disagree over which way to go.

The existence of an explicit decision is an important distinction, because nearly all business cases involve decisions. In many of these cases, however, the decisions are implicit and dependent on another situation. Let's take a case described earlier that involves a problem: the outdoor advertising company. The case implies a decision: What is the best strategy the company should pursue in the future? This decision can only be made after the company's current strategy and how well it works are analyzed.

The decisions featured in cases vary greatly in scope, consequence, and available data. An executive must decide whether to launch a product, move a plant, pursue a merger, or provide financing for a planned expansion—or the president of a country must decide whether to sign a controversial trade agreement. Regardless of the dimensions of a decision, analyzing it requires the following:

- Decision options

- Decision criteria

- Relevant evidence

Identifying decision options is often easy because the case tells you what they are. As soon as you encounter a stated decision, you should look for a statement of the alternatives. If they aren't stated, then the first goal of analysis is to come up with plausible decision options.

The most important part of a decision analysis is determining the criteria. A rational decision can't be made without appropriate criteria. A decision case isn't likely to state criteria—they have to be derived through careful study of the specifics of the case, with the help of specialized methods. The criteria are used to develop evidence to complete a decision analysis. The goal is to determine the decision that creates the best fit between the available evidence and the criteria. In the General Motors case, a possible decision criteria is value to the customer. The reader needs to find evidence indicating which option delivers the greatest value to the customer. (That doesn't settle the matter, though, because there are other criteria.)

One other characteristic of decision analysis deserves mention here. There is no objectively correct decision. The standard for a good decision is the one that creates more benefits than the alternatives and has fewer or less severe downsides.

### Evaluations

Evaluations express a judgment about the worth, value, or effectiveness of a performance, act, or outcome. The unit of analysis of an evaluation can be an individual, a group, a department, an entire organization, a country, or a global region. An annual performance evaluation of an employee is a real-world example. So is a new CEO evaluating the performance of the company she is now heading. An evaluation can also involve the assessment of an act, such as a decision that has already been taken. Here is an example:

> From the perspective of current EU members, do you agree with their decision to enlarge the Union by ten new members?

Finally, an outcome can be the subject of an assessment. The competitive position of a company, for instance, is the outcome of numerous decisions and performances as well as contingencies such as macroeconomic conditions.

Like decision analysis, evaluation requires appropriate criteria. Without them, there are no standards for assessing worth, value, or effectiveness. As in decision analysis, evaluative criteria are inferred from the particulars of a situation with help from specialized methods. Evaluating a company's financial performance over a five-year period can be undertaken with a long list of financial formulas, but the circumstances portrayed in the case come into play as well. The numbers may show that a company has a steadily declining performance over the period, but it still may be doing well because the national economy is slumping and the company is actually doing better than its competitors.

An overall evaluation expresses the best fit between the evidence and the criteria. In the example just given, measured against purely financial criteria, the company is doing poorly. Yet, the evidence pertaining to macroeconomic and competitive criteria alters the evaluation: in a tough market, the company is actually performing better than its peers.

Another requirement of evaluation is that it include both positive and negative sides. A leader has strengths and weaknesses, and both are included in an accurate evaluation. Moreover, there may be aspects of the leader's performance that are ambiguous—he has delegated power widely, but it is too early to tell whether the managers below him can handle the power. And this individual's performance as a leader could be substantially affected by factors outside his control—corporate headquarters has intervened in his promotion decisions and insisted that certain favorites be elevated even though they aren't the best-qualified candidates.

## Rules

Quantitative methods can provide critical information about business situations. For example, say there is a need to compare the value of a company when a specific condition exists—a partnership with another company—and when it doesn't exist. The way to calculate future cash values—one that experts and experience support as reasonably accurate—is net present value. An NPV calculation is done according to a formula. Mathematically, there is a right way to perform the calculation; any other way provides an inaccurate result.

For rules analysis, you need to know:

- The type of information needed in a situation

- The appropriate rule to furnish that information

- The correct way to apply the rule

- The data necessary to execute the rule

Rules analysis exists in virtually every area of business. A breakeven calculation is a rule used in marketing. In manufacturing, quantitative methods are used for process analysis, and accounting and finance consist primarily of rules. The scope of rules is very narrow. For the most part, they are useful only in specific sets of circumstances, but in those circumstances are very productive. There is a correct way to execute or perform the rule, and the output is of one type. A well-defined set of rules is needed to analyze a company's liquidity. Those rules are the most useful in the situation, because they are designed to be. Each calculation specified by a rule has a procedure that must be followed. If it isn't, the result is a meaningless number. Each calculation yields a precise output of a prescribed type (e.g., a percentage less than or equal to zero).

*Qualitative* methods are different from rules. There are often many alternative methods for obtaining the same or similar information. To analyze the quality of leadership in an organization or its competitive strategy, there are a large number of methods to choose from. There is no prescribed method that provides correct information about competitive advantage. In marketing, two different methods can be applied to the same situation, can produce very different results, and can both be useful—or useless. A second difference between rules and qualitative methods is how they are executed. There is a correct way to execute a rule such as the formula for net present value; there is no objectively correct way to execute qualitative methods for analyzing competition.

That is *not* to say that rules analysis lacks uncertainties and ambiguities. Any calculation about the future involves uncertainty. This uncertainty is built into formulas through assumptions, and assumptions involve judgment, not objective truth. Settling on a growth or inflation rate over a certain period of time is speculative. The key is the reasoning behind the choice. Central bankers can be wrong about inflation and growth, and so can the rest of us. Assumptions need to have a reasonable basis, but reasonable people can disagree about them. But note that the argument is about assumptions, not about the rules themselves. (Experts do argue about the fitness of rules and make changes to them, but after they do, everyone uses the changed rule and executes it the same way.)

Sometimes, though, an idiosyncratic assumption has no material effect on the result of a calculation. In the earlier valuation example, you might assume a growth rate that is too optimistic, but if the rate is the same for the calculation with and without the partnership, it should have no effect on the comparison of the end values.

The results of rules analysis frequently provoke sharp differences of opinion. What two people infer from the same numerical results can diverge. Economists are famous for looking at the same set of numbers and coming to vastly different conclusions about them, even though they all agree on the formulas and data that have produced the numbers. The same is true in companies. One executive can read financial numbers as confirmation that a strategy is working, while another can read them as a warning that disaster looms. In short, numbers don't explain what they mean, and they don't make decisions for you.

However, the interpretation of the output of rules is distinct from the rules themselves. If the right rule is applied and correctly performed, and the rule doesn't involve a controversial assumption (like the predicted growth rate of GNP), everyone will come up with exactly the same result. If a qualitative method relevant to a situation is applied to the same set of facts in a way consistent with the generally understood meaning of its concepts, everyone will not necessarily come up with the same result. That is the fundamental difference between rules, as defined here, and qualitative methods.

Rules aren't pursued further in this book. Learning rules analysis means learning a certain category of rules—valuation, for instance—and when and how to use them. That learning is the province of accounting, finance, tax, and other areas that are intensely rule governed. However, it may be helpful to remember that when rules depend upon assumptions, the values chosen for them require an argument. Moreover, the information rules provide has great importance for the analysis of problems, decisions, and evaluations. Accounting rules can diagnose the financial health of an organization. Macroeconomics is invaluable in evaluating a nation's development strategy. Financial rules are indispensable to a decision about whether to sell a company at a given time and price. Rules are a large and important subset of the specialized methods necessary to understand case situations.

## CASE ANALYSIS AS A PROCESS

The way you analyze a case differs from the way anyone else does. There is a difference, though, between personal study habits and a process for analyzing a case. The latter involves more than habits and practices. It concerns how you think about a case. The intention of this section is to suggest a process that has helped case method students become more efficient and productive. This process is designed for case discussion preparation, but it is easily adapted to a process for writing a case essay. (However, the way a case is analyzed for an essay is more prescriptive, since an essay must have certain elements. Chapters 10 through 12 will explain these elements.)

The key to the process is active reading. Active reading is *interrogative* and *purposeful*. You ask questions about the case and seek answers. Questions give a purpose for reading; they direct and focus study on important aspects of a situation. The moment you sense that you are reading without purpose, stop and regroup. It may be a good time to step away and stretch, do some yoga, or walk. Active reading is also *iterative*, meaning you make multiple passes through a case. With each iteration, the purpose of reading changes: you are looking for new information or looking at old information in a new way. Three concepts contribute to active reading: a goal, a point of view, and a hypothesis.

## Goal of Analysis

At first it may seem obvious. What other goal can there be for analyzing a case than to understand it? The problem is that "understanding" is too vague. Another way to think about the goal is, How do you know when to conclude the study of a case? This is an important question. If you don't have a concrete limit, you can drift along for hours, much of it taken up by distraction and undirected effort. Here is a more concrete goal: you are familiar with the information in the case, you have come to a conclusion about the main issue, you have evidence showing why your conclusion is reasonable, and you have thought about other possible conclusions and why yours is preferable to them.

This substantive goal can be combined with a time limit. Allocate a set amount of time—two hours, for example—for each case. At the end of the period, stop and settle for whatever you know about the case. This is a very good way to put constructive pressure on yourself to make the most of the time.

## Point of View

To anchor analysis, take advantage of what's already in the case. Adopt the point of view of the protagonist—the main character. Put yourself in her shoes. Her dilemma should be your dilemma. If it's a decision, set a recommended decision as your goal. When you adopt the persona of the main character, don't assume that you're dealing with a cardboard cutout, a dramatic veneer. Consider the character's strengths, responsibilities, and blind spots. By all means, too, be sensitive to the dilemmas characters find themselves in. Often, a good question to ask yourself is, Why is the person in this dilemma?

## Hypothesis

One of the most useful constructs for resolving the protagonist's dilemma is a *hypothesis*. A hypothesis is "a tentative explanation that accounts for a set of facts and can be tested by further investigation."[2] It is indispensable to science and to any fact-based analytic activity in which multiple conclusions are possible.

A hypothesis offers the advantage of a concrete statement you can test against case evidence. Say that the protagonist of a case must evaluate an individual she has hired—a rising star, but also a person who alienates many people inside the firm and cuts some corners in his relentless pursuit of new business. The hypothesis is that the new hire should receive a high rating despite some flaws in his performance. To test it, you'll have to develop a strong argument, based on relevant criteria, facts, and inferences, that backs a positive evaluation but also recognizes poor performance on other criteria.

Cases don't allow just *any* hypothesis. The available evidence in the case sets the rational limit on the range of hypotheses. A hypothesis that can't be argued from evidence in the case is simply an unsubstantiated opinion. However, there is a range of possible hypotheses about every case. A contrarian's position—one that opposes what seem to be safer hypotheses and can be argued from evidence—can have a galvanizing effect in a discussion, forcing everyone to look at the evidence from an entirely new angle or consider evidence no one else has noticed.

## DESCRIPTION OF PROCESS

The rest of this chapter outlines a process for working on cases. The process has five phases:

1. Situation

2. Questions

3. Hypothesis

4. Proof and action

5. Alternatives

The process is meant to be flexible and adaptable. Experiment with it, using the cases in this book. Many MBA students don't give much thought to their case-study approach, not because it is unimportant but because they don't see anything tangible to think about. Ultimately, the value of the process described below depends on whether it prompts you to think about your own process.

### *1. Situation (5 minutes)*

The most difficult part of a case analysis seems to be the beginning. You have to bridge the gap between no knowledge about the case and knowledge sufficient to form a hypothesis. That gap can look very wide as you begin reading a case thick with detail; it can seem to be all parts and no whole. Earlier in the chapter, I stressed that it is hard to find something when you don't know what you're looking for. To get started, you can structure analysis with a series of questions. The process I advocate is understanding the big picture first and then filling it in with details. Start by asking this question: *What is the situation?*

Usually reading the first and last sections of the case is sufficient to identify the situation. Decisions and evaluations tend to be stated at the beginning. Problems are harder to recognize, and more details about identifying them are provided in chapter 5. A characteristic of a problem case is the absence of any actionable statement made by or about the protagonist. Often, the main character is reflecting on a situation and wondering what to do.

Reading the first and last sections of the case can often provide far more information than just the type of situation. In decision cases, these sections may specify the decision options. That is true of the case "General Motors: Packard Electric Division." If you don't find options at the beginning or end of a case, you should scan other sections. The opening or ending of a problem case may present a partial or complete description of the problem. In all types of cases, the initial and final sections frequently express a tension or conflict important to the analysis. In "General Motors," the first section identifies the decision and a conflict between two functional groups. The two sides of the conflict, with the protagonist in the middle, can be reference points for analysis. Why do the product development people so strongly support an innovative component that they're willing to take a formidable risk? And why are the manufacturing people just as adamant that the company should not go forward with the component in the short term?

After reading the openings and closing sections, you should put the case aside for a moment and consider what you have learned. Is the situation a problem, decision, or evaluation? Do you have any ideas about the causal frameworks or criteria that might fit the situation? Does it seem you'll have to cut through a large amount of information in the case or make many inferences because the information is scarce? Are there any hints in the two sections about causes, criteria, or even a plausible decision or evaluation? Do the hints seem reliable or just a way to throw you off?

## 2. Questions (15 minutes)

Knowing the situation allows you to ask questions pertinent to a problem, a decision, or an evaluation. The most important of these questions is: *What do I need to know about the situation?*

Here are questions specific to each situation:

### PROBLEM

Who or what is the subject of the problem (e.g., a manager, a company, a country)? What is the problem? Am I trying to account for a failure, a success, or something more ambiguous? What's the significance of the problem to the subject? Who is responsible for the problem (usually it is the protagonist) and what might he need to know to do something about it?

## DECISION

What are the decision options? Do any seem particularly strong or weak? What's at stake in the decision? What are the possible criteria? What might the most important criteria be for this kind of decision? Are any of the criteria explicitly discussed in the case (case headings can sometimes give good clues)?

## EVALUATION

Who or what is being evaluated? Who's responsible for the evaluation? What's at stake? What are the possible criteria? What might the most important criteria be for this sort of evaluation? Are any of the criteria explicitly discussed in the case (case headings can sometimes give you good clues)?

You won't be able to answer these questions now. That will take further study. To make this first pass through the text more targeted, it's useful to do a *content inventory*. Its purpose is to locate information that might be used to answer the questions about the situation.

To perform a fast inventory, scan the headings in the text. Read a little of the sections, especially those that seem to have valuable information. Examine the exhibits to get a sense of what they convey. You will learn something about the case—sometimes a great deal more than you might expect. You'll also build a map of the useful content. Because cases often aren't linear in their organization, this map is very important; pieces of information related to the same issue will be found in different sections of the case and in the exhibits.

Use a pencil or pen to mark up the case. Mark high-value sections and circle facts, numbers, and statements of possible importance. Be sure to capture any thoughts about the answers to your questions, and record new questions that come to mind. Note what issues particular exhibits may illuminate, and what calculations might be performed later to yield relevant information.

### 3. Hypothesis (45 minutes)

Armed with a list of things you want to know about the situation and a map of the content, you are ready for this question: *What's my hypothesis?*

This is the most important phase of work on the case. Through close study of high value sections and exhibits, you narrow the possibilities to the one that seems most plausible to you. If there are three alternatives for a decision, test them, starting with the one you suspect has the most promise. Here are some other suggestions for structuring your work at this point:

### PROBLEM

- Make sure you know the problem that needs to be diagnosed. Consider whether the characteristics of the problem suggest causes.

- Think about the frameworks that seem most appropriate to the situation. Quickly review the specifics of the frameworks if you aren't sure of them.

- Pursue the diagnosis by looking at case information through the lens of the cause you are most certain about.

- For each cause, make a separate pass through the case looking for evidence of it.

- If the case has a lot of quantitative evidence, to what cause is it most relevant? If you don't have a cause relevant to the quantitative evidence, formulate one. Work up as much relevant, high-value quantitative evidence as you can.

- In a case with a protagonist, consider whether she is a potential cause. If you think she is, work out how she contributes to the problem.

### DECISION

- Review the criteria you have come up with so far. Which do you have the most confidence in?

- Review the decision options. Do any seem especially strong or weak?

- Apply the criterion that seems to identify the most evidence in the case.

- Investigate the strongest decision option with the criterion you have the most confidence in. Or, if you're reasonably certain about which is weakest, see if you can dismiss that option quickly.

- If the case has a lot of quantitative evidence, which criterion is most relevant to it? If you don't have a criterion relevant to the quantitative evidence, formulate one. Work up as much relevant, high-value quantitative evidence as you can.

- If there are conflicts about the decision between individuals or groups, think about why that is. Look at the decision from the point of view of each of the parties to the conflict.

- If the protagonist is in a difficult position in relation to the decision, consider why that is.

### EVALUATION

- Review the criteria you have come up with so far. Which do you have the most confidence in?

- What are the terms of the evaluation going to be (e.g., strengths/weaknesses)? Do any stand out in the case (e.g., an obvious strength of an individual)?

- Do you already have a sense of the bottom-line evaluation you favor? If you do, what are the reasons for the preference? Pursue those reasons.

- Start by applying the criterion that seems to identify the most evidence in the case.

- Investigate the most positive rating or the most negative with the criterion you have the most confidence in.

- If the case has a lot of quantitative evidence, which criterion is most relevant to it? If you don't have a criterion relevant to the quantitative evidence, formulate one. Work up as much relevant, high-value quantitative evidence as you can.

Taking notes helps you organize and remember information, but it serves the equally important purpose of recording your thought process. Without note taking, you can too easily stray from active reading. Of course, note taking can degenerate into transferring information in the case to a piece of paper or computer screen. Notes on a case don't simply record facts. They capture anything that might lead to answers to the questions you've asked.

It may sound trivial, but I recommend that students try to contain the "highlighter habit." This study aid is well adapted to the lecture model of learning, but it can be a detriment to case study. Highlighting sentences is satisfying because it makes you feel you're doing something. In reality, what you're doing is marking sentences to think about later, and that's a setup for passive reading. You should be thinking about statements *the first time* you encounter them. That said, highlighters can be useful as a tool to differentiate related content: facts about one aspect of the case, for example, or text and numbers that belong to one category of evidence.

A pencil or pen is more conducive to active reading—to write down questions and make notes. When you begin to gravitate toward a conclusion, stop work and write it down. The function of a hypothesis is to give you a position to try out, not a final conclusion, so listen carefully to your intuition.

If you have time, put the case away after this iteration. Even a short break can be useful. There is scientific evidence that our subconscious minds are much better at dealing with complexity than our conscious minds. Turning your attention to something else allows that subconscious capacity to work on the information you have collected.

## 4. Proof and Action (40 minutes)

A hypothesis drives a different approach to the case. You want to prove something, not look for something to prove. Ask these questions: *What evidence do I have that supports the hypothesis? What additional evidence do I need?*

Look at the information you've compiled and identify evidence supporting the hypothesis. Your first priority should be to add to the evidence you have. What is the strongest evidence? Can you add more to it?

Now assess where evidence is missing. Where will you find more—or is there any evidence in the case? Think about any factors you may have overlooked such as a cause, criterion, or evaluative category.

Go back into the case, with the single purpose of bringing out more evidence that aligns with your hypothesis. You don't have to work from the first page to the last. You can go directly to the sections and exhibits you think have what you need. Of course, you can work from beginning to end if that makes you more comfortable. Just be sure to stay focused on what you're trying to prove.

Let's say that you're building an argument for a decision option and one of the criteria is cost savings. You've noted some statements that imply your decision option will save money for the firm and circled numbers that you thought were relevant to savings. Collect those numbers now, and work out calculations to estimate the total savings. You may then have one of those gratifying moments of case study: from those scattered numbers that looked so inconsequential when viewed individually, you've pulled together an estimate that indicates a very large annual savings—and that's just one part of your argument.

Also give some thought to the actionable content of your position. How would you implement the decision you're recommending? What actions does your diagnosis or evaluation call for? Think in practical, real-world, not ideal-world, terms. Don't just sketch out in your mind a broad approach to action. Think about tangible actions and write them down. Finally, give a bit of thought to the order of the actions. An action plan is a program in which actions are taken at a certain time for a reason. It isn't a to-do list.

## 5. Alternatives (15 minutes)

It may seem paradoxical, but the last phase of analysis should be to question your own hypothesis: *What is the greatest weakness of the hypothesis? What is the strongest alternative to it?*

The intention isn't to undermine your hard work but to take a step back and look critically at the hypothesis and the evidence. Every position has a weakness, and you should be the one who recognizes it, not the professor or your peers. Here are some ways to think critically about your work:

### PROBLEM

Can the problem be defined differently? Would that make a difference to the diagnosis? Are there any holes in the diagnosis—could there be causes missing? What's the weakest part of the diagnosis? Could an entirely different diagnosis be made? What would it look like?

### DECISION

What's the biggest downside of the recommended decision? How would you manage the downside? What's the strongest evidence against the recommendation? How would a case for the major alternative look?

### EVALUATION

Have you been objective and thorough about the evaluative findings that oppose your overall assessment? Think how a different overall evaluation might be proved. Have you accounted for factors that the subject of the evaluation couldn't control?

## "BUT WHAT IF MY HYPOTHESIS IS WRONG?"

Students have asked me that question many times. A hypothesis isn't wrong; a hypothesis fails when you can't make a credible argument for it from case evidence. If you find yourself in that situation—and you will sooner or later—first make sure the difficulty lies with the hypothesis and not with your evidence gathering. You may have overlooked important information or not used specialized tools effectively. If you're certain the evidence isn't there, face up to it but realize that the work you've already done isn't wasted.

You now have a good grasp of the case and probably have a good sense of what the evidence is and where it is. Your work with a new hypothesis is therefore likely to move along quickly.

Another way of looking at the fear of being wrong is to ask yourself what the alternative is. I have not heard of a method of case analysis that never leads to dubious conclusions. In fact, making analytic mistakes is invaluable. Through mistakes, we learn more about the thought process called case analysis. And a shaky analysis can sometimes be a symptom of risk taking, which is also an invaluable learning experience.

### NOTES

1.  Michael E. Porter, *Competitive Strategy: Techniques for Analyzing Industries and Competitors* (New York: The Free Press, 1980).

2.  *The American Heritage College Dictionary*, third edition (Boston: Houghton Mifflin Company, 1993).

# CHAPTER 4

# CASE ANALYSIS DEMONSTRATION

The previous chapter describes a case analysis process. This chapter demonstrates how to use the process to investigate a case, "Malaysia in the 1990s (A)." Please read the case first and then reread sections when they are discussed. This process demonstration is not the definitive analysis of the case. Compare your own ideas about the case to those in the chapter. The more you actively engage the analysis and test it against the case, the more learning you will gain for your own approach to analysis.

## 1. SITUATION

You can learn a great deal from the first and last sections of many cases. The first section of "Malaysia" tells us the prime minister must decide how to respond to the charges of Western environmentalists. The situation therefore centers on a decision. The opening section says that the country has been independent for just thirty years at the time of the case. In that period, it has enjoyed "healthy" economic growth and "relative" political stability. The Western environmentalists are decrying rapid deforestation. Their primary threat seems to be a boycott of Malaysian timber products.

The last section ("A Western Timber Ban?") suggests an option: Western timber companies are orchestrating the criticism. The final sentence of the case suggests a more sinister motive: unnamed entities are trying to keep the country poor. In other words, the real issue is East versus West, a developing country versus developed countries. We should note that contention as another issue to look into. Does the case have any evidence to support a conspiracy theory? Before we delve into that, we need to take a step back— already—and think about other questions we might want to ask.

First, are the charges of the environmental groups true? This is a good question because it is fact based. Second, how important is timber to the Malaysian economy? And third: How much would a Western timber ban hurt the country's economy?

Now, we need to think about decision alternatives. In the final section advisers to the prime minister recommend that he reject the criticism and preserve the status quo. By a simple exercise of logic, we can quickly come up with an alternative diametrically opposed to the first: accept the criticism and make the changes necessary to satisfy it. If these are the two extremes, it means that a decision option in the middle is something like this: accept any valid criticism, reject the rest, and make necessary changes.

Here are the decision alternatives and the questions that can organize the initial study:

- Alternatives
  - Option 1: Reject criticism, preserve the status quo.
  - Option 2: Accept criticism entirely, make all necessary changes.
  - Option 3: Accept any legitimate criticism, reject rest, make necessary changes.

- Questions
  - Are the environmental charges true?
  - Is logging economically significant?
  - Would a Western timber boycott hurt?
  - Any evidence to support conspiracy theory about Western timber companies?

By reading just the opening and closing of the case and thinking about them, we already have some promising leads for analysis.

Before moving on, we should critique the options. Sometimes it's possible to draw quick conclusions about them. An Asian country enjoying reasonable economic growth is probably not going to change its policies because distant environmental groups are criticizing it—unless the country is going to suffer dire consequences. Option 1 seems more plausible unless we can find evidence that it will result in serious negative consequences.

## 2. QUESTIONS

Now we should think about decision criteria. Normally, the concepts and methods of an MBA course would be the primary resource for criteria—but that resource isn't available. Instead, I will borrow ideas from a first-year course taught at a business school.

For the Malaysian government, the most important consideration has to be the welfare of the country. The decision should promote the national welfare. But the term "national welfare" is too broad. We need to break it down into specific components. Macroeconomics certainly is a foundation of national well being, and it has the added advantage of being measurable. Other elements of the foundation are social and political dynamics, and they can be measured to some degree. To keep the analysis focused, we want a spare list of criteria. Let's add just one more possibility: Malaysia's international reputation or image. The initial list of criteria (see below) will get us started. We can drop, modify, or add criteria if the initial ones don't yield evidence.

### CRITERIA

- Decision must promote national welfare in these ways:
  - Economic
  - Social
  - Political
- Decision also must support positive international image

Now we scan "Malaysia" and the exhibits and read a little of each section to find relevant content. The following sections and exhibits seem to promise valuable information:

*Factual background*
  - Environmental concerns
  - The concession system

*Economy*
  - Economic strategy
  - Economic performance
  - Exhibits 3, 5, 8, 9, 10

*Social-political*
  - Social conditions
  - Political structure

We will start our investigation with these sections. Other parts of the case may have pertinent information, but at this stage we don't want to overload ourselves.

## 3. HYPOTHESIS

We are now ready to read the case to develop a hypothesis.

## Environment

In "Environmental Concerns," we find that Malaysia has a very small percentage of the world's rain forests, 2 percent to be exact. At the same time, the government admits that the rate of logging activity is currently unsustainable. Our first criterion yields an uncomfortable mix: the country is using up its tropical forests faster than it can replace them, but the contribution to the global problem is small. We could say, at this point, that our work is done. No, Malaysia isn't perfect, but the environmental critics seem to be focused on the wrong country. Still, that doesn't feel like a complete position.

## Economy

Here's what we learn from the sections on the economics of the country.

"Economic Strategy" tells us a lot about the path the government has taken to promote economic growth. The exhibits we flagged tell us even more. Exports are very important to the economy, and timber remains a big part of the export mix. At the same time, a goal of the country's development strategy is lessening its dependence on commodity exports such as logs. The case text and numbers in the exhibits show that the strategy is working. Raw material exports are a declining portion of Malaysian exports, though timber has not declined as rapidly as other commodities. Most of the country's exports of logs go to Asian countries, Japan in particular. A Western boycott of raw timber from Malaysia would probably have little effect, although it might be broadened to include Malaysian value-added wood products, and that could hurt. However, the case doesn't have information on the percentage of value-added wood exports to Western nations.

Foreign direct investment has grown by more than 300 percent from 1980 to 1990, but foreign capital could move on to the next low-wage economy in the region if Malaysian wages continue to increase. That exit might not be as bad as it sounds if the government can move the economy to value-added products and services before the low-wage seeking FDI flows elsewhere.

Two other points about timber harvesting stand out. First, unsustainable logging could eventually harm Malaysia. Environmental degradation imposes costs; in addition, logging would obviously be curtailed or eliminated as the stock of trees declines. It seems that current policies could at some point in the future undermine the future they are supposed to bring about. Second, large-scale production of logs for export continues Malaysia's reliance on commodity exports, a dependence that the government is determined to reduce, if not eliminate.

Political and social well-being are closely linked to economic development. Malaysia has struck a delicate social and political balance based on a bigger pie and an artificially bigger slice delivered to the majority Malays, who have lagged other groups in income, through the New Economic Policy (NEP). Without continuing economic growth and an assurance that the majority will share in it, the risk of instability seems high. At the same time, the NEP should give us pause. It has a positive goal and has produced the intended results, yet the mechanism exacts the costs of inefficiency and is vulnerable to corruption.

Although it may seem too soon, we can already try out a hypothesis. Remember that hypotheses are statements that give purpose to an investigation; they are not hard-and-fast conclusions.

> *Malaysia should make no changes to its basic economic policies for the time being, but the government should monitor logging and take steps if it threatens to hurt long-term development.*

## 4. PROOF AND ACTION

To back our hypothesis, we can build an argument on a framework of several statements:

### FACTUAL CONTEXT

- Malaysia is a very small contributor to tropical deforestation.

- The government admits logging that exceeds agreed upon limits.

### CRITERIA

*Economic*
- Abrupt cuts in raw timber exports will reduce GNP.

- A Western boycott of raw timber would not damage the Malaysian economy.

- But unsustainable logging could hurt the economy more severely if it were continued long enough.

- So can continued dependence on commodity exports and low-wage production.

Establishing the factual context is straightforward. The case states that Malaysia has just 2 percent of the world's rain forests. In addition, logging a tropical forest does not mean that it is permanently barren. Logged land in the tropics can regenerate in twenty-five or thirty years, unlike forests in colder climates.

The financial hit to the national economy that would result from an abrupt reduction in raw timber exports can be proved with numbers from several of the exhibits. The social and political consequences are matters of inference. In the past unrest in the country has been partly driven by economic inequity. Furthermore, Malaysia has not enjoyed the same improvement in living standards as some of its Asian neighbors. If the majority finds itself losing its modest gains, the political consequences might force decisions that prop up the majority's standard of living but injure the overall economy.

Case exhibits provide numbers for Malaysia's raw timber exports that show they are overwhelmingly imported to Asian countries. A Western boycott would presumably have no effect on the Japanese businesses that import most of Malaysia's raw timber. Not only are Japanese firms Malaysia's biggest timber customers, but they also pay the best prices. There is abundant evidence, too, that the government has managed to achieve goals that few developing nations with a heterogeneous population have been able to attain: (1) steady economic growth, (2) an improvement in the standard of living of the entire population, with the largest increase going to the least well off, and (3) a decreasing reliance on volatile commodities. These three related points show how the government's policy seeks to balance various needs, including those of the environment.

Data in the text and exhibits prove Malaysia's steady economic growth. The government's development strategy has propelled the country to an impressive 5.9 percent annual growth rate in the 1980s. The government has adjusted the composition of exports to decrease commodities and increase value-added products; the percentage of manufactured goods has leaped from 28 percent of total exports in 1980 to 67 percent in 1990.

## Social-Political

We have now worked the environmental and economic content in some depth. We should look further into social and political issues to see if they have a bearing on the hypothesis. Exhibits and the section "Social Conditions" inform us that the Bumiputras—the indigenous groups including the Malays and others—have enjoyed 2.7 percent annual growth in terms of household income as compared to 1.4 percent for the Chinese. Rising prosperity across all ethnic groups promotes stability, which is the foundation of economic growth. Although Malaysia has not performed at the level of the "Asian Tigers" such as Singapore and South Korea, it has fared well considering that the Tigers have homogeneous populations and Malaysia does not.

"Political Structure" is brief; perhaps the most significant conclusion we can take from it is that Malaysian politics are a carefully orchestrated balancing of ethnic groups. The majority leads this national coalition but doesn't pursue its self-interest at the expense of other groups. The majority has the political power to mandate policies that essentially confiscate wealth from other groups. In that context, the NEP appears to be a restrained policy.

We can now add some additional points to the framework of our argument:

### SOCIAL-POLITICAL

- Abrupt and sustained reductions in GNP will result in a declining standard of living that would fall most heavily on those with low incomes: the majority Malays.

- If the economic progress of the majority is reversed, the result will be social distress (e.g., rising unemployment) and that could ignite political conflict.

- The majority could demand that the government funnel more wealth to it, disrupting the political system and destabilizing the economy.

The evidence we have compiled is consistent with the hypothesis. If we use just the economic data available to us, we can assert that over time, the export of logs will dwindle. But there are two nagging points. Logging needs careful management to make sure that it can sustain domestic value-added manufacturing, and "careful management" could be viewed differently by Malaysia and Western nations.

Nevertheless, we cannot help but notice that the state of Sarawak is mentioned frequently as a trouble spot for timber harvests. The state has had difficulty managing logging, and there is a cryptic reference to the questionable behavior of Japanese trading firms. In the final major section of the case, we learn that both the state and federal governments invited an international timber organization to assess the situation in Sarawak. To reach a sustainable timber harvest, the group recommended an immediate 50 percent cut in production, but Sarawak hasn't complied, despite assurances that it would.

In the process of proving a conclusion about a case, you may come across an issue that doesn't fit in the argument you are making. That is what is happening here. When this happens, you need to consider whether the issue works against the position you're crafting or is one of the almost inevitable complications case situations throw at readers. The only way to answer the question is further study.

The government belongs to an international organization, has signed an agreement to manage its forests responsibly, and has promised to make a big cut in production. Shouldn't the government keep its word and clamp down on unauthorized logging? The inability to make good on these commitments points to a problem, and it could make foreign investors question putting money into the country. Governments that don't keep their word usually aren't good for business. Malaysia's international image could also take a hit, making other governments less willing to work with the country.

The Sarawak situation deserves a closer look. The state has enjoyed the highest rate of growth in household income in the country from 1976 to 1990, according to case exhibit 7. At the same time, the timber harvest shows a huge increase from 1980 to 1990 (case exhibit 10, section B), and almost all of the harvest has been exported, primarily to Japan (case exhibit 10, section C). The two trends correlate: the people of Sarawak have been making a good deal of money by cutting down their forests at an unsustainable rate and selling them to the Japanese.

How can this happen? Here are some relevant facts and inferences:

- Japanese trading companies appear to be encouraging excessive logging since it provides them with a low-cost source of timber.

- The assignment of logging concessions is not transparent, and there is evidence of blatant self-dealing in Sarawak.

- There is evidence of illegal logging in Sarawak.

- Gross understaffing hampers enforcement of logging limits in Sarawak.

- The state and federal governments appear to be more interested in blaming each other than doing anything about the problem.

Recalling information in "Social Conditions" in the light of the above facts, we can infer that the NEP overlay on the national economic strategy has left the door wide open to corruption. We can make the following inferences:

- Japanese trading companies pay off Chinese businesspeople, the real owners of logging concessions.

- The Chinese pay off their nominal Malay partners required by the NEP.

- The Chinese "silent partners" or the Malay nominal owners pay off the appropriate state and federal officials, who obstruct enforcement and allow the logs to be cut and exported.

Now we need to think about modifying our hypothesis. Is this just an interesting side issue of the case, or is it something more central? Corruption can corrode economic development in multiple ways. We can add to our basic position that the country should deal with the corruption driving logging in some parts of the country:

*Malaysia should make no changes to its basic economic policies, but the government should honor its international commitments and gradually reduce illegal logging.*

This position seems to conform to the evidence, but it may not be realistic given the politics of a heterogeneous population. We do not have much evidence to work with on Malaysian politics—primarily, "Social Conditions" and "Political Structure." Perhaps the country should deal with the corruption associated with logging but move slowly to avoid disturbing the social and political equilibrium brought about by the NEP. The revised hypothesis acknowledges the concerns of external critics but balances that with internal considerations.

## 5. ALTERNATIVES

The criteria and evidence have led us to grapple with the mix of policies that best serves Malaysia's long-term interests. The case attempts to portray the situation from a position of political and ethical neutrality. The criticism of environmentalists in the developed world is reported and not judged as fair or unfair. We are forced to dig into the facts to decide for ourselves, and we find that the criticism may be factually correct, but it doesn't take into account a variety of mitigating factors.

The NEP is not condemned as an obvious violation of free market principles or championed as an engine of economic equality. The case provides data on the NEP that shows progress toward its stated goals. Yet the case also furnishes evidence of negative consequences. Unsustainable logging does not help long-term development. But is it so harmful that the central government should take dramatic steps to curb it? Are there other ways to assist the majority in raising their standard of living without the distortions and dangers of the NEP? Or is the mix of positive and negative factors appropriate to Malaysia's state of development? Should any significant changes be made now when the development model seems to be succeeding for the most part?

Your hypothesis is influenced by your experience, values, and cultural background as well as by the evidence. The case can be viewed as a conflict between critics from wealthy developed nations who can afford the luxury of environmental concerns and leaders of a developing nation who are trying to improve the lives of their people. The perspective can be reversed: groups in the West are trying to protect the environment in all parts of the world, not just developed nations, because that is in the best interests of the global population. As much as possible, we should try to recognize the importance of both the world ecosystem and the best interests of millions of people living in a developing country.

We have gone far enough to demonstrate a case analysis. Your responsibility would be to decide on a final position—a recommendation to the prime minister—and to have evidence at hand to support the recommendation as convincingly as you can. But it's also important for the learning process that you also have in mind questions provoked by study of the case. Each of them can be a path to further learning, for you and for everyone else in a case classroom.

## CONFIDENCE IN A CONTENTIOUS WORLD

It is not easy to prove something. There are situations in which an audience has a low threshold of proof, but generally, with an internal audience in a company, a group of potential investors, or an MBA class, proving a controversial position is hard work. To be persuasive you need to be able to perform an adequate analysis of the situation.

Developing a proof requires multiple skills. Yet confidence has a lot to do with it too. You need to keep in mind the standard of proof for a position on a case: reasonable and actionable, not scientific certainty. In other words, *are you confident that your argument takes into account the major pieces of evidence in the case?* as opposed to, *are you satisfied that your argument is true and excludes all other possible arguments?* Many new case method students tacitly assume that the standard of proof for an interpretation of a case is the scientific one. They try to build an airtight proof, working against a standard they can never achieve because the case content simply does not allow it.

A second point to keep in mind is a variation on the test of optimism versus pessimism: Is the glass half full or half empty? Students can focus obsessively on the half-empty part of the glass: what they don't know about the case. You are far better served by focusing on what you *do* know about the case and working from that to create more knowledge.

# CHAPTER 5

# PROBLEMS

What explains the success of one company and the missteps of another? In the U.S. airline industry, older "legacy" carriers such as United and American have experienced monumental difficulties, while some newer airlines like Southwest and Jet Blue have thrived. Why has Jet Blue fared far better than United? How can we explain these business results? We assume they aren't arbitrary—that it was just luck or circumstance that produced the outcomes. If that were true, business schools wouldn't exist. Some kind of logic underlies the end results. But what is that logic?

An entire category of case situations poses this question. Problems are outcomes or results of actions, processes, activities, or forces that we don't fully understand. Many problems concern business pathology: managers who perform poorly, change efforts that fail to achieve their goals, and companies that don't realize expected financial results. Understanding business success is just as important. Problem situations also fall between the poles of robust success and abject failure.

For the reader, cases about problems can be difficult because they simply describe a situation. Case protagonists and other significant characters tell us about a situation. Sometimes they have an acute awareness of the problem, and sometimes they have none at all. Although his company has had a sensational year, the president of a drug company knows he will have to adapt its strategy quickly to enjoy more good years. In a case set in Mexico, the main character, a top executive, is absolutely confident about the future of a business on which the firm has placed a big bet, but when we "look over his shoulder," we see a host of issues to be worried about. In cases involving success, characters often don't understand the relevant success factors, don't disclose them, or disagree about them.

Whatever the proportion of successful outcomes to unsuccessful ones in a case, you need to pull them apart and trace their causes. Problem diagnosis, especially of business pathology, leads to a critical second phase: figuring out how to fix the problem. It does little good to understand problems if there is nothing that can be done about them.

Problem analysis has five elements:

- Problem definition

- Diagnosis

- Cause-effect analysis

- Concepts and frameworks

- Actions

## PROBLEM DEFINITION

Recognizing problems can be tricky simply because they are rarely defined in a case. You can't begin a causal explanation until you know the problem that needs to be explained. A problem definition organizes, concentrates, and describes the critical effects that the main character in the case should be most concerned about. When preparing a case for discussion, you probably aren't going to write a formal definition but noting its major attributes is worthwhile. Here's an example:

Failed change effort:

- Second unsuccessful try

- The change is important to company

- Manager could lose job if third try fails

- She doesn't know reasons for failure

A *problem*, as defined in this book, requires a diagnosis based on *cause-and-effect analysis*. A *diagnosis* is a summary statement of the important causes. The problem situation in a case presents effects as well as information and data that make possible the diagnosis and a causal explanation: these causes acted in a certain way to produce these effects.

Problem analysis has a fundamental stability. The actions or activities that caused the effects of interest have been completed. The effects are not moving targets, and the case provides a record of them. As we will see, this is important because cause-and-effect analysis is about reasoning backward. Contrast this to cases involving decisions. Decisions are about the future and therefore cannot have the same level of certainty as cases set in the past. Complexity usually characterizes problem analysis. First of all, effects have to be pulled apart from causes. Second, complex effects imply multiple causes.

## CONCEPTS AND FRAMEWORKS

Cause-effect analysis relies on causal frameworks appropriate to the problem. Such frameworks allow us to make statements like "Allies and alliances assist leaders in making change" or "External and internal consistency are crucial to an effective strategy" and use these insights to investigate situations where they apply. Specialized methods—business frameworks, theories, and formulas—fill this role. One of the first things you need to consider when you recognize a problem is what causal frameworks are relevant to it. In a course, the professor may designate a framework to employ, or you may have to choose one or more from those you have learned.

## ACTIONS

Problem analysis yields actionable content—often a great deal of it. The problem definition about a failed change effort given above will lead to an analysis that has many actionable points such as in this example:

*The manager needs to build allies and networks in the field so that people get to know and trust her. She should use the networks to obtain feedback on her proposal so that it reflects conditions and needs of the distribution centers.*

You should reflect on your analysis and formulate actions that will improve the current state as it is described in the problem definition. Case discussions often take up action plans, and case examinations often call for them.

## RECOGNIZING A PROBLEM SITUATION

Let's consider some ways to identify problem situations. The case "Allentown Materials Corporation: The Electronic Products Division (Abridged)" begins with these two paragraphs:

*In July 1992, Don Rogers took a moment to reflect on the state of his organization. He had become the Vice President and General Manager of the Electronics Products Division (EPD) at Allentown Materials Corporation following his predecessor's untimely death two years before. The EPD faced a number of problems, and Rogers was not sure what he needed to do. He felt increasing pressure from headquarters. EPD was expected to continue to meet the corporation's 10% average annual growth rate and aggressive profit targets, despite increased competition in the electronic components industry. The division's performance had declined in 1991 and 1992 and most component manufacturers anticipated that they were competing for a shrinking total market. In addition,*

*EPD's reputation for delivery and service had slipped, and their number of missed commitments was very high. Rogers commented:*

> *I have had some difficult times in my division over the past two years. Our business is becoming fiercely competitive and this has led to a decrease in sales. To deal with the downturn in business we have reduced the number of people and expenses sharply. This has been painful, but I think these actions have stemmed the tide. We are in control again, but the business continues to be very competitive. Morale is low; there is a lot of conflict between groups that we can not seem to resolve. There is a lack of mutual confidence and trust. The organization is just not pulling together and the lack of coordination is affecting our ability to develop new products. Most of my key people believe that we are having conflicts because business is bad. They say that if business would only get better we will stop crabbing at each other. Frankly, I am not sure if they are right. The conflicts might be due to the pressures we are under but more likely they indicate a more fundamental problem. I need to determine if the conflict between groups is serious, so I can decide what I should do about it.*[1]

EPD is obviously a troubled organization. Notice the long characterization of the organization in the second paragraph. It provides some additional insights, including the presence of conflict and differing opinions about its root cause. Key managers attribute it to poor business conditions, while Rogers believes "a more fundamental problem" might be responsible. He does not suggest what that problem might be. You might not notice that the second paragraph consists of Rogers' opinions. As the head of the division, he may have a vested interest in portraying the situation in the best possible light. Yet blaming external factors is a way of avoiding responsibility. Does Rogers seem to be doing that?

Nothing in the opening of the case suggests a decision or an evaluation. Rogers needs to make some decisions, but he isn't ready to make them: "Rogers was not sure what he needed to do." This kind of uncertainty is a characteristic of problem situations. The protagonist is aware of a condition and has something important at stake, yet he doesn't have an explanation for the condition that can give him a basis for taking action.

Here is a disguised excerpt from the opening of a case:

> *In early 2000, Karl Biddleman, an assistant credit analyst for a European furniture manufacturer, StyleHouse, was reviewing the company's accounts receivable. He noted major changes in the accounts of Softline and Stella, two well-established furniture retailers. Both had large overdue balances. He decided he should bring the accounts to the attention of the credit manager.*

The excerpt suggests a routine business situation: a supplier with two delinquent customers. No decisions can be taken until Biddleman understands the two delinquent customers better. Then he can begin to answer questions:

- What should he tell his boss about the two customers?

- What should he conclude from the financial statements of the two retailers?

- Are their situations similar or different, and should StyleHouse treat them the same or differently?

This case is like a detective story that requires financial analysis to solve. When applied well, the analysis reveals the stories of two retailers pursuing very different courses and offering very different risks to their supplier, which in turn can lead to different decisions about how to handle the retailers. Precisely what decisions are most appropriate can be the subject of an interesting debate.

Please read the following disguised excerpts from two cases. The first is taken from the last section of a five-page case.

*With new managers, a recent restructuring, and the sale of Finesse Products, Cristine felt confident the company would return to profitability. It was her belief that the auditors would give the company a clean bill of health. However, in their report, they questioned whether Finesse was a "going concern." Such a qualification could be the kiss of death for relationships with lenders and suppliers, not to mention customers.*

The second excerpt is the third paragraph of a seven-page case.

*The Trout School was in trouble when Hart became principal. The previous year there had been several violent incidents, and the school had to shut down once because of a student demonstration and once because of a contract issue with the teachers. Academically, performance in the lower grades was marginally better, but the upper grades showed a decline. There was no question that the school was failing to achieve its goals.*

The first excerpt sets up a problem that turns on a difference of opinion. On one side is a company that has apparently made changes to put its financial house in order. On the other are auditors who have taken the grave step of questioning the company's ability to survive. The reader's task is to apply financial methods of analysis to gather an accurate reading of Finesse's current financial condition and its prospects for the future. The auditors might be right, and the company may need to be liquidated. If the company is right, it will need to provide a convincing case that the auditors have mis-read the data. Or the interpretation may fall in the middle, indicating seri-ous financial trouble but not the potentially terminal condition indicated by the auditors.

The second excerpt about the Trout School is an example of a case that defines the problem: "There was no question that the school was failing to achieve its goals." Even so, we need to be clear about the specific nature of the failure. A school's primary mission is to educate, and if test scores are an adequate measure of educational effectiveness, the school is indeed failing its students. We need to go further in the definition of the problem, how-ever. The degree of failure is serious because the school can't guarantee physical safety, and classrooms were shut down at least once. The reader's task with this case is to pinpoint the root causes of the problems and suggest ways to correct them quickly.

As mentioned earlier, you are rarely going to find a neat and inclusive definition of the problem in a case. The Trout School example is one of the exceptions. To trace causes, of course, you need to know what effect they produce. Your first step in a problem case is therefore to describe or define the problem. A general definition of a problem situation is something like this: What are the characteristics of the situation confronting the main char-acter that she should be *most* concerned about?

## MANY CAUSES OR FEW?

The problems in cases are complex. EPD, for instance, employs nearly a thousand people who work in different functions. Each of these employees has his or her own set of experiences and skills, and each contributes, for better or worse, some of both to the company's presence in a market, which in turn consists of customer and competitor organizations. The problem at EPD is therefore going to have multiple causes, and the same is true of other problem cases.

A question essential to diagnosis is, How many causes are sufficient? The first limit on the number of causes is the case itself. We'll see in some detail how the evidence in "Allentown" translates into a causal account. One limit is the small amount of information available about the changes in the mar-ket and the technologies involved in EPD products. Another is the dearth of financial data.

Despite the limits, evidence in a case can be the basis for many causes. In a business school course, you may learn various theories and be tempted to try to apply them all to a single case. You might think that more causes lead to a more comprehensive analysis. However, proliferation of causes leads quickly to confusion. A long list obscures the really important causes.

Another limit on the number of causes is translating the analysis into action. A causal account needs to be convincing, but it also needs to be actionable. An analysis that asserts many causes isn't going to be useful to the people responsible for doing something about a problem because it creates impossibly large and complex tasks.

The analysis should focus on those causes that have the greatest influence or impact on the problem. Diagnosing and fixing 85 percent of the problem is better than diagnosing 99 percent of it but failing to fix anything. There may be case method instructors who grade by counting causes, but I recommend that you follow the advice of a medieval thinker, William of Ockham, who devised the principle now known as "Ockham's razor": don't multiply entities (causes) unnecessarily.[2] In other words, strive for the least number of causes sufficient to account for the principal effects.

## HARD TIMES AT EPD

This chapter began with two paragraphs from "Allentown Materials Corporation: The Electronic Products Division (Abridged)." We will use the full case to explore how you can analyze a problem situation. Please read it now; otherwise, you'll learn little from the discussion that follows.

### *1. Situation*

The first section of "Allentown" lays out most of the major issues. Rogers is the general manager of a division in trouble. The industry in which it competes is much more competitive than it used to be, and the division's financial performance has slumped in the last two years. Yet corporate headquarters has set "aggressive profit targets." Within the division, conflict is ubiquitous and functional groups aren't coordinated. The last section of the case informs us that an annual meeting devoted to major organizational issues is approaching. We can infer that Rogers needs some answers before then.

Another element of the case can be missed because it is only implied: Rogers himself. The case is written from his point of view. Everything we know about the case we learn from him. But we shouldn't look just at what he's concerned with. We should take a step back from Rogers' point of view and look at him. He has been on the job for two years, yet he doesn't have any answers. His lack of insight is therefore an issue. As we explore the case, we should look at his contribution to the crisis.

Taking into account the first section only, we know Rogers is concerned about the recent financial numbers, but he can only influence them indirectly, through internal change. Of the issues mentioned at the beginning, he certainly should be concerned about:

- Outmoded competitive strategy

- Financial issue

- Rampant conflict and low morale

- Lack of coordination

- Stalled product development function

- Pressure from corporate

This seems like a decent problem definition to start with; of course, we can modify it as our work progresses.


## 2. Questions

The inventory of a case involving a problem looks for information relevant to the problem definition. An inventory of "Allentown" doesn't turn up specific sections that seem to be potentially more valuable to the analysis than the others. In addition, the case isn't particularly long, although it has a great deal of detailed information. The most sensible approach seems to be to read the case from beginning to end, taking notes that help us trace causes.

The problem definition implies essentially the same two questions about each of the characteristics:

Does the case contain enough information to provide a causal explanation of the characteristic?

If so, what is its cause?

We can rule out two areas of investigation after reading the case. Although the competitive landscape has changed and EPD's competitive strategy may be outmoded, we don't find information to support an investigation of strategy. Likewise, there is no information for analyzing financial causes. The case only provides a few numbers about the financial performance of the division. On the other hand, there seems to be information relevant to the other facets of the problem.

An academic course would no doubt include business concepts and methods useful for diagnosing this situation. As an example, leadership theories define the characteristics of an effective leader, and they could be our reference for studying Rogers' leadership. A great benefit of specialized concepts and methods is that they give you things to look for in a case. The sample analysis that follows employs some common principles of leadership and organizational behavior to diagnose the problem. The analysis would be richer if more use were made of specialized concepts and methods. However, that would require you to become familiar with them, and that isn't the point of this demonstration.

### 3. Hypothesis

Forming a hypothesis for a problem situation means developing a diagnosis. The diagnosis expresses the problem and its most significant causes. In practical terms, you develop a hypothesis for a problem by accumulation: you identify a possible cause, test it for substantial supporting evidence, and, if you find it, include the cause in the hypothesis.

The initial sorting out of causes, effects, and extraneous information can make establishing the first cause difficult. A helpful distinction is external versus internal—causes that operate outside the unit of analysis (such as EPD) and those that operate inside it. The location of causes varies in cases. You should be aware of this and be sure to consider the case in terms of where to look for causes. In a strategy case, there will be internal causes (e.g., the strategy itself and how aligned it is with the strategy) and some external ones (e.g., the industry, the market, and competitors).

In "Allentown," the competitive changes in the market are an external cause—and are a good place to start the analysis because you don't have to infer them. They are stated in the case. The change in the terms of competition and the new emphasis on product development—a function in which EPD is weak—subject the organization to competitive and economic stress. Corporate's insistence on aggressive profitability when the division is struggling is another negative influence.

In this case, though, the larger group of causes seems to be internal. Cause-and-effect analysis is reasoning backward, from effect to cause. In "Allentown," we think Don Rogers is one of the causes of the division's performance, so we have something on which to base a hypothesis and a starting point for exploring internal causes. Even if we conclude he is not a significant cause, working backward from him will teach us much about the situation.

### 4. PROOF AND ACTION

The proof of a diagnosis begins when we can identify a possible cause. Our hypothesis is that Rogers is a cause. Let's see if there is evidence to support that.

Rogers has definite personal strengths. He's technically knowledgeable, very bright, personable, and seemingly without hidden agendas. However, as a manager and a leader, he has weaknesses that are frustrating his own good intentions. He apparently didn't foresee the coming shift in the terms of competition, which suggests he's not especially close to the sales force. Now that the shift is obvious, he hasn't rallied the division to face the huge change from the predictability of a near monopoly to the demands of real competition. No one in the division, including Rogers himself, seems to have a sense of urgency about responding to the change.

Further, he doesn't listen in meetings and isn't curious about the views of division personnel. That deprives him of valuable information that could help him lead the division. Rogers isn't holding his managers accountable for their goals. Given his background, it isn't surprising that he remains involved in technical issues, but he doesn't seem to have the same interest in the other functions of the division. He is often absent working on corporate projects—despite the fact that his division is in serious trouble. The product development process, which is the key to the future of the business, is broken, and Rogers is not actively trying to fix it. He didn't even attend the monthly product development meetings, which were gridlocked by conflicting viewpoints, until his desperate marketing manager asked him.

Rogers transferred the divisional headquarters back to corporate, removing himself and the marketing people from close contact with other EPD groups. He also split marketing off from sales and product development. All of these organizational moves have backfired. Rogers needs to be physically present to learn about and lead a fractious organization. Market conditions require marketing to be closely coordinated with sales and the plants and everyone to be in close communication.

Rogers appears to have been suspicious of people and programs associated with his predecessor. He replaced a number of the top managers with people from outside the division, thus losing the experience and knowledge of the old managers and sending a message to the remaining employees that he doesn't have a high regard for people promoted by Bennett. These actions are a prescription for low morale. And he ended an organizational development project that addressed a number of the difficulties EPD is facing.

Two other inferences can be made about Rogers. Probably his biggest weakness is that he has very little awareness of the many issues that are hurting EPD's performance. He has little chance of having any impact on the problem unless he's motivated to look more closely at the organization he is supposed to be leading. The other conclusion comes from the case account of Rogers' experience. He was promoted to vice president and general manager because of his technical expertise, not his management experience or leadership abilities. In that respect, he isn't a good fit with the needs of the division.

With the evidence we have found, we can say Rogers is a cause of the problem. Now we need to look for more causes.

*Corporate Mistakes.* The fact that Rogers wasn't well qualified for the job raises the question of why he was promoted. That question leads us to think about the role of the corporate headquarters in Allentown.

Rogers' lack of management experience isn't his fault. We can infer that corporate didn't provide Rogers with any special training or support in his new position, and did nothing to help the organization cope with the sudden loss of their hard-charging former leader, Joe Bennett. They endorsed Rogers' new management team, which is sorely lacking in experience, and set unrealistic financial targets that the division is in no condition to achieve. As we look at corporate's actions closely, they appear to be a significant cause. Note that the case provides relatively little information about those actions, and the references are scattered.

Now we have two evidence-backed causes, Rogers and corporate.

*Culture and Conflict.* The information about Joe Bennett enables us to compare EPD under him and under Rogers. Bennett was the founder of the division and a smart, creative businessman. He moved his headquarters out of Allentown—we can speculate that he wanted to ensure that he was in complete charge of the division. He made all the important decisions and used everyone else to implement them. In other words, EPD was strictly a top-down organization, with an authoritarian leader at the apex and "political and manipulative" managers underneath.

Rogers had worked at Allentown and returned the EPD headquarters there after he was named the general manager. Allentown has a culture built on "close-knit family" relationships. Hierarchy isn't important, and people at all levels communicate freely and informally. The difference between the corporate and divisional cultures couldn't be starker. At EPD Rogers seems to believe that the division should run in the same collaborative manner as corporate. Nevertheless, the division is still the company that Bennett shaped. Besides the emphasis on hierarchy and bad habits such as politics and manipulative behavior, the EPD departments have no interest in working together. They aren't a close-knit family—that is certain. Thus the clash of cultures is a cause that may work in tandem with Rogers' management failures.

So far we haven't made much use of the information in the overviews of each of the major EPD departments in the section "Review of the Functional Departments in 1992." Because they take up nearly half of the length of the case, the descriptions must have significance for the analysis, unless their main purpose is to distract us. A good deal of the detail doesn't seem essential and could bog us down if we tried to work all of it into the analysis. After reading all of the descriptions, we need to take a step back and ask if there are issues that seem to apply to all of the departments—or if there are issues specific to the departments that could be significant.

*Misalignment.*   There are some issues in common, and they are easy to miss among the clutter of particulars. Every department or function is in conflict with the others. In fact, EPD seems less like an organization than a collection of warring tribes. Some of this can be explained by cultural collapse: the top-down organization has lost its linchpin, the authoritarian leader. Another factor is at work, however. All of the functions are misaligned in several dimensions. First, their incentives are different. Second, there are no clear definitions of responsibility and accountability. Third, there is a discrepancy and inequality in the perceived importance of the functions in the division and at corporate, as well as big differences in the experience and length of service of key personnel. And finally, the functions are physically dispersed in a way that doesn't make sense for the work that needs to be done.

I'll end the analysis here, although we haven't touched on all possibilities. Our argument of primary causes looks like the following:

### PROBLEM

- Declining performance

- Rampant conflict

- Lack of coordination

- Stalled product development function

- Poor leadership

### EXTERNAL CAUSES

- New terms of competition

- Corporate mistakes

### INTERNAL CAUSES

- Rogers' mistakes and limitations

- Cultural differences

- Conflict

- Misalignment

We can safely assume that more causes remain to be identified in "Allentown." A particular leadership paradigm would use an entirely different set of terms to diagnose Rogers' actions and Bennett's legacy. Another framework might highlight the aspects of organizational structure that give rise to the problem. These different perspectives are complementary, not competitive, however.

*Actions.* The diagnosis of the problem at EPD is a blueprint for action. Every cause is a target of change. Action planning should include steps for all of the causes except the new competitive terms; we don't have enough information to suggest changes to the division strategy. Because Rogers is the leader of the division, much of the action planning focuses on him. He is an important part of the solution to internal conflict and misalignment. To improve the latter, he can begin the process of changing incentives so that they motivate people to work for the same end and move people back from corporate into EPD facilities, including himself. He can also work on changing the organizational culture, but that will take time.

But Rogers' first steps probably should center on himself. Because he seems to have no clear sense of his strengths and weaknesses, he needs to assess both. Hiring a coach would give him an unbiased outside perspective. He can make a start on bringing everyone at EPD together by calling for—perhaps demanding—a shared urgency. The division is headed in the wrong direction, market conditions aren't favorable, and everyone's job could be at stake. That situation doesn't seem to be on anyone's mind, and Rogers should make sure it is front and center. Rogers needs to break out of his self-imposed isolation to cultivate allies and involve the division in the shaping of a vision. He should use his relationships at corporate to get them to ease off and lobby for their support of the changes he must make.

And these are just a few of Rogers' action items that you would want to consider. The hardest part of articulating a plan for Rogers and the division would be to keep it from becoming voluminous.

## ALTERNATIVES AND OPEN QUESTIONS

Beyond causes, the analysis of "Allentown" could delve into the comparative influence of the causes. In other words, Which causes make the greatest contribution to the problem? In this area, sharp differences of opinion are likely.

Each time I read the case, I become more convinced that corporate has the largest share of the responsibility for EPD's troubles. Rogers' many mistakes are of course not attributable to anyone else, but he would never have been in a position to make them if corporate executives had understood the division and its needs better. They condoned Bennett's one-man operation, probably because he produced consistently good numbers. A succession plan for Bennett's eventual departure didn't exist, apparently, and that is further evidence of senior management's detachment from this business unit.

On the other hand, from the information on the EPD departments, we can discern weaknesses within each of them. The overall picture makes one wonder whether an experienced leader with a realistic view of the organization could do better than Rogers in just two years. Bennett created an organization at the extreme of one-man rule. He had to have controlled hiring and promotion, as he did everything else at EPD. It's possible that people willing to work in an organization that gave them no authority and didn't need creative thinking might not be the people who would want to take on the new conditions of the market. Under any circumstances, the transition to another leader wouldn't have been easy.

The larger point is that for all the clarity we can realize through careful study of this case, the grey areas persist and warrant more study, reflection, and debate.

### NOTES

1. Michael Beer and Jennifer M. Suesse, "Allentown Materials Corporation: The Electronic Products Division (Abridged)," Case 9-498-047 (Boston: Harvard Business School Publishing, 1997), 1.

2. Paul Vincent Spade, "William of Ockham," in *The Stanford Encyclopedia of Philosophy (Fall 2006 Edition)*, ed. Edward N. Zalta, http://plato.stanford.edu/archives/fall2006/entries/ockham.

# CHAPTER 6

# DECISIONS

Cases involving an explicit decision are a staple of management education. By *explicit decision*, I mean a case built around a stated decision—one not implied or subordinate to another issue such as a problem diagnosis. That's an important distinction to keep in mind, since almost every business case can be talked about in terms of a decision. The following is a sentence from the first paragraph of the sample case for this chapter, "General Motors: Packard Electric Division."

> *The Product, Process, and Reliability (PPR) committee, which had the final responsibility for the new product development process, had asked [David] Schramm for his analysis and recommendation as to whether Packard Electric should commit to the RIM grommet for a 1992 model year car.*[1]

David Schramm has to make a decision about the recommendation he will give a company committee, and the rest of the text is concerned with his choice—this is what is meant by a decision situation. Cases of this type have as much to do with how to make a decision as they do with a particular decision. They may teach you about sales or hedge funds, but they'll also teach you about the process of deciding.

Decision analysis has five elements:

- Options

- Criteria

- Analysis of options

- Recommendation

- Actions

## OPTIONS

A decision requires concrete options; otherwise, there is no decision to be made. Not all cases define decision options, but many do. If your first reading of a case is lockstep linear—from page one to the end—you may not learn the options until the very end of the case. That diminishes the usefulness of your first reading. You can't begin to consider what decision may be appropriate and what you need to know to choose it unless you know the choices.

Cases often don't provide the options in early sections, or they appear to but omit significant additional information. Here are the critical sentences from the opening of a marketing case:

> *In 1990, the Nestlé Refrigerated Food Company (NRFC) contemplated the introduction of a refrigerated pizza product to the U.S. market . . . Cunliffe [the decision maker] sought to further opportunities for Nestlé's growth in refrigerated pasta. Prior to launching a pizza product, however, he knew he had to take a hard look at the numbers to ensure its business viability.*[2]

The opening seems to propose a simple yes-no decision: launch a refrigerated pizza product or not. Later, the case adds a twist. The decision has a second level: Should the company launch a refrigerated pizza with one topping or provide a kit with multiple toppings? If you don't skim the case before beginning a serious analysis of it, you won't be aware of this complication and will have to reread the case in light of it. At the same time, you need to consider whether this complication is meant to distract you from concentrating on the basic decision: Should this company launch a refrigerated pizza product at all?

The sentence quoted from "General Motors: Packard Electric Division" refers to an innovative new part that would substitute for the current one used in automobiles. A reader who goes straight through this case doesn't discover the three specific options Schramm is pondering until the last section of the case text.

When you realize the case you are reading is a decision situation, you need to hunt for the decision alternatives. In the instance of the pizza case, you would be well advised to think for a moment about the priority of the decisions suggested in the case. Launching a new type of pizza might be the wise thing to do for NRFC and duplicate its first-mover success in the refrigerated pasta product category. It might also be a mistake. However, if you become embroiled in the decision about alternative pizza products without first making the fundamental choice, you may be missing a large part of the case. Of course, the two decisions might actually be aspects of a single one. In the RIM grommet case, you need to know the particular options the company is considering as soon as possible. The opening of the case implies a yes-no decision, but at the end, you find there is an option in the middle. It may be a terrible choice, but you need to know it exists and understand whether it meets your criteria better than the other options.

# CRITERIA

A rational decision can't be made without criteria. For example, to decide whether to extend more credit to a retailer, a supplier might use the following considerations to make the decision:

- The retailer must be in sound financial condition.

- It must be well managed.

- It must have a good credit history.

- It must have long-term value to supplier.

The criteria you use for resolving decision situations depend on both specialized tools and the circumstances of the case. "Sound financial condition" is not very meaningful until financial metrics such as cash flow and capital structure give it concrete meaning. "Long-term value to the supplier" is similarly abstract, but sales history as well as information about the retailer's future prospects and the overall market give the words tangible meaning.

Criteria profoundly influence decision making. They should be relevant, they should be kept to the minimum necessary for a sound decision, and they should be able to relate a significant amount of the available evidence to the options. First of all, they have to be relevant to the decision and the situation. Relevance is defined by circumstances of the case. Some criteria will crop up frequently—cost and profitability are two. Others will be very specific to a case or category of cases. A case we will study later in this chapter has as a criterion the reliability of a new manufacturing process. Second, decision analysis should use the minimum number of criteria necessary for a credible recommendation. Too many criteria are just as much a liability as too few. Too few criteria lead to an inadequate recommendation and a weak evidence base. Too many criteria produce so much fragmentation and confusion that a clear-cut recommendation becomes impossible. And finally, just because a criterion is relevant to the decision doesn't mean that it's useful. It must be able to connect substantial evidence to the decision being considered.

Some guesswork is involved in choosing criteria. You should be alert to clues in the case about which criterion may yield the most informative results. Say the case about the supplier's credit decision has little text, one exhibit on the market, and several financial exhibits. The case is telling you that the most fruitful criterion may be the one involving the analysis of financial data. Still, you should not forgo applying other criteria that you believe are relevant, even if initially there doesn't appear to be a lot of information to work with. Sometimes a criterion will help you pull together related pieces of evidence that are hard to recognize because they occur in different sections of the case and in the exhibits.

## ANALYSIS OF OPTIONS

Once you know the decision options and have selected some of the criteria (you don't need all of them to start work), you begin looking at the case information in relation to the criteria. Gradually you will bring into focus the decision option that seems to create the best fit between the criteria and the facts.

Let's say you are trying to decide whether to extend additional credit to a retailer. "Sound financial condition" is one of the standards. Using data from the case, relevant financial tools supply information on the financial health of the company. Say the numbers indicate the retailer has a serious short-term cash shortage. Then you find it has an operating loss for the previous year, apparently because it has reduced prices to clear existing inventory. None of this seems to be good news, but the case notes a mild recession has been in place over the last few years, and numbers from an exhibit show an industrywide drop in sales. Now we look at data on capital structure and see that this particular company has kept its balance sheet largely free of debt. It has prudently maintained the capacity to borrow to cover operating losses in circumstances like the ones that now prevail. Moreover, the recession is ending. The weight of the financial evidence seems to indicate that managers of the company are operating wisely under difficult circumstances.

So the criterion "sound financial condition" aligns the evidence with the decision to grant additional credit. Nonetheless, the criterion does have negative findings. (See exhibit 6-1 for a summary of the positive and negative factors.) Merely applying criteria and business methods doesn't make

**EXHIBIT 6-1**

### Criterion: sound financial condition

| Negative factors | Positive factors |
| --- | --- |
| • Reduced cash flow | • Reduced inventory during period of slow sales |
| • Current operating loss | • Little debt; high degree of financial flexibility |
|  | • Recession ending; sales should increase |

the decision. You still have to interpret the results. Often, you will face mixed results within each criterion, as with the financial standard we just applied. And the results of different criteria may clash. Let's say the financial condition and management criteria confirm a decision to extend credit, but on the credit history standard, the retailer doesn't look good, and its long-term value to the supplier is uncertain. You have a decision of your own: Which of the criteria are most important and is the evidence associated with them strong?

In a time-constrained situation, as in a written examination, you need to commit to a hypothesis as quickly as you can. In such situations, you need to conserve as much time as possible for writing. You need to be alert for the fact threshold that allows you to commit to a hypothesis about the decision. *Fact threshold* simply means that you have enough evidence that fits a decision option to give you confidence in the option. Your task changes then—from testing for the criteria-evidence fit with a decision to aligning as much evidence as possible with your preferred option.

## RECOMMENDATION

The object of decision analysis is to recommend the best choice among the available options. As a hypothesis, a specific recommendation gives you a way of thinking about the case facts that isn't available when you don't make a commitment. It sharpens your focus and poses the challenge of proving it. When you have succeeded in aligning what you believe is persuasive evidence with a decision option, the hypothesis becomes your recommendation.

The advocacy of a decision doesn't mean you cover up its downside. In fact, acknowledging the downside enhances the recommendation by helping the decision maker anticipate and prepare for it.

## ACTIONS

The purpose of a decision action plan is to implement the decision as effectively as possible. That single goal distinguishes decision action plans from problem and evaluation action plans, which frequently have multiple goals.

Developing implementation steps can be frustrating because the case can provide little explicit information directly related to the steps. Some creativity can help fill the void. So can recognizing conditions in the case relevant to implementation. In the "General Motors" case, the innovative product that is the subject of the decision is certain to cause problems for the manufacturing operation of the company. Whether the product is introduced immediately or deferred for a year, those problems remain. So, the action plan for any of the decision choices has to include steps to resolve them.

## THE RIM CONTROVERSY

"General Motors: Packard Electric Division" concerns a wholly owned supplier to the automotive giant, General Motors, and an innovative new component with an odd name, the "RIM grommet." Please read it now; otherwise, you'll learn little from the discussion that follows.

### 1. Situation

The opening paragraph is a minefield for the inexperienced case method student. The very first sentence has a reference to a glossary in the appendix. The diligent reader can easily become immersed in the glossary, studying the terms in order to understand them when they are used in the text. The next paragraph has a reference to Exhibit 1, a GANTT chart. The exhibit is just as much a time sink as the glossary. The two have one other thing in common: they are meaningless at this point. They can double or triple the time it takes to get through the opening section. The opening of this case is one of the best illustrations of why worrying about the big picture before immersion in the details can make case analysis cleaner and faster.

By jumping directly to the back of the case, a reader can quickly confirm that the situation is a decision. The final section, "Schramm's Options," lists his three alternatives. What difference does it make whether you read the opening and concluding sections of the case first or read the case from beginning to end? If you start from the beginning, you read the entire case knowing only that Schramm must make a decision. You'll be looking for decision options while absorbing information pertinent to the decision. At the end of the case, you find that the work you have done on choices has been a waste of time. When you read the opening and concluding sections together, you can organize your reading of the case around the options. You won't always find decision alternatives neatly packaged at the end of the case, but they'll often be stated somewhere in it.

One strategy for making decision analysis easier is to see if you can defer or eliminate one of the choices. The number *three* has a strange magic. In cases, you'll often find that decisions have three choices. By eliminating one, you can simplify your work. Comparing two alternatives is far easier than comparing three.

## 2. Questions

Let's take stock of what we know and can infer from just the first and last sections of the case text. We know that two groups have conflicting views. Schramm's decision options correlate with the conflict. One option represents the views of each party, and one is a compromise. When you read the description of the compromise, "parallel development," it sounds complex. It would create even more SKUs and therefore increase engineering time and cost, two problems the parties are trying to solve. It would force Packard Electric to accommodate two separate assembly operations, putting even more pressure on manufacturing. And it might be difficult for Packard's customer, GM, to handle two different versions of the same part. The decision maker, Schramm, certainly has to wonder whether the new process would receive the commitment it needs from manufacturing if the old process was still running. The compromise option seems, well, compromised.

Of course, there is an entirely different way of assessing the options. An exclusive commitment to the new component might be too risky, with both Packard Electric and the customer paying a high price for a flawed manufacturing process. In that light, delaying adoption of the part for a year could be the lowest-risk option, allowing time to perfect the process and get yields up. Or the middle way could be repositioned, with the RIM the first-line product and the old component available as a backup in case of problems with the RIM.

The two different scenarios can confuse the analysis. Rather than investigating all three options at once, we can start by concentrating on the two "pure" options, to forgo the RIM grommet for the upcoming production year or commit to it completely. To investigate these two alternatives, a couple of questions seem critical:

- What are the advantages of the RIM grommet to Packard and its customers?

- What are its disadvantages?

These seem to be questions we should answer. But it would be helpful to have a more specific meaning for "advantages" and "disadvantages." The opening and closing sections have enough information to be more specific:

- The new component must offer significant value to the customer. The component seems to have some value because the customer wants it.

- It must have a positive impact on Packard Electric costs, at least in the medium to long term. The first and last sections don't mention cost, but it's always a good idea to consider it.

- The problems it causes for PEs and the customer's manufacturing processes must be manageable.

To be more useful for case analysis, the possible criteria can be converted into questions:

- How much value does the RIM offer the customer?

- How much can the RIM reduce PE costs?

- How bad are the manufacturing problems associated with the RIM and can they be solved before the new model year?

## 3. Hypothesis

Surveying the case, we find several sections that seem to offer information we will need:

- "Packard Electric's Products"

- "The RIM Grommet"

- "Views on the RIM Grommet"

We are trying to answer specific questions about the new product. We have a purpose and want to achieve it as quickly as possible. You can read only the sections listed above, or you can read the whole case, being careful to insulate yourself as much as possible from irrelevancies. If you maintain a disciplined focus, you can read a case in any way you chose. The best approach is to experiment and see what works best for you.

Reading the three sections listed earlier, we learn the following points, which raise further questions:

### VALUE

- The RIM better accommodates increasing electrical content of vehicles.

- It provides a better water seal (reduces dealer costs/increases end user satisfaction).

- Does increasing electrical content and better quality have value to GM beyond the obvious?

### COST

- Cost savings on water seal repairs (can this be quantified?)

- Big reduction in SKUs

- Big reduction in engineering time

- Can total savings be quantified?

MANUFACTURING

- Requires additional investment, new technology, and workforce training

- Dramatically reduces SKUs

- How hard are the manufacturing-related problems?

It may seem premature, but we have enough information now to put forward a hypothesis: *Go with the RIM grommet for the upcoming model year.* Now case analysis can focus on the evidence for the hypothesis.

## 4. Proof and Action

Building a proof from this case isn't easy. The exhibits are hard to interpret. Also, they address two different issues, one of which is never directly mentioned or addressed. The exhibits that apply to the implicit issue serve as "noise" for analysis of the first issue, the RIM grommet. Finally, the case has various traps designed to appeal to the conscientious student, and these create additional noise that distracts the reader and obscures the important data and information. The exhibits are much easier to work with when you know what you are looking for. From the three high-value sections, we can conclude that the RIM grommet has many advantages, some fairly obvious, some not.

- The RIM has double the wire capacity of the old component, which is critical because the electrical content of automobiles is increasing at a rapid pace.

- The component is a better seal against water than the old component. Water leakage has been the subject of customer complaints and is costly for dealers to repair. It may also reduce end user satisfaction and brand loyalty.

- It is less prone to breakage.

- It simplifies the customer's manufacturing process and allows more design flexibility to include desirable vehicle features.

- The best proxy for customer value is the fact that GM is willing to pay a premium for the RIM.

- The RIM part will lower Packard's overall costs by reducing initial design costs, the number of Engineering Change Orders (ECOs), and the number of SKUs.

Despite these clear advantages, they would be more forceful if they were backed by estimates of possible savings. A financial argument without numbers is *not* convincing. Throughout, the case refers to costs and furnishes some numbers that can be used to prepare estimates. The analytical work is to pull out numbers, group them in the proper category, and calculate savings. There seem to be four categories of cost savings:

### REDESIGN

IHG, the old part, has to be redesigned every two to three years, with $30,000 in engineering costs, totaling $43,000 with retooling. RIM development has $5,000 in engineering costs, for a total of $12,000 with tooling. RIM needs less frequent redesign. Also flexibility makes it suitable for different model cars. If RIM is redesigned at half the frequency of the IHG, or every 6 years, cost savings will be $71,000 ($43,000 × 2 − $12,000).

### ENGINEERING CHANGE ORDERS

Because of flexibility, RIM will reduce ECOs by an unknown percentage. Current ECO costs are huge: $24,000,000 per year ($50 per hour × 500 engineers × 50 percent time or 960 hours per year). A mere 25 percent reduction will amount to an annual savings of $6,000,000!

### SKUS

The number of SKUs will decline from 45,000. Assign an arbitrary cost per year to maintain an SKU of $5.00 and assume an SKU reduction of 50 percent. Annual savings are $112,500.

### IHG VERSUS RIM REPAIR COSTS

- IHG
  - IHG defect rate is 12 percent at the Mexican plant in week 52 of production. With a production cost of $4.40 and 70,000 units in volume, the loss is $36,960.
  - Defect rate at assembly is 1 percent in week 48 after kick-off. With 2 hours of labor at $45 per hour and 70,000 units in volume, the loss is $63,000.
  - Dealer records in 1989 list 250 repairs related to IHG. Losses are $35,000 (4 hours labor × $35 per hour × 250).

- Overall, annual repair costs for IHG are $134,960.

- RIM
  - Repair cost for RIM is $180. RIM is more reliable. With the defect rate reduced to half that of IHG, repair costs will be $63,000.
  - Repair cost savings from RIM will be $71,960.

## TOTAL ESTIMATED SAVINGS FROM RIM

- $6,296,000 per year.

The ECO category turns out to be the bonanza for RIM advocates. Even if the savings are much less than the estimate, the total annual savings attributable to the RIM are large.

When we expand the analysis to other sections and exhibits, we find additional evidence to support the hypothesis. For example, the second section, "Packard Electric Background," reveals that GM has been losing market share to Japanese manufacturers. Thus, the RIM grommet innovation can have a small but meaningful role in enhancing GM's competitiveness. It can increase the build quality (less leakage and breakage) and allow more electrical content. The combination of higher quality and greater product functionality contributes to GM's competitiveness in an increasingly global market.

The emotional or attitudinal significance of the RIM situation may be greater than its technical and financial virtues. GM is the parent company of Packard Electric, and it is showing signs of a competitive stress, losing 11 percent of market share in nine years. Meanwhile, PE has had a healthy growth rate. Is PE complacent about the importance of innovation to its continued success and that of the parent company? You certainly don't get the impression that there is a sense of urgency about it.

An action plan for the immediate adoption of the RIM would make the manufacturing issues an urgent priority. The product development engineers should assist manufacturing to make the RIM process scaleable and reliable, the two principal production issues. Schramm should set an example by putting himself on a cross-functional team responsible for RIM manufacturing, and all the product development engineers involved should go out of their way to cooperate with the manufacturing team.

The potential cost savings of the RIM justify hiring more engineers. PE might even consider buying the small vendor that makes RIM machines and have their people focus exclusively on working out the process and increasing reliability. The action plan would set a schedule with milestones. Given the circumstances, the team in charge should identify the plan's most serious risks and develop a contingency plan to deal with them. The cost savings can also justify budget reserves to fund the contingency measures.

And there is no question that regardless of the RIM decision, PE must do something about product development, starting with the casual or even indifferent attitude toward innovation. A major part of the action plan should propose a new structure for product development and an effort throughout PE to educate employees on the importance of innovation.

## 5. Alternatives and Open Questions

Value to the customer and cost strongly support Schramm's first option. Is it then the right answer to this case? Strictly speaking, the decision isn't about whether to commit to the RIM, although Schramm fears that it may fall by the wayside if the company doesn't push ahead with it for 1992. The decision is about *when* to commit, and that is still controversial and can be argued from different points of view.

In this case, the manufacturing criterion identifies a problem with an immediate shift to the RIM technology. The new fabrication process is not yet ready for full-scale use, and there are serious questions about reliability. The manufacturing operation has no experience with it, and the plant must be retooled. Only one vendor produces the kind of RIM machine PE needs, but it is so small that it probably can't provide much support to PE to solve process issues.

Although the case suggests that these problems are not insurmountable, nothing leads us to believe that they will be solved in time for the upcoming model year. Because of the frosty relationship between the product development and manufacturing engineers, they might not cooperate. Manufacturing definitely has legitimate grounds for being unhappy. They didn't promise anything to the customer, but they are mainly responsible for making good on Product Development's promises. Finally, breakdowns and failures in RIM production could cause grave difficulties for GM that it can ill afford. The middle option of parallel manufacturing processes can be argued as a safer approach than a complete commitment to the RIM for the upcoming model year. Staying with the old part for a year might be the safest of all the options. Someone favoring this option might ask, Is a one-year delay really a serious problem, considering the risks of immediate adoption?

In the "Allentown" case studied in the last chapter, the failed leadership of the main character is undoubtedly a cause of the problem. Yet people can disagree about the extent of his responsibility in relation to other causes such as the executives at corporate headquarters and the sudden change in the terms of competition. Don't assume that because you have arrived at a fact-based conclusion about a situation—even one as strong as the argument for the RIM grommet—that everything is settled and all loose ends have been tied up. There is uncertainty in all case situations, and there will always be different ways of looking at it and different ideas about how to deal with it.

## NOTES

1. Steven C. Wheelwright and Geoffrey K. Gill, "General Motors: Packard Electric Division," Case 9-691-030 (Boston: Harvard Business School Publishing, 1999), 1.

2. Marie Bell and V. Kasturi Rangan, "Nestlé Refrigerated Foods (A): Contadina Pasta & Pizza," Case 9-595-035 (Boston: Harvard Business School Publishing, 1994), 1.

# CHAPTER 7

# EVALUATIONS

Evaluations are judgments about the worth, value, or effectiveness of a performance, act, or outcome of some kind. In a case, an evaluation can be explicitly stated. "Rob Parson at Morgan Stanley (A)" concerns the dilemma Paul Nasr faces in evaluating Parson, a star performer who has nonetheless racked up "among the most negative" evaluations from peers, subordinates, and superiors Nasr has ever seen.[1] Evaluations can also be implied as in "Empresas ICA and the Mexican Road Privatization Program." Members of ICA's board of directors are giddy with the prospects of the road concession business in Mexico, believing that "the company's continued success seemed secure for years to come."[2] The case implicitly begs a question: Is building and operating private toll roads as certain an opportunity as the board believes it is? Readers need to assess how good the business is now and will be in the future, using the facts present in the case.

An evaluation isn't a collection of pros and cons or strengths and weaknesses. To be actionable, an evaluation needs a concisely expressed bottom-line conclusion:

- The company's strategy was effective until new entrants were able to deliver the same service at lower prices.

- Despite a few setbacks and false starts, Carrie Liu has exercised excellent leadership since being promoted.

- On balance, the finance minister's decision was the best one available, although it does have significant risks.

## ELEMENTS OF AN EVALUATIVE ANALYSIS

Like any conclusion about a case, evaluative statements need to be backed by an analysis. The analysis must include factors that support the overall evaluation and those that do not. The latter condition is likely to be true of every evaluative case and analysis. In the real world, perfect performances and flawless acts aren't frequent occurrences. In fact, the negative side of an evaluation can be the most valuable. A performance appraisal of an individual is a familiar example. If you were to respond to "Rob Parson at Morgan Stanley (A)" with a positive evaluation of him, you would need to include and account for the bad reviews he has received. If you took the opposite position, you would want to acknowledge his strengths. One reason to cover weaknesses in the assessment of performance is to help the subject improve, whether it's an individual, a work team, or an organization.

An evaluation has six elements:

- Criteria

- Terms

- Evaluative analysis

- Bottom-line judgment

- Qualifications

- Actions

## Criteria

Clear and appropriate criteria are critical and have a powerful impact on evaluation, just as they do on decision analysis. Everything said about decision criteria in chapter 6 applies to criteria used for evaluations. They should be:

- Relevant to the performance and situation

- The minimum number needed for a credible result

- Productive when applied to the case

The two sources of criteria are the situation in the case and specialized methods. Interestingly, the assessment of various types of business-related performances has attracted much study and research. To pick criteria for a business-related evaluation, theories and frameworks specific to a performance or act are often available. In fact, it may be challenging to decide which one to choose. In an academic course, a mandated theory may spare you that choice. Relevance to the case situation will exclude some frameworks or parts of them, but be careful that you don't try to use as many as possible under the assumption that more means better. Remember that employing many criteria usually leads to an incoherent analysis. As a rule, you should use the fewest criteria necessary to capture the essential issues.

Criteria that can be quantitatively measured are a good place to start an assessment. They can provide a useful initial reading of the situation and a concrete foundation on which to build. A place to start work on "Empresas ICA and the Mexican Road Privatization Program" would be financial analysis of the road concession business to evaluate its profitability.

## *Terms*

Appropriate terms are needed to express an evaluation. Performance appraisals often have multipoint scales for expressing the effectiveness of an individual, but in cases you are probably more likely to use terms like "good" and "bad" or "effective" and "ineffective." You will often need additional terms that fall between the two primary terms. For instance, an element of a company's market strategy might have both positive and negative effects. You may also need a term that allows you to describe aspects of a performance or act that are ambiguous. You can't always neatly classify everything as positive, negative, or in between. A manager might take actions that aren't effective or ineffective leadership because the results aren't yet in, for example.

## *Evaluative Analysis*

Evaluations are organized according to criteria such as "economic consequences" or "impact on collaborators." Discussion of each criterion is divided into the terms being used, such as "advantages" or "disadvantages." The analysis works its way through the criteria, building up evidence for the positive and negative sides of each. A one-sided analysis or one that dismisses any factor opposed to the overall evaluation simply isn't fulfilling the task. The comparative *quantity* of positive and negative evidence doesn't decide the bottom-line judgment—the comparative *importance* of the criteria and evidence does.

## *Bottom-line Judgment*

An evaluation without an overall or bottom-line judgment is like a decision analysis that doesn't include a recommendation. An evaluative analysis has a conclusion, just as decision and problem analyses do. Otherwise, it is merely a group of statements about the subject. In cases and the real world, bottom-line judgments are essential because they make the evaluation actionable. An assessment of Rob Parson might point to ways he can be more effective within the firm and thus increase his value to it (and, not insignificantly, reduce the stress on him and others that results from the turmoil he seems to provoke). The optimism of the ICA board about road concessions may be justifiable, but a fact-based evaluation could call attention to vulnerabilities the board should be aware of and prepare for.

## *Qualifications*

Qualifications state factors that are not part of the evaluation but that have a significant effect on it. A qualification could be a condition that needs to exist to make the overall evaluation valid. A marketing program judged as effective could be subject to this qualification: "As long as the company is willing to support a separate sales force for it, the program will be an asset." A qualification about a national policy could state: "The national government needs to keep tight control over inflation for the policy to have the intended effect."

## *Actions*

In both the real world and in cases, the result of an evaluation can drive meaningful action. A manager can be promoted or not; a company can change a strategy or maintain the status quo; the leadership of a country can safely follow up a decision with a series of measures or backtrack quickly.

## LOOKING AT BOTH SIDES

Fact-based evaluation demands thoroughness, a careful accounting against the criteria that shows where the subject of the evaluation measures up to the chosen standards and where it doesn't. Evaluation is very different from the other types of analysis. In problem diagnosis, you are concerned with locating and proving the primary causes of a problem; you don't, and shouldn't, provide a discussion about why a cause might not account for the effect. In decision analysis, you are concerned with recommending the best option and proving it; you should acknowledge the major downsides of your recommendation and respond to them. Evaluation, though, needs to encompass everything relevant to a performance, act, or outcome—good, bad, in between, and ambiguous.

Case-based evaluation encourage two habits of thinking that are invaluable to business school students:

- It enforces analytical honesty, making you pursue a more complex persuasive task than simply advocating a single point of view with no or very few qualifications.

- It requires you to consider the import of evidence opposed to your overall evaluation.

## RESISTERS AND RESISTANCE

"Allentown Materials Corporation: The Electronic Products Division (Abridged)" (see the case reprinted in this book) concerns a troubled organization as seen through the eyes of its head, Don Rogers. The case is used in chapter 5 to explore a problem situation. If you haven't read the case, please do so now. The following discussion requires familiarity with the case.

### 1. Situation

"Allentown" is a problem situation. Rogers, the protagonist, describes the many adversities of the division he's leading. A great deal of the case has to do with Rogers' actions (and inaction) in the two years he's been in charge at the Electronic Products Division (EPD). Because the case has much information about Rogers' performance, we can also look at it as an evaluation: How effective a leader is Don Rogers? Cases about performances, acts that have already taken place, and outcomes can be evaluative when a question asks for that type of analysis.

### 2. Questions

For the assessment of Rogers' leadership, we can choose simple terms: "effective," "ineffective," and "uncertain" or "ambiguous." Simple terms, and few of them, give clarity to assessments.

I said earlier that for business-related evaluations, many theories and frameworks are available. Few facets of business have been studied as intensely as leadership. Rather than introduce a leadership theory here, I'll designate some commonsense standards of leadership as well as borrow a piece of a well-known framework.

A leader of a division of a company should be accountable for its business results, and the case provides some information about them. However, because many variables other than leadership affect financial results, they don't qualify as a criterion. Instead, they can be used as partial and indirect evidence for the quality of leadership.

A leader surely needs some special skills. She should be able to communicate and motivate. She should be able to translate business knowledge, technical knowledge, and an awareness of the environment into decisions that further competitiveness. Organizations always confront obstacles, and their leaders must be able to detect them and mobilize people and resources to find a way around them. In addition, from what we learn on the first page of the case, EPD seems to need change. John Kotter's eight-step process is a handy framework for evaluating how well Rogers leads change. The eight steps are:

1. Establish a sense of urgency.

2. Form a powerful guiding coalition.

3. Create a vision.

4. Communicate that vision.

5. Empower others to act on the vision.

6. Plan for and create short-term wins.

7. Consolidate improvements and keep the momentum for change moving.

8. Institutionalize the new approaches.[3]

We'll group the steps under "Change skills" and employ only those that fit the circumstances.

We should see if any qualifications ought to be included in the evaluation. We do this not only to be faithful to the facts but also to ensure that actions taken on the basis of the evaluation accomplish what they are supposed to. It makes no sense to try to improve a leader in an area of performance for which he isn't responsible. Let's say some employees create conflict and the leader can't control them. But let's also say that the employees are the favorites of senior managers, and they ignore the leader's thoughtful attempts to work out the conflicts. If the meddling of the senior managers isn't taken into account, the assessment of the leader will be distorted and could lead to actions that have no impact on the situation or make it worse.

We start, then, with three criteria to assess Rogers and state them as questions:

• How good are his leadership skills?

• How well does he overcome obstacles?

• Are his change skills effective?

In addition, the analysis will be open to qualifications.


## 3. Hypothesis

Each of the evaluation criteria is a kind of analytic filter on the case situation. When we look at the case facts through the lens of relevant standards of performance, information should pop out.

The performance of the division isn't good. Sales are down 10 percent in the two years Rogers has been in charge, and operating income is down 160 percent. A number of factors are behind these numbers. The market has just recently become more competitive. Joe Bennett, the previous leader, created and maintained a near-monopoly and apparently didn't have to cope with much change in the competitive landscape. A major triggering event, the end of the Cold War, surprised even expert observers, as did the rapid growth of the PC market. There is no evidence that corporate executives saw the change coming and prepared Rogers for it. Clearly, if Rogers' leadership is a cause of the plummeting business results, it isn't the only one. Nevertheless, the business results combined with the issues cited early in the case suggest a hypothesis that Rogers has not performed well.

## 4. Proof

Our task in this phase is to make our way through the case gathering evidence on each of the criteria. Given the hypothesis, we will expect to find mostly negative evidence.

*Leadership Skills.* Rogers does have strengths in this category. He has an appealing personality and is liked and trusted. He's smart, his business-related knowledge is wide and deep, and he's good at oral communication. He is forthcoming with information and is able to elicit the same in people he works with. This combination of knowledge, skills, and personal characteristics should be a solid foundation for working with people, encouraging a free flow of information, and making technically sound decisions.

On the other hand, his skills deficiencies are serious. He doesn't listen in meetings, and this may be a clue to his stance toward the organization as a whole: he isn't curious about it. If, after two years, he's just beginning to realize that there may be a problem with conflict, he must have had blinders on. From the descriptions of the product development meetings, we know that Rogers has had concentrated doses of clashes between key functions and a rampant lack of accountability. The case furnishes evidence that Rogers isn't comfortable dealing with actual or potential conflict.[4] That is a clear disability for a leader. Rogers is said to have a good intellectual grasp of managerial issues, but he's had limited hands-on management experience. An example of his inexperience is his unawareness of the bad fit between his leadership approach and that of his predecessor. Managers and employees working under Bennett were conditioned to have him make all the decisions, and presumably he enforced accountability. Rogers is supposed to be bringing the culture of corporate—informal, nonhierarchical, and collaborative—to EPD, but he doesn't appear to be doing anything toward that end, despite the fact that the two cultures are polar opposites.

Although Rogers exhibits some strengths in this category, overall he is weak in leadership skills.

*Overcoming Obstacles.* The foundation of overcoming obstacles is an awareness that obstacles exist. Rogers has taken positive steps to fix the division's service and delivery. His review of the functional areas proves that he has a body of facts to work with, and yet we're left to wonder why he can't connect the dots.

Two large obstacles are the conflict among the major functions and the absence of accountability or responsibility. The conflict arises in part from the misalignment of all the major functions. The goals and incentives of the functions are often incompatible, and there are large differences in the experience of personnel. In addition, and crucially, no one regards problem solving as their responsibility—it's always the other guy's issue.

Rogers has unwittingly made the situation at EPD worse through both acting and failing to act. The sharp conflict and the misalignment of functions are described in the case through his eyes. He's aware of the conflict— how could he not be?—but he has not acted to contain it. A qualification may be in order, however. No one is coming forward and helping him understand what he's seeing and experiencing.

Rogers has made his own mistakes, unwittingly amplifying the potential for conflict. Marketing and sales would benefit from being housed together, so that they can each learn from the other and work directly together; but Rogers has separated them and moved marketing to corporate. From a distance, it's much easier to sustain self-justifying criticism of others. Rogers has moved his office to Allentown instead of remaining elbow to elbow with the people he's supposed to be leading. He also separated the product development group from its manager, which can't help that group's struggles to push out new products. Finally, Rogers has ended the organizational development program started by Bennett just when it was most valuable to the organization. The flimsy logic for his decision suggests another agenda that hobbles leaders: the attitude that if their predecessor initiated a program, it must be flawed.

Overall, Rogers is dangerously weak at overcoming obstacles.

*Change Skills.* EPD is subject to two different but powerful changes in leadership and competition. They are likely to have recovered from the sudden loss of Bennett, but their adjustment consists of far more than the acceptance of loss. An autocratic leader has been replaced by one who seems to want a participatory model, but the employees have yet to hear a clear statement about that and so continue to operate as they did, except there is no dominant figure to make the decisions and suppress conflicts. With the new leader unwilling to decide for them, they seem unwilling to take the risk. Add in the dismal financials, and the need for change is compelling.

Thus, Rogers' change skills carry a lot of weight in the evaluation. Significant change needs motivation, and that is partly accomplished with a sense of urgency. To give that motivation direction, a vision is necessary. There is no evidence in the case that Rogers has tried to confront employees and managers with their dire circumstances. As for creating and conveying a vision, the four major functions described in the second half of the case all seem to be pursuing different goals, and the product development meetings are an arena in which the agendas collide. Rogers needed allies when he stepped into the job. Having replaced most of the divisional management, his choices are candidates for a guiding coalition, supplemented with key people who worked under Bennett. Instead, from what we can tell in the case, Rogers is a bit of a loner; in addition, he's frequently away on corporate business, cutting down on the time he has to cultivate allies in the division.

On this criterion, Rogers is again weak.

## 5. Qualifications

No leader controls all the forces that influence an organization's performance. The facts suggest Rogers was promoted for the wrong reasons: for his intelligence and technical expertise, not for his management and leadership abilities. Corporate promoted Rogers into a position he wasn't prepared for and therefore deserves some of the responsibility for his performance. For Rogers to learn on the job, corporate should have seen to it that he had some preparation—ideally, some formal training before he took up his new position and mentoring or coaching afterward. It's not in corporate's interest to have a sink-or-swim attitude toward its top managers, and yet that is the attitude they seemed to have taken with Rogers.

You also must wonder why Rogers isn't more attuned to the change in business conditions. Corporate has been in a position to monitor industry trends and financial indicators. They require a formal monthly review of financials at each EPD plant. Nevertheless, they have insisted on aggressive profit targets that are unobtainable by the division in its current condition. EPD has been a reliable contributor of revenue to the parent company, and the sudden loss of divisional operating income should have set off alarm bells at headquarters. In that light, corporate's active encouragement of a physical separation between Rogers and his staff and the operating groups is inexplicable.

The disconnect between corporate and the division is pronounced. It could mean that corporate executives are poor managers themselves or are distracted by other concerns. Whatever the cause, the lack of understanding at the parent company and their actions regarding EPD have made a large, if hard to discern, contribution to Rogers' track record.

Exhibit 7-1 shows Rogers' "report card":

**EXHIBIT 7-1**

**Evaluation of Rogers' leadership**

| Criteria | Evaluation |
|---|---|
| Leadership skills | Weak |
| Overcoming obstacles | Very weak |
| Change skills | Weak |
| Qualifications | External factors contributed to poor performance |

We can conclude with this bottom-line assessment of Rogers' performance: he is an ineffective leader, although some strong forces outside his control have hurt his performance.

### 6. Actions

As for action, Rogers himself says on the first page of the case that he needs to do something. On the last page, the statement is repeated, and we learn that he is about to meet with his managers to discuss problem areas. The meeting is a golden opportunity to begin the process of change EPD needs. An action plan will speak to the weak areas revealed in the course of the evaluation, and Rogers' first step could be using the meeting as a platform for acknowledging the major problems, conveying a sense of urgency, and asking the managers to work with him to find solutions. It will be important for him to show the group that he is listening, not just giving them airtime and then imposing his solutions. Following Kotter's steps, the management group is a natural place to start building a coalition and shaping a vision that reflects the new realities of the business.

In the longer term, Rogers needs to be much clearer about the major obstacles that will take time to surmount. Changing the culture of an organization doesn't occur overnight, but it should be high on the list of long-term actions. So should the alignment of incentives to get everyone pulling in the same direction. Each category of the evaluation yields its own concerns that should be pursued in the action plan. The exception is business results, which are moved indirectly through measures based on the evaluation.

## ALTERNATIVES AND OPEN QUESTIONS

"Allentown" can be read as the story of an ill-suited individual predictably failing in trying circumstances. Rogers can be seen as a case study of the Peter Principle, which wryly suggests that in hierarchies, individuals tend to be promoted to their level of incompetence, meaning they end up one level beyond their abilities.

Nonetheless, this picture of personal failure can be debated in a number of different directions. How much responsibility does corporate deserve for promoting someone with the skills and knowledge necessary to succeed? Weren't they aware that the organization Bennett shaped, with their tacit approval, could have a very difficult transition to a leader more compatible with the corporate culture? The managers Rogers has brought in from outside don't seem to be tackling the organizational problems in their areas. No one seems to have approached Rogers about their concerns and frustrations. Glen Johnson, the chair of the contentious product development meetings, is so troubled about the meetings that he regrets having taken a job at EPD. He doesn't share his concerns with Rogers, though. Rogers isn't getting valuable information from his management group that could alter his perceptions of the people in the division and their interactions and give a more meaningful context to the things he has observed.

Many people, not a mere few, seem to lack an urgent sense of personal responsibility and accountability. Did Bennett hire employees that he thought would do what they were told? Did he worry at all about whether employees had a healthy sense of accountability because he enforced it through fear and force of personality? Could it be that the division is largely staffed with individuals who have worked too long in an authoritarian structure?

Thus, responsibility can be allocated differently according to how you read the situation and draw conclusions from the evidence.

### NOTES

1. M. Diane Burton, "Rob Parson at Morgan Stanley (A)," Case 9-498-054 (Boston: Harvard Business School Publishing, 1998), 1.

2. Willis Emmons and Monica Brand, "Empresas ICA and the Mexican Road Privatization Program," Case 9-793-028 (Boston: Harvard Business School Publishing, 1992), 13.

3. John Kotter, *Leading Change* (Boston: Harvard Business School Press, 1996), 33-34.

4. Michael Beer and Jennifer M. Suesse, "Allentown Materials Corporation: The Electronic Products Division (Abridged)," Case 9-498-047 (Boston: Harvard Business School Publishing, 1997), 4.

PART II

# DISCUSSION

# CHAPTER 8

# HOW TO DISCUSS
# A CASE

Case discussions can be exciting and revelatory, or they can be aimless and seemingly pointless. They can be data driven and fast paced or vague and plodding. They can also embody every one of these qualities in the course of an hour or two. The variables that influence the path and quality of a case discussion include the instructor, the students, the case, and a host of other possibilities such as the physical setting, the time of day, or the proximity to exams. This chapter deals with the only variable you can control: yourself. It is highly selective, concentrating on a few points that can be particularly helpful to students new to the case method.

Discussion skills are important because business school students often spend significant classroom time talking about cases. Case discussions are a principal means for learning in business programs. They teach the application of concepts and methods such as those in marketing, strategy, negotiation, and entrepreneurship—the knowledge most students identify with professional business education. They also help you learn how to think about business issues on your own and as part of a group. In the long run, you may find the learning about *how* to think is at least as important as the learning about *what* to think.

## COLLABORATION

Case discussion skills are grounded in the special qualities of the case method. The purpose of a case discussion is to construct meanings for a case based on evidence drawn from it and to recognize the uncertainties inherent in all of the meanings. This purpose can be at odds with your previous educational experience.

In a conventional classroom, experts share their knowledge with students, who take it in and, through examinations and other means, demonstrate they understand it. Students participating in case discussions for the first time can view it as a disguised rendition of the old learning model, and make a number of wrong assumptions:

- Cases are stories that have embedded in them the knowledge students previously received directly from a text, an expert, or both, and are therefore containers in which the truth is hidden, or a long word problem with a right answer.

- Case analysis is the process of finding the correct answer.

- Case discussion is the opportunity for students to show the instructor they have found the right answer.

Students who feel confident in their "right answers" will be eager to speak, and those who have less confidence want to avoid participation. Those who speak see themselves as being in a competition to prove to the professor that they have found the truth. They have no compelling reason to listen closely to other students because only the instructor is certain to know the answers. So class "discussion" is really serial exchanges between individual students and the instructor.

These beliefs are understandable—and at odds with the case method. Setting them aside and adapting your academic skills will help you become a full beneficiary of case discussions.

Case discussions aren't opportunities to recite knowledge learned elsewhere. They are opportunities to use knowledge and intuition to generate new knowledge. Everyone in a case classroom has to give up the comforting idea that a case is a container of truth. A case is a description of a situation, usually a complex one, that has multiple meanings, some of which can be contradictory. Of course there is truth in a case. The numbers that describe the financial performance of a company over the last decade are fact; they cannot be changed at will. However, the explanation of why the numbers are what they are is open to debate and so is the crafting of a strategy most advantageous to a company.

In a case class, you have to do something that may not feel comfortable at first: take responsibility for your own view of a case, develop an argument for it, be prepared to explain the argument, and listen to others who disagree with you. This very public process can be nerve-wracking for anyone, but it becomes less and less so as you become accustomed to being the focal point of the discussion—although only for a short time—and see how disagreement can enhance your learning.

It's very important that you set reasonable expectations for your performance in a discussion. The standard comment is not a piercing insight expressed with a debater's skill. Providing a fact straight from the case when it is needed in the discussion is valuable. So is asking a supposedly "dumb" question—the same question many of your peers have but are hesitant to ask. In fact, students often say that the right question at the right time can be the most powerful contribution anyone can make. No one wants to make a habit of voicing comments that don't contribute to the discussion, but the range of constructive comments is very wide. If your remark reveals a misconception about the case, the "mistake" is often the same one some of your classmates have made. Bringing it into the open can lead to a clarification that might not have happened if you hadn't spoken up.

Collaboration is what the case method is about. It succeeds or fails on students' willingness to take risks and contribute to the evolving understanding of a case situation. When only a few them are willing to take risks, the method falters; if the entire group participates, the method can succeed to a degree that no one in the room expected. In the case method, the burden, the responsibility, and the privilege of learning rest primarily with the students, not the instructor, a complete reversal of the lecture learning model.

Students and instructor in a case discussion classroom are like a team. For a team to perform well, every member needs to contribute. A soccer team made up of individuals, some wanting to showcase their individual skill and others wanting to stay as far away from the action as possible, cannot succeed—and neither can a case discussion class. The coach (like a case instructor) can guide and support the team—but can't kick a goal or save one.

## CLASSROOM RISKS

Every student in a case classroom shares the risk of exposure. There are also personal factors that can heighten the level of perceived risk:

- The language spoken in the classroom may be not your first language, and you don't feel you are as nimble in a free-flowing discussion as native speakers. You fear tripping over words, mispronouncing them, and thus making it hard for your classmates to understand you. Worse, you may fear someone will laugh at you.

- You may have to contend with gender differences that can make speaking in a group seem extremely risky. Or you may struggle with cultural norms that conflict with the realities of case discussions such as a high value placed on public consensus and a complementary prohibition of public disagreement. You may have learned a style of academic expression that emphasizes indirection and implication over assertion and explanation. Some international students may have to cope with a full agenda of language, cultural, and rhetorical complications.

- You may enter business school with a degree in an unrelated field, have little practical experience in business, and believe the combination puts you at a disadvantage.

- You may have a general intellectual fear that you are in over your head, that you are an admissions mistake.

If you have fears like these, you share them with many other students. It's natural and constructive to manage the risk you perceive. There are effective and ineffective ways to do that. The latter can be enticing, so let's explore those first.

### Reducing Risk—the Wrong Way

Every new student would like to make sure she has something valuable to say in class. Reducing the necessity of thinking and speaking on the fly is an apparent means to that end. This can be accomplished in a number of ways.

*Canned Comments.* You can stockpile points about a case before class—points you think can be delivered as high-impact comments. The points usually aren't organized into a coherent interpretation of the case. They're simply a list of statements about various facets of the case you expect to come up in class. The broad coverage is appealing because it seems to put you in a position to say something regardless of how the discussion develops.

Walking into the classroom, you feel a new confidence. You believe you are now equipped to make a quality contribution. However, in the next few classes the discussion takes paths you didn't anticipate; despite the broad coverage of your prepared points, the discussion doesn't match up with anything on the list. Then, finally, a class does take shape the way you thought it would. You scan the points for the case as the conversation moves along. Unfortunately, they are either preempted by other students or don't quite fit into the discussion, and you're hesitant to adapt points extemporaneously—the very situation you're trying to avoid. Frustrated as time slips away, you feel you must present a point even if it isn't relevant to the current topic. After all, you're certain you have valuable insights into the case and therefore expect the group will change the course of the discussion to pursue what you bring up. So you share one of your points when called on. You say it well—but it still sounds like a rehearsed comment.

The instructor says nothing. Her reaction is hard to read, but she doesn't appear to be impressed. The other students are also quiet—too quiet. The next student to speak steers the group back to the issue that was being discussed before you spoke. The instructor encourages that, ignoring your comment.

Vvivi Rongrong Hu, an MBA student, sums up this scenario in a few words: "A great comment at the wrong time is the worst thing!"[1] An excellent but ill-timed comment impedes the discussion and will probably be pushed aside. Everyone loses because the value of the comment is lost, and the timing of the comment reflects poorly on the speaker.

*Speeches.* A related risk-reduction technique is the preparation of a speech. This option may seem to be even safer than a list of points. You choose a key issue in the case and write out an extended comment. With a script to work from, you won't forget any of the facts or your reasoning. You also won't have to search for words to express yourself because you have already found them. Again the challenge is to find the right moment, and again the reality is that the moment hardly ever arrives. That's fortunate, too, because no matter how hard you try to disguise it, a speech will sound like a speech.

The worst effect of canned comments is the one it has on you. Your engagement with the class is a constant attempt to fit *their* conversation to *your* thinking, and that removes you from class discussion. In the end, your own learning suffers the most.

*Delay and Assess.* Another risk-reduction technique seems modest and prudent: delaying entry into the discussion until you feel at ease with the cases, the give and take of discussion, your classmates, and the professor. This "break-in period" doesn't mean you don't work hard on the cases. You study them carefully and pay attention to what class members are saying; and, as you compare the comments to your thinking about the case, you're assured that you're equal to the task. You may find that you are anticipating some of the comments; you may even discern important issues or evidence missing from the discussion.

However, the longer you remain silent, the harder it is to join the conversation. The cumulative effects of nonparticipation can be subtle. A regular participant builds a backlog of collaborative effort and credibility with the group. Both are helpful in creating good will toward the individual, which lowers the felt risk of participation. Good will also acts as a cushion for the inevitable errant comments everyone makes.

With no participation track record, a student becomes essentially invisible to classmates and the professor and lacks a reserve of good will in the group. It's also possible that some classmates may feel a touch of resentment that they are taking risks while the silent student avoids them. If a student's lack of participation goes on for a long time, she usually comes to believe that only a very high-quality comment will establish her as a full participant. The lofty standard eliminates the option of an easy entry into the discussion, such as providing a case fact. If the student doesn't find a way of breaking free from her self-imposed standard, a spiral effect can develop: the longer the silence or sporadic participation continues, the higher the ante is and the more difficult it becomes to speak, which simply pushes the ante higher still.

The student could be lucky. Classmates who have had discussions with her outside class may urge her to speak up in class and try to boost her confidence: "When we talk after class, you have a lot of interesting things to say about the case. There's no reason you can't do that in class." The instructor may suggest ways to jumpstart participation. Still, you should not count on others to solve the problem. The best way out of the dilemma is to make sure you don't create it.

### Reducing Risk—The Right Way

Some discomfort is unavoidable with the case method. Better than two thousand years ago, Socrates was making Greek students uncomfortable with pointed questions and relentless logic. The case method entails a level of risk for all participants—including the instructor. You should be realistic about that but remind yourself that everyone, not just you, shares it. Risk isn't purely negative, either. It is a motivator to do the hard work the case method requires.

However, don't exaggerate the risk. An artificial sense of risk leads straight to fear, and fear makes you a poor listener and robs you of the confidence to speak. What is the worst that can happen if you do speak? Making superficial comments, getting facts wrong, or misunderstanding what the professor or a classmate has said can certainly be embarrassing, but these moments inflict no permanent damage on active participants because everyone makes the same mistakes at one time or another. After one of these remarks, the discussion simply moves on. By the end of class, it's likely that no one will remember the comment. In fact, silence is more damaging than comments that misfire. As Maureen Walker, associate director of MBA Support Services at Harvard Business School, notes, "Silence *is* saying something."[2]

*Speak Up Early.* The most valuable advice about case discussion is this: participate as early as possible, ideally in the first class. Speaking up early not only reduces the nervousness of being in the spotlight. It also assists you in setting realistic expectations for yourself. MBA student Chris Cagne gives this advice:

> *Be brave! It is very hard in the first class to spell out the brilliant solution of a case or even make a comment with a high level of quality. It is highly likely that in the very beginning, your comments will just be OK or worse. But this is only another barrier that you have to overcome to enhance the quality of your comments. Never stop talking in class because in the last class you said something silly.*

Chris is suggesting that class participation itself is a learning process. No one is born to be an effective case discussion participant. Thus, another reason for becoming involved early: to learn how to be a good participant, you have to participate.

*Be Prepared.*  Because the discussion of a single case can have many variations, it isn't feasible to prepare for every possibility—even if you could identify all of them. To be a real contributor, your preparation should be thorough yet flexible. The case analysis process described in chapter 3 can be a foundation. It consists of a series of phases, each with a different purpose. This gives you a plan of attack, which makes your studying more efficient and makes you less susceptible to the confusion a case can induce. The early steps of the process are the most important because at that point you know little about the case. They prompt you to ask basic questions about the case.

What should you know when you go into the classroom? Here is an answer from chapter 3:

> *You are familiar with the information in the case, you have come to a conclusion about the main issue, you have evidence showing why your conclusion is reasonable, and you have thought about other possible conclusions and why yours is preferable to them.*

You might not have worked out a complete argument for your conclusion, but you will want specific evidence, not just an idea of what the evidence may be or one piece of it. If the case has both quantitative and qualitative evidence, you should draw on both. Surprisingly, doing a few of the most basic calculations required for the analysis of a case can be an excellent platform for participation.

An MBA graduate, E. Ciprian Vatasescu, found a role for himself in case discussions by using numbers to build a point of view:

*To my immense surprise, people sometimes don't bother to do back-of-the-envelope calculations and build their arguments on intuition. That's why, when you throw in a simple calculation, it can change the discussion radically.*

No case has perfect information or data, just as no real-world situation does. Every case has significant ambiguities and grey areas. You ought to be aware of them and give some thought to their implications for the main issue of the case.

In class, you may never be called on to present a recommended decision and then give your argument for it in detail. Nevertheless, the work you do to understand a rule, decision, problem, or evaluation; to identify types of evidence; and to make choices about how to analyze the evidence takes you deep into a case and provides knowledge that can be adapted to whatever discussion takes place. Preparation that yields some understanding and raises salient questions serves you far better than prepared points or disconnected notes.

## PUT LIMITS ON YOUR PREPARATION

Careful preparation is the foundation for effective class participation, but you shouldn't overprepare. The last part of the statement may seem odd. In an academic setting, is it possible to study too much? As far as case analysis is concerned, the answer is emphatically yes.

Don't fall into the trap of believing that the more hours you put into a case, the better prepared you will be. The first time I encountered a business case, I had no idea what was going on in it. I spent a very long time reading and rereading it and got almost nothing out of it except exasperation. But I at least was very familiar with the text. By the time I finished—"gave up" is a more accurate term—I had practically memorized it! You can always justify long hours studying a case by telling yourself that knowledge is proportionate to time. Maureen Walker disputes that justification. She says those long hours will just make you sleepy, not more knowledgeable. Rastislav "Rasto" Kulich, an MBA graduate, feels that balancing preparation and rest is one of the most important contributors to good classroom participation.

Open-ended study of a case means you aren't making choices about the allocation of your scarce time. Setting a limit on case preparation has several benefits: it puts a healthy pressure on you to use the time well; it helps you keep your life in balance and stay fresh; and it encourages you to pay attention to how you analyze a case. Case analysis is a skill just like class participation. You can develop that skill the hard way, by spending large chunks of time on a case until disappointing results, fatigue, or both convince you to seek a better way.

An alternative is to make decisions about an analytic approach at the beginning of case study and make necessary changes as you gain experience with cases. Much of this book is dedicated to informing decisions about how to analyze cases. One of the decisions is a time limit. If you have two or more cases to prepare, two and a half hours per case is a good place to start; aim to gradually reduce that to two hours per case. If you're preparing only a single case, you can afford three hours; paring the time down to two or two and half hours is a reasonable goal.

## READ ACTIVELY

Reading passively is one of the most potent obstacles to efficient (and fruitful) analysis. Reading with the vague objective of "understanding the case" can lead directly to passive reading—reading without thinking. Passive reading is insidious because you may not be aware you're doing it. To ensure you read actively, you should begin with an explicit process for analyzing a case. Chapter 3 provides a model that you can try out and modify or replace over time.

## RECOGNIZE THE SOCIAL FACTOR

I have been around business school students for better than sixteen years and have always been impressed by their ability to party. I admit my attitude was negative; I thought a lot of students were too serious about partying and not serious enough about learning. It never occurred to me that building a social network is important to case discussion until Agam Sharma, a business school student, pointed it out.

A case classroom can be an intimidating place. The material used for discussion isn't easy to work with. Case discussion can be hard to join, and cases can provoke strong differences of opinion. Students can feel intimidated by those who differ with them. And conflicting views on cases that involve issues such as ethical values can sometimes seem to have a personal edge. Add in competition for grades, and the discomfort students feel can mushroom.

Classmates who get to know each other outside the classroom can change the atmosphere inside it. A group of strangers competing for grades can become a group of acquaintances and friends who recognize that they're competing but also understand they're collaborating for the benefit of everyone who takes part. Students surrounded by classmates who clearly respect them will probably be at least a little more willing to take risks in discussions. The listeners are probably going to be more empathetic toward the speaker, more willing to help out if they can when a classmate stumbles while trying to make a point, and more understanding when the classmate's contribution doesn't help the discussion. The often subtle but damaging influence of stereotypes about gender, personal appearance, and many other characteristics can be muted when people get to know each other as they are instead of what they are projected to be. A classroom friend can encourage a reticent student to speak up or to take bigger risks with his comments.

Bowling, card games, class dinners, sports—there are plenty of ways for classmates to get to know one another without the stresses present in the classroom. An awareness of how social ties can help in the classroom is particularly important for students who believe social activities are simply a distraction from solitary study.

## REMEMBER HOW TO LAUGH

Business schools can be very serious places. Students new to them, though excited to be there, can also be anxious about how they will perform. The seeming high stakes of case discussion can feed the anxiety, and anxiety can stifle an individual's sense of humor. Graduates of case method programs have some advice: remember how to laugh. Listen to Rasto Kulich:

> *The ability to lighten up is very important. Many students, especially internationals, are very intense and tense and take themselves too seriously. That makes them stiff in delivery and rigid in responding to audience reaction or comments. Humor, especially the self-deprecating kind, is very much appreciated and often needed. Students' ability to spice up the discussion or laugh at themselves will help them improve audience attention and increase acceptance of their comments.*

No one is advising you to memorize some jokes and incorporate them into your comments. But, for many reasons, spontaneous and natural humor belongs in the room.

## LISTENING *IS* PARTICIPATING

When asked to give advice about case discussion, MBA students repeatedly mention the role of listening. In the two years of business school, students spent far more time listening than speaking in a case discussion. Here is what one student says about this underrated skill:

> *Always listen carefully to the other students' comments and the professor's questions. It's not only important to get the essence of different perspectives, but also to help you follow the flow of the case discussion.*

A business school graduate describes how he listened in case classes:

*It is a great exercise to listen to comments in class and decide whether you agree or not with what people are saying. If you have a good argument to support your agreement or disagreement, it is time to raise your hand and talk!*

Listening *is* participation (as long as it isn't the only thing you do). You listen to keep up with the discussion and find opportunities to contribute. A quality comment isn't possible if you haven't been listening with care. A good comment fits the context of the ongoing conversation at the moment it is made. A few moments later, the comment will be redundant; a few moments earlier, it would be illogical.

A good case discussion isn't just the sum of a linear series of related but separate discussions. A comment or observation from early in the discussion can take on an entirely different meaning or significance near the end. A line of thinking about a case can commence, recede into the background, and then reappear. A comment made in the middle of the discussion can answer a question asked at the end. A good case discussion has richness and complexity that demand adroit and sustained listening.

Beyond helping you find your place in the discussion, listening is absolutely vital to learning. In a lecture, listening imports knowledge. The process doesn't demand much of the listener, who can also compensate for lapses of attention by borrowing someone's notes. In a case discussion, listening furnishes other peoples' thinking and puts it in juxtaposition to your own thinking. Learning comes from this dynamic, which isn't linear like the learning compiled from a lecture. You can take a view into class that remains unchanged throughout, but it is just as possible that the view will be overturned or changed somewhere along the way. The class can work its way through a case and settle on a narrow range of conclusions about it and that effort can be negated suddenly by a different view. Students can walk out of class frustrated but realize later that they learned more by pursuing a false lead than they would have if they had taken a direct route.

Listening in case classrooms isn't a skill to be taken for granted. Listening intently for 60 to 120 minutes to an unpredictable conversation is a task many students have to adjust to because little in their prior experience has prepared them for it. They have to *learn* how to listen. Interestingly, complacency and anxiety lead to the same end. Complacent students aren't listening because they don't realize that the discussion is generating knowledge continuously. Anxious students can't listen because there is too much going on in their heads. Finding a place between the two extremes is part of case classroom learning.

## REFLECT ON WHAT YOU LEARN

Business students are busy people with more going on in their lives than studying and going to class. As they leave a classroom, their minds have probably already moved on to something else besides the discussion that just took place. Nevertheless, by taking a little time after class to think about the discussion before the memory of it fades, you'll capture more of the value of the classroom experience. Yusuke Watanabe, an MBA graduate, recommends a post-discussion practice that has both a short-term and long-term payoff:

> *Make sure you write down two or three takeaways for each case and reflect upon them later. It will take only three to five minutes to write them down. Writing down takeaways will make you remember the virtual experience much longer.*

In the classroom, you'll note some of the broader lessons emerging from the discussion, but recognizing them can be difficult when you're immersed in the point-to-point movement of the discussion. Moreover, some of these lessons don't take shape completely until the end of the discussion—or after class, if you take a few moments to reflect on the discussion as a whole. Think expansively and sift out the points that seem to have value beyond the particulars of an individual case.

The short-term benefit is greater clarity about the issues that link one case to another and lends coherence to a course. That clarity is a resource for subsequent case analysis, class participation, and examinations. According to Yusuke, there is also the potential for long-term value: "A lot of . . . graduates tell me that these takeaways will become your personal bible for leadership."

## BE PATIENT WITH YOURSELF

The goal of this chapter is to help you get the most out of case discussion. More could be said, but I want to err on the side of too little instead of too much. Learning the case method is challenging enough without being bombarded with "indispensable" advice.

Set an objective of a comment in the first class of every case course. Remember that the context of every class comment is listening. Go into the first class to listen to what people are saying, not to wait your turn. When you listen actively, responses come to mind organically, and when they do, don't evaluate whether they are good enough. Just raise your hand.

Along with the willingness to take the plunge, you need patience. Don't regard your early comments as a vehicle to prove your brilliance to peers and the professor. While you become accustomed to the art of case discussion, keep performance anxieties at bay by taking a long-term view. Effective collaboration is the product of useful contributions over a period of time, not occasional bravura performances.

I repeat this advice as a conclusion because I have said it many times to incoming MBA students, and so have others who have worked with students longer than I have. We have seen the positive results, and we have seen the troubles that we were trying to prevent come to pass. But the best authority on this subject is someone who recently completed two years of business school, a marathon of five hundred cases. Yusuke Watanabe urges you not to be "afraid to make the obvious comments and stupid question." He continues:

> *Discussion is all about confidence. If you are a shy person and don't speak upfront in the semester, it will become harder and harder to speak. You will start pressuring yourself to come up with great comments and not speak until you have one. Things just get worse. Ask the stupid question, make the obvious comment . . . The stupid question is usually everyone's question. Once you start talking, you will feel comfortable, and your mind will become clearer, and you will come up with better and better comments*

### NOTES

1. All student quotes from e-mail responses to the author, 2006.

2. Maureen Walker, "International Orientation, Class of 2006," slide presentation to entering MBA students, Harvard Business School, July 2004.

PART III

# WRITING

# CHAPTER 9

# HOW TO WRITE A CASE-BASED ESSAY

Writing about a case is very different from talking about it. You collaborate with others in a discussion, bringing to bear everyone's background and case preparation along with the instructor's knowledge and facilitation skills. But you usually work on your own when writing about a case. You have to perform the entire analysis yourself as well as organize and express your thinking for a reader.

However, the difference between talking and writing about a case runs deeper still. Audiences have much more exacting expectations of a text than they do of spoken comments. Logical gaps and the back-and-fill tolerable in a discussion are a major problem in an essay, confusing readers and undermining the writer's credibility. Audiences don't want a transcript of the writer's thinking as it evolved. They want to know the end product of the writer's thinking, expressed logically and economically.

## CHARACTERISTICS OF A PERSUASIVE CASE ESSAY

Writing about a case builds on the process of analyzing a case. The case situations described in previous chapters can be used to organize essays. An essay arguing a decision is organized in a different way from one offering a problem diagnosis. The structure of problem, decision, and evaluation essays is described in chapters 10 through 12, respectively. The chapters also include cases and sample essays about them. The essays are based on the writing of MBA students.

To convince a reader that a conclusion about a case is valid, the writer must offer credible evidence linked directly to the conclusion. This fact helps explain the characteristics case-based essays have in common:

1. Answers two questions—What? Why?—and often a third—How?

2. Makes a position statement (What?)

3. Uses evidence to persuade the reader (Why?)

4. If needed, provides an action plan (How?)

## Three Questions

Contrary to what many MBA students think, most professors don't want essays filled with lengthy case summaries and lists of insights and observations. They don't want you to prove to them that you have read the case carefully by telling them everything you know about it. They want you to answer whatever questions you have been asked about a case—and to answer them as efficiently as you can.

The parts of a case essay can be organized around three simple questions: What? Why? How? The position statement responds to What? and the argument answers Why? How? refers to action: How should the recommended decision be implemented? How can the problem be fixed?

Exhibit 9-1 sums up the organizing questions for a case-based essay.

## Position Statement

A sharply focused position statement organizes the entire essay. Without one, the essay has no purpose or direction as far as the reader is concerned. The most common failing of the case exams I have seen over the years is that the writers try to look at a situation from all angles, suggesting many meanings but committing to none. I use only one negative example in this book, but it's instructive to look at an essay that complicates the reader's task from the beginning. It was written as a response to the decision situation described in "General Electric: Major Appliance Business Group (Abridged)," a case used in chapter 11.[1]

**EXHIBIT 9-1**

### Case-based essay Q&A

| Question | Answer |
| --- | --- |
| What? | Position statement (expresses a conclusion) |
| Why? | Argument |
| How? | Action plan |

*A. Decision*

*I recommend that the Project C (PJC hereinafter) management team go to the board of directors and ask for an additional capital authorization structured as follows:*

> *+10% = $2.8 million for the management information and support systems, which don't require formal approval.*

> *+5% = $1.5 million for the skills training in technical problem solving, which would require formal approval.*

*Moreover, I recommend that the PJC team not drop the $1 million investment in the integrated computer control room, as it is crucial for the division's processes.*

*I would not support the additional capital spending of $1.5 million in the factory environment because it doesn't bring direct benefits. I see it only as an attempt to get union buy-in. The union's support can be gained differently, by reinforcing job enhancement and enrichment programs.*

*I am also against adding an additional iteration in the product development (PD hereinafter) process. This will only delay the process without clear benefits, setting the precedent for further delays from the engineering teams. Strict deadlines will encourage innovation and commitment.*

The case is about the development of a new GE dishwasher. The two previous machines have missed their sales targets. Jack Welch has challenged the managers of the product development process (Project C) to set a benchmark for a world-class operation and introduce a product that beats the competition. The managers have to decide which, if any, of five additions should be made to the project and how much more investment and time they will require. The opening you have just read renders a decision on each of the five proposed additions, but the decisions don't seem to have anything to do with one another, and the writer's reasons for advocating or rejecting them are either vague or not stated.

The first paragraph of another essay on the case is a revelation: it relates the decisions to a larger issue. This writer recommends five different decisions, *but* they are linked together.

*The Project C management team should persuade senior management and the board of directors to increase the budget by 15 percent, or $4.2 million, and extend the time for completion by four months. Four of the five changes should be added to the project, leaving improvements in GE's management information* *and support systems for a later stage. The strategic importance of Project C to GE's success in the dishwasher industry demands meeting all of the project objectives, and the four changes are critical to meeting them. Failure to do so would put at risk the initial investment and overall competitiveness in the dishwasher industry.*

When you finish this paragraph, you have no doubt about what the writer thinks. This excellent example of a position statement also asserts a single reason for all of the decisions.

Stating your position at the beginning has several advantages. First, the reader expects you to answer the question you have been asked. Why make the reader wait for it? Second, critical readers evaluate an argument as they go along. Professors do this in order to award a grade. Others do so to judge how convincing the argument is and what implications it may have for their thinking and for action. Readers can't evaluate an argument, however, until they know what it's trying to prove. If your conclusion appears at the end of the essay, they must go back to the beginning and compare the proof to the position. Their reading will be more efficient if they know the position before the proof. Finally, and probably most important, a position statement at the beginning of an essay provides a statement of intention for the reader—and for you, the writer. That statement of intention can be your reference point as you compose.

In this paragraph, the writer states a position and expresses an intention about the organization of the essay:

*Rogers took over an organization that rewarded the politics of self-interest and expected leaders to be virtually dictatorial. They had lost Bennett, the tyrant who made the division work. The market is also changing. The division's problems stem from three sources: a lack of a new vision, Rogers' leadership weaknesses, and a misaligned organization.*

The last sentence gives both the reader and the writer an agenda for an argument: prove that vision, an individual's leadership weaknesses, and misalignment are the primary causes of an organization's troubles.

Opening with a position statement does have a downside. It can be difficult to write the conclusion of an essay before you write the essay itself. Depending on your writing process, starting with the conclusion may be a problem because you develop one as you write. However, that is a high-risk way to write when time is short. Better to write a partial position statement to get started and then add to it, e.g., name two causes of a problem that you are sure of and then add the one or two more that become clear later. A second disadvantage of an early position statement is that it can make the writer seem aggressive and arrogant to readers. On certain occasions and in certain cultures, it may be best to defer a position statement until you have proved it. However, there are many situations in which you can reasonably assume that knowing your conclusion will help the reader. A case-based exam is one of those situations. If you have any doubts, ask the professor.

## Evidence

Using evidence well is probably the most crucial skill for a writer of case essays. Illustrating how to use evidence is difficult, though, because it requires familiarity with the case that furnishes the evidence. I hope to provide enough of the case context so that you can understand how each of the following examples of evidence works.

The first example uses qualitative and quantitative evidence. It is discussing one of the five proposed additions to the dishwasher product development effort called Project C described in "General Electric: Major Appliance Business Group (Abridged)." The value engineering cycle needs more time and money, both touchy issues at GE since late rollouts and quality problems have plagued prior models. In fact, sales of the Project B machine were 30 to 40 percent lower than expected because of the bad quality of the A model. The first sentence is the recommendation.

*(1)* After PermaTuf A and B failed to meet the desired goals, one additional prototype cycle or iteration before market rollout seems to be a very sound measure. *It will ensure high product quality and will also lower warranty and service costs. The most critical part of implementing this change is the project delay of three to four months. However, the value engineering cycle would increase product quality, lower costs, gain market share because of product improvements, and ensure that Project C does not run into the same problems as A and B. Although it is possible to delay this change for one or two years after the launch, by then it might be too late. The product's reputation could already be jeopardized, and it would be extremely difficult to convince both the sales force and customers that the product is the improved version they expected in the first place. In addition, senior management has been very clear: "Do it right the first time."*

*The total cost is $1.2 million. By year 3 (1985), the added cost of the proposals will be recovered through additional contribution from Project C. By year 7 (1989), Project C by itself will increase contribution 70 percent compared with total contribution in 1979. With each year after the launch of the new model, more and more of the increased revenue from the project will fall directly to the bottom line.*

Exhibit 9-2 summarizes the evidence in the paragraph. The author cites many advantages of value engineering, and there is quantitative confirmation that it will increase contribution over the long term. The two paragraphs are a good example of how qualitative and quantitative evidence can be used to reinforce each other.

The second example uses primarily quantitative evidence. One lesson of the example is that merely citing numbers will not persuade a reader; writers have to tell the reader what they mean in the context of the argument. Another is that several numbers that align with a similar conclusion are more persuasive than one or two. In some situations, you won't have much quantitative data to work with. In those instances, every piece of quantitative evidence has a high value. If you have a finance background, this second example will be familiar ground. If you don't, the context will help you follow the logic of the paragraph. The case is about a manufacturer and two retail customers that owe it a substantial amount of money. An analyst is assessing the likelihood that the retailers will be able to repay the debt. The evidence (in brackets) backs the conclusion (not italicized).

*Liquidity: Smyth & Company has a [current ratio of 2.53], and the [acid test shows that its current assets minus inventories can cover 1.26 times its current liabilities]. This is a good sign that the company can cover its short-term liabilities, such as the accounts payable it owes Mercury Enterprises. Nevertheless, when we look at the accounts receivable, the collection period has worsened. In 1998, Smyth & Company took on average [82 days to collect its accounts receivables] versus an average of [62 days in 1996]. At the same time, the [days payable measure also increased from an average of 53 days in 1996 to 70 days in 1998], a good sign. However, the [accounts payable did not increase as much as the collection period], putting pressure on the company's cash flow since [the gap between the time Smyth & Company gets paid versus*

**EXHIBIT 9-2**

## Project C: yes on value engineering

| Disadvantages | Advantages |
| --- | --- |
| • Imposes delay in launch | • Addresses major problem with Projects A and B |
| • Adds cost | • Reduces warranty and service costs |
| | • Creates greater customer satisfaction |
| | • Increases sales force confidence in product |
| | • Eventually increases market share |
| | • Pays for itself and increases contribution |

*the time it needs to pay its bills increased from 9 days to 12].* Although currently the acid test and current ratio show good liquidity, key liquidity measures like accounts receivable and accounts payable are deteriorating and will start to impair Smyth & Company's ability to pay its short-term payables with Mercury Enterprises.

This part of the essay makes clear, authoritative use of numbers. The author states evidence favorable to the retailer (the acid test and current ratio), compares the positive data to the negative, and finds the negative more compelling. The acknowledgment of evidence contrary to the author's conclusion doesn't weaken the argument but enhances it (and the writer's credibility) by assuring the reader that all of the relevant data has been considered.

Case-based essays use the results or outputs of specialized methods as evidence to prove conclusions. In the example above, the words in brackets express the outcomes of the quantitative tools the writer has employed. The paragraph is constructed around significant calculations and what their results mean. Without financial tools, the writer would have nothing meaningful to say about liquidity.

The final example employs only qualitative evidence. The overall argument concerns the organization featured in "Allentown Materials Corporation: The Electronic Products Division (Abridged)," the case discussed in chapter 5. The evidence (in brackets) supports the first sentence.

The current organization cannot succeed because it is [misaligned], and Rogers has to take much of the responsibility. *He made organization [changes that ran counter to the division's past and were not guided by a clear vision]. New product development has suffered because Rogers made [changes that did nothing to fill the void left by the brilliant but controlling Bennett]. He moved the division headquarters to corporate, which has a [very different culture from the political and conflict-ridden division]. Sales and marketing were separated with [no consideration for their complementary nature. Sales is not simply selling, but the source of market information]. The marketing people can't collaborate effectively with sales, because [they do not have the skills needed to do their job (they are all recent graduates or have one or two years of experience)], yet [he is not coaching and helping them]. They need the market expertise of sales.*

The paragraph is worth rereading to understand how the writer accumulates evidence sentence by sentence, all of which points to the conclusion expressed in the first sentence. Students have sometimes criticized paragraphs like this as being mere catalogs of case facts. This one isn't for three reasons. The facts have been carefully selected from various parts of the text; they are combined with inferences that connect the facts to a conclusion; and they all support the same conclusion.

The paragraph above uses methods very different from the quantitative ones employed for the analysis of liquidity, but they are used for the same end: to prove a conclusion. The primary concept of the paragraph, misalignment, is derived from organizational behavior. The bracketed words are the products of leadership and organizational behavior frameworks.

Please note one more feature of the three examples of the use of evidence. Each contains a sentence telling the reader the conclusion the evidence justifies. That sentence controls the meaning of the other sentences and is, in effect, a position statement for a paragraph. The sentence can occur at any point in a paragraph. The safest place to put it is at the beginning. The statement can also come in the middle or at the end, as it does in two of the examples. In both, though, the preceding sentences anticipate the content of the position statement, which pulls together all the statements and thus ensures coherence.

## Action Plan

The action plan complements and completes the argument of a case-based essay by answering the question How?

- How do you solve a problem?

- How do you implement a decision?

- How do you improve a performance?

Exhibit 9-3 shows the division of labor between an argument and an action plan. The general purpose of action plans is to improve or advance the situation as it is presented in the essay through a coherent series of actions.

**EXHIBIT 9-3**

### What action plans do

| Case situation | Argument | Action plan |
| --- | --- | --- |
| Problem | Prove cause-effect relationships that account for problem | Solve problem: fix weaknesses and reinforce or increase strengths |
| Decision | Recommend best decision | Implement decision: show the best pathway to achieve desired outcome |
| Evaluation | Provide detailed evaluation of performance, act, or outcome | Improve performance or outcome; implement or change decision |

The argument of a case-based essay precedes the action plan because there is nothing actionable until there is a fact-based understanding of what is to be done. In other words, the argument creates both the necessity for action and the actionable content. Aside from different content, there are two specific reasons for separating an argument from an action plan: organization and reader comprehension.

A case argument and an action plan have entirely different organizing principles. Logic determines the order of an argument. An argument for a decision, for instance, is organized according to the reasons supporting the recommendation. On the other hand, an action plan is *chronological*—it unfolds in time. There is no way to reconcile these two very different organizing principles—and there is no reason to try, although many students do. When a writer tries to combine an argument and action plan, something has to give. Either the logical structure of the argument has to be thrown out in favor of chronological order, which makes no sense for an argument; or the chronological order of the action plan has to be sacrificed to the logical plan of the argument, which then makes it impossible for the reader to know the order of the proposed steps. The second reason for the separation is the reader. Moving back and forth between argument and action destroys coherence and thus the reader's ability to understand the argument or actions.

## ELEMENTS OF AN ACTION PLAN

An effective action plan has these five characteristics:

- Sets goals based on the argument

- Addresses the actionable content of the argument

- Consists of specific steps

- Has realistic short- and long-term steps

- Identifies and responds to the major risk to the plan

### Goals

An argument doesn't provide explicit goals for action. A diagnosis argues the principal causes of a problem but doesn't say how those causes can be acted upon to improve the situation. An argument for a decision doesn't say how the decision is to be carried out. A goal statement at the beginning of the action plan summarizes the desired end state of the plan. The goal can be simple and have one or several parts:

- *Goal:* Transfer production to an appropriate vendor as soon as possible, with a target of one year to begin transfers and two years to complete them.

- *Goals:* Corcoran's team should persuade senior management to accept the recommendation, align stakeholders, and execute each proposal.

A goal statement can be more involved:

- *Goals:* His short-term objective should be to develop a clear vision, redesign the organization to enable it to realize the vision, and create a clear plan for getting there. Long term, he needs to create a customer-facing organization. He needs to reestablish stability rooted in a vision and culture of continuous improvement and cooperation.

The last objective is typical of essays on problems and evaluations. Both usually specify multiple factors that require some kind of action. You should be wary of complex goal statements, though, for they can quickly become too complicated to be useful.

## Actionable Content of Argument

The argument is the source of all the actionable content. The plan translates that content into tangible action. Every major actionable issue in the argument should be represented in the action plan. An argument that asserts three major causes of a problem should have an action plan that deals with all three causes. But an action plan shouldn't deal with an issue that isn't addressed in the argument. This is an easy mistake to make. While drafting an action plan, writers can come up with ideas that haven't been covered in the argument (e.g., a new criterion for a decision) and insert them into an action step. The discrepancy is readily apparent to readers and suggests to them that the argument is incomplete.

## Steps

A plan consists of a series of actions to be taken over a period of time. To be useful, the steps need to provide specifics. Here is the first step of a decision implementation plan:

*Establish a rock-solid consensus among senior executives and agree on transition dates and process. Form a multidisciplinary team to vet vendors and manage the transition.*

The next example is part of a plan in a problem diagnosis essay:

*Next, they need to create a vision—a vision that is simple, important to all the groups, and easily acted upon. Manufacturing is only concerned about low cost while other groups are concerned about new products, causing conflict when they work together. The vision needs to be measurable to allow short-term wins. For example, measurements of delivery and service can show that a vision focused on customer needs is working. Next, the vision needs to be communicated throughout the division. The conflicts in the division take place at all levels, and it is important to get everyone aligned and committed.*

The description of actions should strike a balance between generalities and excessive detail. A generality doesn't tell the reader enough:

*Select manufacturing partners.*

This statement doesn't answer questions such as, What kind of partner should be considered? What are some of the criteria for making the decision? On the other hand, an action step can indulge in unnecessary specifics:

*To select manufacturing partners, Stott should schedule a meeting with Whistler's manufacturing managers in the next week to discuss the criteria to be used for partners. He should prepare an agenda in advance that covers considerations like the track record of potential partners in outsourced manufacturing, how well their manufacturing experience matches up with Whistler's needs, and how well their management team works with Whistler's. Stott should give a lot of thought to how Whistler can quickly research track records of companies in South Korea. What contacts does Whistler have to investigate the companies? How much importance should it give references? Is there anyone in the country who is reliable and equipped to do the research?*

As a guide, ask yourself what readers want to know. Vague steps give readers no idea how they would be implemented. Minute details bog readers down and cause them to lose sight of the important details of a step.

## Organization

Action plans are carried out in time. Some steps come first, some come later, and others come much later. You have to show the reader the order of the proposed steps in time. An action plan isn't a to-do list, which records items randomly. Most substantial action plans need both short-term and long-term steps. Some may even require a medium-term category. Exhibit 9-4 lists criteria for deciding where a step should fall in the time sequence of a plan.

EXHIBIT 9-4

## Criteria for action plan steps

| Position in sequence | Criteria |
| --- | --- |
| Short term | • Urgent |
| | • "Low-hanging fruit" (easy) |
| | • Necessary for longer-term steps |
| Long term | • Dependent on prior steps |
| | • Complex, need time to accomplish |

The short-term part of a plan begins with the most urgent actions. What is the first thing that needs to be done to implement a decision or improve a performance or solve a problem? The first step tells the reader a lot about the attention you've paid to the sequential logic of the plan. Short-term steps can also be actions that are easy to perform. Is there something the protagonist can do quickly and easily that will immediately improve the situation? Finally, short-terms steps can be the foundation for later steps.

Long-term steps almost always depend on short-term steps. There will be no implementation of a proposal requiring senior management approval until they are convinced that it is the right thing to do. Winning their approval is therefore a step that comes before any steps to put the proposal into effect.

Be *realistic* about the time it takes to achieve actions and make that clear to readers. Actions that are complex, sensitive, or involve a large number of people are usually long term. Changing the entire incentive system of organization will take months or years. Even some fairly simple actions, such as a single change in a company's strategy, may play out over a long period of time.

### Risk

Every action plan has an element of uncertainty and risk. *Nothing* ever goes entirely as planned. You are well advised to identify the chief risk to the plan and propose measures to manage it, but don't agonize over the risk of every step. Rather, ask the question, What's the worst thing that could go wrong with the plan? Then ask, How can the risk be contained or eliminated?

## NOTE

1. "General Electric: Major Appliance Business Group (Abridged)," Case 9-693-067 (Boston: Harvard Business School Publishing, 1992).

# CHAPTER 10

# PROBLEM ESSAYS

Problem situations in cases are outcomes or results of actions, processes, activities, or forces that we don't fully understand. They concern both business pathology (e.g., managers who perform poorly) and success (e.g., a company strategy that results in market leadership). Problems also fall between the poles of success and failure. They include some of the most difficult and intriguing interpretive tasks case method students must perform. (For more on problem situations in cases, see chapter 5.)

This chapter and the two that follow have the same purpose and structure. They outline the structure of an essay appropriate to a problem, decision, or evaluation and provide one or more examples of a persuasive essay based on the work of MBA students. At the end of the three chapters, you will also find templates to help you plan an essay.

The sample essay in this chapter was written in response to questions about the case "Allentown Materials Corporation: The Electronic Products Division (Abridged)." To benefit from this chapter, please read the case and the essay. (Note: "Allentown" is also used in chapter 5 so you may have already read it.)

## HOW TO ORGANIZE A PROBLEM ESSAY

An essay on a problem situation has four parts:

1. Problem definition

2. Diagnosis

3. Proof of causes

4. Action plan

The problem definition and diagnosis are much shorter than the other two parts, and yet they are pivotal to a successful essay. Together, they comprise the essay's position statement, and everything in the essay flows from it. Readers look for a position statement because it furnishes a purpose for their reading.

Problem cases can be hard to write about because they involve multiple effects and multiple causes. Confronted with cases like these, you can feel compelled to compile a lengthy list of causes. Typically that results in an essay offering little proof of each cause, and the sacrifice of depth for breadth diminishes the persuasiveness of the essay. To resolve this dilemma, observe a version of the 80-20 rule: 20 percent of the causes explain 80 percent of the effects. Explaining 80 percent of the problem with several causes backed by detailed proof is more convincing to readers than explaining 99 percent with many causes backed by superficial proof.

## Problem Definition

The problem definition should express the effects or outcomes identifiable in the situation that the main character in the case should be most concerned about. The sample essay opens with this paragraph:

> *Don Rogers faces an array of difficulties. The EPD Divison's performance is currently declining and their reputation for delivery and service has been slipping. Employees have low morale, don't trust those from other groups, and are participants in unending conflict.*

The paragraph states what Don Rogers needs to solve. The Allentown division's financial performance and reputation are in decline, and the organization suffers from a variety of serious internal issues that have a bearing on its poor performance. This paragraph may seem to be no more than a case summary, but nowhere does the case state a problem; it simply catalogs many things that appear to be going wrong. Defining the problem means organizing, concentrating, and describing the key effects or outcomes that constitute it. The definition also declares the type of problem that needs to be solved. The problem in "Allentown" concerns the behavior and performance of people, not marketing, strategy, or manufacturing.

## Diagnosis

After the problem has been defined, the next task of the essay is to summarize the diagnosis—the principal causes of the problem. To pinpoint causes, common sense and intuition are helpful, but they aren't sufficient. Causal analysis can only be performed with frameworks appropriate to the situation. The sample essay uses widely accepted concepts of leadership and organizational behavior. This is the diagnosis:

> *Many of these issues can be traced to the underlying culture of the division, the differing leadership styles of Bennett and Rogers, poor decisions by Rogers, and the lack of alignment among different groups in the division.*

The sample essay provides a clear and compact expression of the diagnosis, naming four causes: culture, leadership styles, Rogers' decisions, and misalignment.

It takes courage to say that a problem has just a few major causes. It can seem much safer and truer to a complex situation to assert many causes. But the writer's work is to clarify complexity by reducing a problem to its few most influential causes—and the the sample essay does this well.

## Proving Causal Links

Showing the reader why the diagnosis is valid takes up most of a problem essay. After the diagnosis, the sample essay explains the evidence that connects the four causes to the effects or outcomes that define the problem. No cause is left out, and no causal proof is short on evidence. The sections of the proof have the same organization as the diagnosis. This is a small but important symmetry in an argument. Readers expect that the order of the elements of a position statement will be the order of the proof that follows. If there is a difference, readers will wonder why. They expect everything in an essay to be purposeful, and when it isn't, reader comprehension is reduced.

Now let's take a closer look at how the proof in the essay works. Please read paragraphs two and three of the sample essay:

### Cultural Differences

*Rogers is under pressure to align the division more closely with the rest of the corporation, but their cultures are very different. Allentown is a close-knit family in which hierarchy doesn't matter. People discuss problems face to face, there is formal and informal discussion among people at all levels, and people interact socially. On the other hand, Bennett shaped EPD's culture to suit his leadership. He created a hierarchy with himself at the top holding all the power and making all the decisions. There is little cohesiveness and no discussion of problems, a great deal of politics, and all meetings are formal. The two cultures are currently incompatible and trying to convert one to the other is bound to cause conflict.*

### Leadership Differences

*The cultural difference is due to the leadership of Bennett, who ran the division from infancy until Rogers took over two years ago. Bennett wanted the division to be separate from Allentown so that he could be in complete charge. He was powerful and a micromanager with a strong will, yet he also had a desire to try new things. He was motivated, respected, and experienced. However, he was also feared and was an authoritarian leader who made all the big decisions.*

*This style left no room for other leaders, only managers. He did, however, focus on organizational issues with the program he started.*

*Rogers is more consultative, yet he doesn't seem to have a well-defined approach to leading. He involves people in his decisions and shares information. He is bright, communicates well, and is liked and respected. However, some of these qualities cause people to question his leadership. He is looked upon as soft and unwilling to take on much conflict. He doesn't listen and spends too much time on corporate assignments, both of which limit his knowledge of EPD. He is not very experienced, which can lead to a lack of credibility. Rogers' leadership style conflicts with the realities of the organization Bennett created, and his weaknesses reinforce the difference.*

In this early stage of the argument, the writer is trying to connect two causes—a clash of cultures and a clash of leadership styles—to effects described in the case. The writer notes that Rogers has a mandate to change the culture of the division so that it conforms more closely to that of the corporation. No one has thought very deeply about this task because changing a culture is difficult under any circumstances and is even more difficult when the change is so great. Rogers seems to be operating as if people in the division will behave differently simply because their new boss expects them to.

In the next paragraph, the writer contrasts the leadership styles of the past and present chief executives. Bennett was an authoritarian leader who shaped the organization to serve his way of leading. His choice succeeded because of his creativity and intelligence—and the willingness of division employees to work in a system that severely limited their autonomy and denied them any power. Rogers has arrived on the scene with a commitment to a model of leadership that isn't entirely clear but is more open and consultative than Bennett's. His style is probably better suited to the new competitive environment, but Rogers has not taken into account the division's recent history and hasn't done anything to bridge the large gap between two different approaches to leadership.

Now let's analyze the paragraphs according to the types of statements they contain with an eye toward identifying a pattern of argument. The two paragraphs from the sample essay are broken into lists of sentences and labeled as evidence or conclusions:

*Cultural Differences*

*[Conclusion] Rogers is under pressure to align the division more closely with the rest of the corporation, but their cultures are very different.*

- *[Evidence] Allentown is a close-knit family in which hierarchy doesn't matter.*

- *[Evidence] People discuss problems face to face, there is formal and informal discussion among people at all levels, and people interact socially.*

- *[Evidence] On the other hand, Bennett shaped EPD's culture to suit his leadership.*

- *[Evidence] He created a hierarchy with himself at the top holding all the power and making all the decisions.*

- *[Evidence] There is little cohesiveness and no discussion of problems, a great deal of politics, and all meetings are formal.*

*[Conclusion] The two cultures are currently incompatible and trying to convert one to the other is bound to cause conflict.*

The pattern that emerges is a movement from conclusion to conclusion, with facts that prove and connect the two conclusions. Not all conclusions are of equal weight, however. Some of them are primary, part of the backbone of the overall argument, and others are subordinate, providing a logical bridge to a more important conclusion. The initial sentence of the paragraph is a conclusion that is refined and connected to the problem in the last sentence. Rogers' mandate to make EPD like Allentown causes conflict between him and the division, and that conflict exacts a cost in the division's performance.

Let's look at the paragraph as a list:

*Leadership Differences*

*[Conclusion] The cultural difference is due to the leadership of Bennett, who ran the division from infancy until Rogers took over two years ago.*

- *[Evidence] Bennett wanted the division to be separate from Allentown so that he could be in complete charge.*

- *[Evidence] He was powerful and a micromanager with a strong will, yet he also had a desire to try new things.*

- *[Evidence] He was motivated, respected, and experienced.*

- *[Evidence] However, he was also feared and was an authoritarian leader who made all the big decisions.*

- *[Evidence] This style left no room for other leaders, only managers.*

- *[Evidence] He did, however, focus on organizational issues with the program he started.*

- *[Evidence] Rogers is more consultative, yet he doesn't seem to have a well-defined approach to leading.*

- *[Evidence] He involves people in his decisions and shares information.*

- *[Evidence] He is bright, communicates well, and is liked and respected.*

- *[Evidence] However, some of these qualities cause people to question his leadership.*

- *[Evidence] He is looked upon as soft and unwilling to take on much conflict.*

- *[Evidence] He doesn't listen and spends too much time on corporate assignments, both of which limit his knowledge of EPD.*

- *[Evidence] He is not very experienced, which can lead to a lack of credibility.*

*[Conclusion] Rogers' leadership style conflicts with the realities of the organization Bennett created, and his weaknesses reinforce the difference.*

Once again, the paragraph moves from an initial conclusion to a more definitive one. By reducing it to the conclusions, we can distill the paragraph's contribution to the proof of the diagnosis: The cultural difference is due to the leadership of Bennett, who ran the division from infancy until Rogers took over two years ago. Rogers' leadership style conflicts with the realities of the organization Bennett created, and his weaknesses reinforce that difference.

This argument ties together the differences in culture and leadership style as essential factors accounting for a major disconnect between the new leader and the division. It makes clear how ill suited each is to the other. Nevertheless, the two-sentence argument wouldn't be convincing without an evidence base. The two paragraphs consist of many evidence statements and only four conclusions. There is no standard ratio for a proof, but this example illustrates that conclusions are earned with a substantial number of relevant evidence statements, and these statements constitute a large part of the argument.

## Problem Action Plans

The task of the action plan for a problem essay is to improve situations involving poor performance, sustain those involving high performance, or do both. The action plan in the sample essay seeks to improve EPD's performance. (For more information on action plans, see chapter 9.)

The sample states the goals of the action plan and sorts the steps into short term and long term. The plan addresses the major issues of the diagnosis: culture, leadership styles, Rogers' misguided actions, and misalignment. The action plan reverses some of Rogers' most harmful decisions such as the geographical separation of EPD people and cancellation of the organizational development program. Many of the steps prescribe a revamped approach to leadership, starting with the very first short-term step. Writing steps to cover the entire diagnosis is probably the biggest challenge of the action plan for a problem situation.

The next biggest challenge is to order them in time. The writer shows good judgment in selecting early steps that are urgent (creating a vision and fixing product development), easy (restarting the organizational development program), and necessary for the long term (listening to people and cultivating allies).

The long-term steps are more complex and thus take longer to achieve (change of incentives), build on prior steps (better communication), or both (changing the EPD culture). The exact order of individual steps usually isn't critical. The first few long-term steps, for instance, could be placed in a different order. But the overall chronological order of steps should have a clear logic. Among the short-term steps, Rogers' assessment of what he needs to do belongs before any of the others because they flow from the assessment. Creating a vision from the thinking of people throughout the division belongs before other steps to stimulate cooperation and collaboration because it gives everyone a common goal.

The essay finishes with a consideration of risks. Two major ones are identified, but more could be added. In fact, it would be possible to think of a risk for every step. However, an action plan is subject to the same principle as an argument: less is more. The action plan should account for the least number of contingencies that account for the majority of the risk.

No consideration of risk is complete without measures to contain or eliminate it. In an exam situation, it is easy to concentrate on describing risks—and forget to say how they can be handled. Be sure to include effective responses.

## PROBLEM ESSAY

*Case:* "Allentown Materials Corporation: The Electronic Products Division (Abridged)." Reading the case before the essay will help you understand the chapter comments about the paper.

*Writing task:* Explain the two-year decline of EPD and suggest measures to reverse it.

Don Rogers faces an array of difficulties. The EPD Division's performance is currently declining and their reputation for delivery and service has been slipping. Employees have low morale, don't trust those from other groups, and are participants in unending conflict.

Many of these issues can be traced to the underlying culture of the division, the differing leadership styles of Bennett and Rogers, poor decisions by Rogers, and the lack of alignment among different groups in the division.

### Cultural Differences

Rogers is under pressure to align the division more closely with the rest of the corporation, but their cultures are very different. Allentown is a close-knit family in which hierarchy doesn't matter. People discuss problems face to face, there is formal and informal discussion among people at all levels, and people interact socially. On the other hand, Bennett shaped EPD's culture to suit his leadership. He created a hierarchy with himself at the top holding all the power and making all the decisions. There is little cohesiveness and no discussion of problems, a great deal of politics, and all meetings are formal. The two cultures are currently incompatible and trying to convert one to the other is bound to cause conflict.

### Leadership Differences

The cultural difference is due to the leadership of Bennett, who ran the division from infancy until Rogers took over two years ago. Bennett wanted the division to be separate from Allentown so that he could be in complete charge. He was powerful and a micromanager with a strong will, yet he also had a desire to try new things. He was motivated, respected, and experienced. However, he was also feared and was an authoritarian leader who made all the big decisions. This style left no room for other leaders, only managers. He did, however, focus on organizational issues with the program he started.

Rogers is more consultative, yet he doesn't seem to have a well-defined approach to leading. He involves people in his decisions and shares information. He is bright, communicates well, and is liked and respected. However, some of these qualities cause people to question his leadership. He is looked upon as soft and unwilling to take on much conflict. He doesn't listen and spends too much time on corporate assignments, both of which limit his knowledge of EPD. He is not very experienced, which can lead to a lack of credibility. Rogers' leadership style conflicts with the realities of the organization Bennett created, and his weaknesses reinforce the difference.

## Rogers' Bad Decisions

Many of Rogers' decisions have been misguided and have had bad outcomes. He has mistaken aligning the division with the corporation as something that can be done structurally and geographically as opposed to culturally. He has moved the headquarters back to Allentown as well as the market development group. He left the product development group at the plant but consolidated control under Ted Moss in Allentown. He has also replaced many of the division managers with people from Allentown, who are viewed as outsiders. Furthermore, he has split up the sales and marketing groups.

All in all, he has put even greater gaps between functional groups that not only needed to be more aligned but also lacked cohesiveness in the first place. Finally, he cancelled the organizational behavior project, perhaps because it was a Bennett legacy, even though it was having a positive impact.

## Misalignment

All of this has caused misalignment in the division. No one clear direction or vision exists. The incentives of the different groups and the people in them (plant managers versus sales force) are not aligned and there is no coordination or information flow among them. The division views corporate as slowing them down and feels they have no influence to get things done. This leads to big problems in the newly critical function of product development. There is no coordination in the group and any department can kill projects without the knowledge of the others. The meetings they hold twice a year are a disaster. There is a separate meeting for the two products they produce, even though the sales force is integrated. People are filing in and out of meetings, and many of the people with the needed information are not there. There is no discussion of why these things happen and the reasons for the problems. Many conflicts arise, and people just agree to disagree. Everyone advocates, no one listens, and nothing gets done.

## Action Plan

Rogers needs to change his own priorities, align the groups within the division, and transform conflict into collaboration.

### Short Term

First, Rogers must understand what he needs to do. He needs to shed responsibilities not directly related to the division. A change process needs a full-time leader. Rogers needs to grasp the difficulty of the required changes and ask for corporate support. He needs to learn much more about the division by changing his tendency to talk; he needs to just listen.

From day one, he should build a sense of urgency in every corner of the division. Employees seem to be completely disconnected from what's happening in the market. He should address all the key people in the division and walk them through the bad business results. He should read a list of issues that need to be solved and put his leadership at the top of the list. He will need to keep repeating this message.

He should use his contacts at corporate to lower financial targets in the short term to take unnecessary pressure off the division. This action should also indicate to the division that Rogers intends to lead more assertively.

As part of his effort to mobilize the organization, he needs to recruit a group of allies to shape changes, promote buy-in, and direct the change process. His allies should be from all of the functional groups.

To get everyone working toward the same goal and leverage the sense of urgency, he and his allies should develop a vision that is simple, inclusive, and actionable. The vision should express the major traits of the new culture he is trying to create. They should solicit opinions from everyone, regardless of level. When work on it is finished, the vision should be communicated and constantly reinforced. It's important that every employee not only knows the vision but also understands it and is committed to it.

Rogers then needs to channel the frustration many people are feeling into the energy and commitment necessary to fulfill the vision. Rogers needs to sustain a sense of urgency by reminding everyone of the deteriorating financial performance, the new competitive demands, and the necessity of everyone working together.

Rogers needs to fix product development quickly. He should create a product development group with members from all of the functions who have the needed skills and knowledge. The group should have a clear set of goals and be held accountable. Anyone who doesn't agree should be dropped from the group or fired. The group needs to meet more frequently than twice a year and should have an effective leader. Currently, Johnson is not happy with the position. If the changes don't make a difference to him, he should be replaced.

Rogers should reverse his decision to drop the organizational behavior program, especially since the final phase deals with coordination issues.

### Long Term

He should bring all of the EPD functions together in one place. Getting everyone to work together is far more difficult, if not impossible, when functions are split apart.

Changing EPD's culture can only be accomplished in the long term. However, many of the short-term steps will alter old ways of thinking and acting. Most of the long-term steps will also contribute to cultural transformation. Rogers should emphasize the cultural values of the vision statement on a regular basis.

The incentives of all EPD groups should be aligned. Currently, manufacturing and sales are at cross-purposes. They should be compatible with the long-term strategy of the division, as expressed in the vision.

There needs to be better communication in the division. EPD is a silo operation, with each function aware only of its own concerns.

The division lacks leadership at all levels, and Rogers should work to develop new leaders. Younger employees not steeped in the old culture may be the best candidates.

Rogers should seek the continuing support of corporate for the changes he needs to make and keep them informed of progress.

### Risk and Response

Two major contingencies could throw up barriers to the change process. First, corporate could be uncooperative, not seeing the need for sweeping changes and refusing to lower financial targets or provide extra resources. Second, a large number of EPD people might try to undermine change.

Rogers must make a strong case for change to corporate and be sure he has the backing of key people. He should give a detailed picture of the troubled division and emphasize that without change, the division might actually fail.

In anticipation of internal resistance, Rogers needs to canvas widely in the division and make sure he includes employees in planning change. He should let every employee and manager know that the division's survival is at stake and work relentlessly to secure buy-in. He should also be prepared to get rid of people who try to block the changes—especially managers, who are in a position to influence other individuals.

## PLANNING TEMPLATE FOR A PROBLEM ESSAY

This template will help you build a problem essay.[a] It follows the organization of a problem essay, but you don't have to use it in that order. The important thing is to capture your ideas as they occur to you.

### Position Statement: Problem and Diagnosis

State the problem of the case. Try to state it in a single sentence and then expand it in a few more sentences—if they are necessary. Then summarize the diagnosis: the primary causes of the problem. The terms of the diagnosis should reflect the frameworks you are using. (Note: You can't start work on the position statement until you know the problem and have one or two of its principal causes. The statement can be revised as you work.)

| Problem: |
| --- |
| |
| |
| Diagnosis: |
| |
| |

## Proof of Diagnosis

List the primary causes of the problem and note the evidence for each. Identify the fewest number of causes that account for the majority of the problem. Be sure to use the appropriate frameworks. Note action steps as they occur to you. Don't be concerned about the order of the steps.

| | Evidence | Action plan ideas |
|---|---|---|
| Cause: | | |
| | | |
| | | |
| | | |
| Cause: | | |
| | | |
| | | |
| | | |
| Cause: | | |
| | | |
| | | |
| | | |
| Cause: | | |
| | | |
| | | |
| | | |

## Action Plan

The general purpose of a problem action plan is to improve the current situation by acting on the causes of the problem.

### Goal(s)

State the goal(s) of the plan—the major outcome(s) the steps are supposed to bring about.

| Goal(s) |
|---|
| 1. |
| 2. |
| 3. |

### Action Steps

Write the steps of the plan without worrying too much about their order. When you finish, write numbers in the first column to indicate the final chronological order of the steps. The second column can help you think about steps as part of phases (e.g., consensus, communication, and improvement).

*Short term*

| Order in essay | Phase | Step |
|---|---|---|
|  |  |  |
|  |  |  |
|  |  |  |
|  |  |  |
|  |  |  |
|  |  |  |
|  |  |  |
|  |  |  |
|  |  |  |
|  |  |  |
|  |  |  |
|  |  |  |
|  |  |  |
|  |  |  |
|  |  |  |

*Long term*

| Order in essay | Phase | Step |
|---|---|---|
| | | |
| | | |
| | | |
| | | |
| | | |
| | | |
| | | |
| | | |
| | | |
| | | |
| | | |
| | | |
| | | |

### Major Risks and Responses

Identify the major risks that could undermine the plan. Propose responses that will eliminate or contain them.

| Risk | Response |
|---|---|
| | |
| | |
| | |

a. Tehila Lieberman contributed substantially to the development of the essay planning templates.

# CHAPTER 11

# DECISION ESSAYS

The stereotype of the manager is an individual who sits in a corner office and calls the shots, making one decision after another until it's time to go home. You aren't likely to find that stereotype in cases. The decisions portrayed in cases involve tough issues and require judicious thought. They involve competing and conflicting interests, and the decision maker often has little time to think through the options because the situation has blossomed into a crisis.

Another popular stereotype portrays business decision making as equal parts intuition, guts, and toughness. The opposite stereotype is the numbers-driven technician making decisions according to a spreadsheet. The reality isn't as colorful. Serious decisions are best made with careful analysis as well as intuition and the willingness to act. That process doesn't make for good television or celebrity business books. It does make for good decisions, though. (For more on decision situations in cases, see chapter 6.)

This chapter has two sample essays that respond to questions about the cases "General Electric: Major Appliance Business Group (Abridged)" and "Whistler Corporation (A)." Please read the cases and the essays now. You won't benefit from the chapter without reading them.

## HOW TO ORGANIZE A DECISION ESSAY

Decision essays have six elements. The following list arranges them in the state-and-prove order explained below.

1. Recommended decision (position statement)

2. Decision options

3. Decision criteria

4. Proof of recommended option

5. Critique of options

6. Action plan

The pivotal element is criteria. They must be chosen carefully for their relevance to the specifics of the decision, and they must be clearly conveyed to readers. Criteria can range from the extremely technical, as in a finance case, to broader ones such as a strategic imperative. The first sample decision essay uses two fairly narrow criteria, and the second essay uses three broader standards. The variation in the circumstances of the case situations explains the difference. Decision criteria are contingent on the needs of a particular situation; they aren't derived from rules that apply to every situation.

Although a good decision essay will include all six parts, their order can vary. The state-and-prove model just presented is generally the safest because it begins with a recommendation, which tells the reader what the essay will prove. It also gives the writer a clear-cut purpose. The state-and-prove model is well suited to situations in which writing time is constrained, as it is during academic exams. Sample essay 1 in this chapter, which deals with the case "General Electric," is a decision essay built on this model. However, the state-and-prove may seem biased and aggressive to some readers in some situations—for instance, the culture of the writer and reader frowns on the direct assertion of a position. The model may also lead the writer to pay insufficient attention to the reasons why the other options have been rejected.

A second approach, the prove-and-state model, organizes a decision essay as follows:

1. Decision options

2. Decision criteria

3. Critique of other options

4. Proof of remaining option

5. Recommended decision

6. Action plan

This organization is *inductive* because it leads the reader to a conclusion through a process of elimination. Alternative options are shown to have weaknesses that rule them out, leaving one preferred option to be proved. The sample essay on the "Whistler" case follows the prove-and-state model. If there is reason to believe that readers don't want a conclusion expressed before it is proved, this is the model to use. Some expert readers may prefer that students follow an apparently empirical path to a decision. That means stating the options and criteria and then applying the criteria to each option. This approach can be quite convincing (see exhibit 11-1). The reader feels

**EXHIBIT 11-1**

## Decision essay organizations: pros and cons

| Organization | Pro | Con |
|---|---|---|
| State-and-prove | • Reader knows what you think | • Less "scientific" and more dogmatic or aggressive in appearance |
| | • You know what you have to prove | • May invite insufficient attention to rejected options |
| | • Forces immediate move to proof | |
| | • Less risk you'll run out of time | |
| Prove-and-state | • To reader, essay seems objective and scientific | • More risk you'll run out of time |
| | | • More risk you'll stray from intended organization |

that each possible alternative has received equal consideration. Of course, you must know exactly what you want to prove to write a convincing state-and-prove essay. The appearance of complete objectivity is precisely that, an appearance, but it can have a powerful impact on the reader.

The drawbacks of the prove-and-state approach mostly concern time management. In an exam situation, if you aren't careful, you can take too long getting to the recommendation and have too little time to prove it adequately. Also, without a stated recommendation and reasons for it at the beginning of the essay, you can stray from the intended organization.

### Recommended Decision

The essay on "General Electric" has to deal with five decisions, three options, and three criteria. Juggling that many elements while trying to reach a coherent decision poses a stiff challenge. Applying the three criteria to the entire package of decisions and sifting through three options for each can result in a very long essay or one that loses its way—or both. The essay handles the complexity adroitly. It states a recommendation in the first paragraph (not italicized):

> *The Project C management team should persuade senior management and the board of directors to increase the budget by 15 percent, or $4.2 million, and extend the time for completion by four months. Four of the five changes should be added to the project, leaving improvements in GE's management information*

*and support systems for a later stage.* The strategic importance of Project C to GE's success in the dishwasher industry demands meeting all of the project objectives, and the four changes are critical to meeting them. *Failure to do so would put at risk the initial investment and overall competitiveness in the dishwasher industry. The unsuccessful launch of PermaTuf increased the importance of Project C to save the division's reputation and meet future growth objectives.*

The non–italicized sentence is the position statement. An early position statement leaves no doubt in the reader's mind about the direction of the essay. The rest of the paragraph summarizes the reasons for the position. In the body of the essay, readers will expect an argument showing how the recommended decisions are linked to the reasons.

The Whistler essay, which uses the prove-and-state model, also puts forward a recommended decision, although the statement of it occurs near the end of the essay:

*Whistler's long-term competitive advantage resides in design and engineering. The best decision will enable the company to concentrate on its core strengths and free up resources for expanded new product development. Whistler needs to follow the lead of its competitors and achieve the lowest possible unit cost through outsourcing.* The second option is therefore the preferred decision because it satisfies both criteria.

## Decision Options

There is no decision without alternatives, and readers need to know what they are. This part of a decision essay often isn't difficult to fulfill. Many decision cases explicitly state alternatives. The "General Electric" case lists them in the fourth paragraph. In "Whistler," they are spread over the second and third paragraphs. Neither case specifically refers to decision options or alternatives, however. You need to know what you're looking for in the case.

Note that both cases present three options. That's true of many case decision situations. That number has a certain logic to it; three possibilities allows for two opposite solutions and one in the middle. Both the "General Electric" and "Whistler" cases use this symmetry. Exhibit 11-2 shows the alternatives in both cases.

The middle choice can be attractive because it seems to be a compromise. But the middle way isn't necessarily a real compromise. Splitting Whistler's manufacturing between domestic and offshore plants may be in the middle, but it isn't a compromise. The solution doesn't have any effect on Whistler's

**EXHIBIT 11-2**

**Range of decision options**

| Case | Extreme | Middle | Extreme |
| --- | --- | --- | --- |
| General Electric | Pursue none of the changes | Pursue some of the changes | Pursue all of the changes |
| Whistler | Reengineer domestic manufacturing | Move more production offshore | Move all production offshore |

increasing manufacturing woes. Moreover, even if the in-between option is a legitimate compromise, that doesn't make it the best choice.

## Decision Criteria

The most common, and the most damaging, weakness of essays on decisions is vague criteria. Many writers simply aren't aware that to make a reasonable argument for a decision, they must have explicit and relevant criteria. Having said that, finding relevant criteria can be arduous. The two sample essays provide tangible examples of writers who have made good choices about criteria.

The writer of the GE essay has what appears to be the easier task. The case lists criteria in the first paragraph, although they are called "objectives":

- Achieve worldwide dishwasher industry leadership in product quality and profitability.

- Achieve world-class leadership in process quality, productivity, and quality of work life.

- Achieve increased job security through high-quality, low-cost products that gain increased market share.

The writer has reasoned that the proposed changes should serve the objectives of Project C, so the objectives should be used as the decision-making standards. Still, a hurdle suggested earlier in the chapter remains. With five possible changes, three options, and three criteria, there are in theory forty-five different combinations to consider. However, the options refer to all of the changes, not each one, and that helps reduce the complexity of the task. The writer then does something clever. He essentially reduces the three criteria to one: whether they contribute to competitiveness. This doesn't make the argument for a recommendation easy, but it does simplify it. Competitive success is defined by the three objectives:

- Low-cost products
- Profitability
- Productivity

The writer's task is to determine whether the proposed changes help to realize these characteristics. But the adoption of the changes is constrained by two factors: budget and time. The Project C team has set a target of $2.8 million in additional investment for the changes because the team can authorize a 10 percent increase in budget without the approval of senior management. The time constraint is the team's desire to stay as close as possible to the original schedule. These considerations need to be added to the competitive criteria. The full set can be expressed as a series of questions:

### COMPETITIVENESS

- Does the change contribute substantially to competitive success?

### COST

- Does the total cost of the proposed changes exceed 10 percent of the budget?

- Can the additional cost of the recommended changes be justified?

### TIME

- Can the total additional time added by recommended changes be justified?

These questions reveal the logic of the criteria drawn from the case. Note the decision logic: the competitiveness question needs to be answered first. If the answer to the question is no, the other two questions are moot. If the answer is yes, then the next two questions have to be answered.

The writer probably didn't articulate each of these questions in his mind, but the essay reveals that he was working with their core concepts. When there is sufficient time, it can help both you and readers if the decision logic that flows from the criteria is included in a document.

The writer of the Whistler essay employs these criteria:

*To make his decision, Stott should use two criteria:*

- *The strategic importance of radar detectors to Whistler.*

- *A manufacturing solution best suited to that importance.*

These standards are not explicitly stated in the case. Inferring criteria from case facts may be the hardest task of both decision and evaluation essays.

Where did the criteria for the Whistler essay come from? The story told in the case has two dimensions: the radar detector market and Whistler's manufacturing function. The case gives far more attention to manufacturing than to the market, and that imbalance can entice you to follow the lead of the text. But a manufacturing strategy decision can't be made without reference to the company strategy. The two need to be aligned, and that insight allowed the writer to choose relevant criteria.

The last paragraph and exhibit 2 in the case provide most of the information related to the company strategy. On that criterion, there doesn't seem to be much room for controversy. The market is in long-term decline, and, like its competitors, Whistler's competitive advantage doesn't reside in the low-cost production of commodity electronics. On the manufacturing criterion there is plenty of room for differences of opinion. The writer of the essay has skillfully developed an argument around this criterion to show that his recommendation is the best choice. When criteria aren't stated in a case—and they often are not—they come from case analysis.

Sometimes you have to determine how to measure the criteria you have chosen. The strategic standard employed in the Whistler essay can be applied directly to the case facts. The second criterion, a manufacturing solution best suited to the strategic importance of radar detectors, requires further specification when used to investigate the option of investing in process re-engineering. The writer understands that the only way to resolve the question of whether domestic production fits the declining strategic value of radar detectors is to calculate the comparative costs of reengineered domestic production versus offshore production. In chapter 12, the sample evaluative essay provides another example of criteria that are broken down into quantitative metrics such as GNP, unemployment rates, crime rates, and the percentage of households living below the poverty line.

Notice that the Whistler criteria have to be applied in a specific order, like those for the GE decision. The strategic importance of the product has to be resolved before a complementary production solution can be formulated. You'll find that criteria in many decision situations have to be used in a particular order. However, criteria can also be independent of each other and be applied in any order.

Two other characteristics should be noted. First, the number of criteria should be small. It is tempting to apply many to a complex situation, but an argument that juggles numerous criteria usually falls apart. Second, effective criteria tend to be broad, not narrow. The more general the criteria, the more inclusive they are—up to a point. Criteria that are too abstract will yield very little useful information about the decision. The trick is to hit the right level of abstraction.

## Proof of Recommended Option

A decision argument has a simple structure. The criteria are applied to each option, and the argument shows how good the fit is between the option and the information in the case. The argument proves the fit with evidence. Here's a section from the GE essay:

> *2. Skills training in technical problem solving*
> *Implementation of this change will empower employees and* rapidly increase product quality, process quality, and productivity. *Training would have an immediate effect on worker* involvement in, ownership of, and commitment to the success of the project. *Like the factory initiative, it could have a snowball effect,* prompting skilled workers to propose process improvements. *This change would also increase the attractiveness of working in the plant,* reinforcing the first change. Increased costs would be offset by the reduction of labor-related costs that would be incurred if the change was not implemented. Total cost would be $1.5 million. This change has no impact on the project's schedule.

Look back at the discussion of the criteria for the "General Electric" case earlier in the chapter. The non-italicized words are the key results of applying the criteria to the case information about this change.

This paragraph from the Whistler essay also shows criteria in action:

> *Because the* radar detector market is dropping off and is now all about cost, *it has* little strategic value *to Whistler. The solution that fits that reality is the one that* offers the lowest unit cost. *Reengineering is attractive because it corrects so many of the mistakes the company has made in the past. However, it is* uncertain—at best—that the domestic plants will ever be able to compete on cost with offshore vendors. *Therefore, reengineering isn't a good option for Whistler.*

The non-italicized words again show how the criteria have been applied and also the order in which they have been applied. The coherence that results from having clearly stated and logically applied criteria is the foundation of an essay's readability and credibility. It gives readers what they need.

## Critique of Options

An expected part of a decision essay is proof of the recommended option. But the proof of one option doesn't necessarily mean that the others have no merit. You persuade readers more readily when you prove that the other options are less desirable. The Whistler essay provides extended examples of negative proof. The "Transfer only low-end products offshore" alternative is dismissed with an argument that concludes as follows:

> *In the end, Whistler's costs are 33 percent higher than those of offshore plants, a severe competitive disadvantage. Moving more of the volume to Korea would narrow the difference only slightly and leave untouched and unsolved the problems in its domestic manufacturing operation.*

To arrive at this conclusion, the writer relates the lengthy history of bad decisions behind the problems of the manufacturing process. He points out the major flaw in the alternative: it will leave in place all the accumulated production problems. The writer could have limited the negative proof to a statement that the process is broken and the option won't fix it. The proof in the essay is more convincing because it gives the reader a detailed picture of the biggest manufacturing problems and where they came from.

The critique of options extends to the recommended alternative. That may seem like a very bad idea. Nevertheless, no decision is without a weakness or downside. Understanding the major ones permits decision makers to be prepared for them and, ideally, limit or eliminate their effects. The writer of the Whistler essay is frank about the decision to outsource manufacturing:

> *Whistler will be incurring a risk by entrusting an entire function to an outside organization. . . . The biggest disadvantage, though, is the closing of the domestic plants and the human cost that will exact.*

But the writer also puts forward measures to manage the downsides—for example, softening the impact of the plant closures. A decision essay can succeed with readers without raising the topic of a decision's downside, but the essay is stronger if it does.

## Decision Action Plans

The purpose of a decision action plan is to implement the decision as effectively as possible. The plan has a single goal, and that distinguishes it from problem and evaluation action plans, which usually have multiple goals. (For more information on action plans, see chapter 9.)

The action plans included in the two sample essays each declare simple goals. Beyond the obvious objective of executing the decision, they set conditions easily inferred from the situation. The Whistler goal emphasizes speed in light of the fact that the company is losing $6 million a year. The GE goal stresses achieving consensus and commitment since the dishwasher division has a history of budget overruns, late launches, and underachievement.

Recognizing conditions relevant to decision implementation and working them into the action plan is key.

Writing an action plan for a decision can be frustrating because the argument and the case often provide little information useful for implementation. This is different from problem and evaluation essays, which generally provide abundant actionable content. Some creativity can help fill the void and so can the experience gained from classroom discussions of action plans. The criteria for action plan steps in chapter 9 will aid you in brainstorming.

Removing the details of the steps reveals a logical organization more specific than short term and long term. The GE plan has four phases:

1. Consensus

2. Leadership and communication

3. Execution

4. Monitoring and reporting

The Whistler document has two more phases, but the argument suggests both since they are primarily devoted to handling the downside:

1. Internal consensus

2. Communication (managing the downside)

3. Selection

4. Transfer

5. Outplacement (managing the downside)

6. Monitoring

When creating a decision action plan, it may be helpful to think in basic phases like the ones above. An equivalent to an outline, the phase concepts can stimulate your thinking about specific steps. Persuading senior management, for instance, is an obvious short-term phase of the GE action plan, as are selection, transfer, and outplacement in the Whistler plan. They give you a good start on filling out the plan.

Both action plans have short sections on risk management that deal with worst-case scenarios. The writer of the GE essay wants the Project C team to be prepared in case senior executives won't go along with a budget increase that exceeds 10 percent. He would drop what he considers to be the least critical change that reduces the budget to the 10 percent limit. The Whistler plan focuses on two risks and considers one as more serious: turmoil in the company after the plant closings and layoffs are announced.

Although there's no assurance that the contingency plan will contain trouble, a plan is well worth the effort even if it only partially succeeds.

---

### DECISION ESSAY 1

- *Case:* "General Electric: Major Appliance Business Group (Abridged)." You need to read the case before reading the essay to understand the chapter comments about the paper.

- *Writing task:* Recommend a decision to Corcoran, tell him why it's the best option, and draft an action plan.[a]

The Project C management team should persuade senior management and the board of directors to increase the budget by 15 percent, or $4.2 million, and extend the time for completion by four months. Four of the five changes should be added to the project, leaving improvements in GE's management information and support systems for a later stage. The strategic importance of Project C to GE's success in the dishwasher industry demands meeting all of the project objectives, and the four changes are critical to meeting them. Failure to do so would put at risk the initial investment and overall competitiveness in the dishwasher industry. The unsuccessful launch of PermaTuf increased the importance of Project C to save the division's reputation and meet future growth objectives.

#### Options

The Project C management team has identified five possible project modifications:

1. Improving the quality of the factory environment

2. Skills training in technical problem solving

3. Revisions in GE's management information and support systems

4. Adding a value engineering development cycle

5. Drop (postpone) construction of the integrated computer control room

Although any combination is possible, the team tended to agree on three options:

1. Not to pursue any changes now

2. Go ahead with some of the modifications (limiting options to $2.8 million to avoid the need for approval)

3. Pursue substantial additional capital authorization sufficient to cover all of the modifications

### Selection Criteria

Project C has three primary objectives:

- Achieve worldwide dishwasher industry leadership in product quality and profitability;

- Achieve world-class leadership in process quality, productivity, and quality of work life; and

- Achieve increased job security through high-quality, low-cost products that gain increased market share.

In addition, Corcoran must evaluate the proposed additions on cost and schedule:

- Total cost should be as close to $2.8 million as possible.

- Time added to the schedule should be minimal.

#### 1. Improve the Quality of the Factory Environment

This change will mostly enhance quality of work life. However, by improving that, productivity, process quality, and therefore product quality will be raised along with increased job security. The main impact of this change will be increasing employee motivation and their pride in being part of this project, a critical factor for its success. Although it will challenge other divisions because employees will demand similar facilities, Project C can take GE operations to a world-class level and have a snowball effect; other divisions will want to follow their lead. Together, these two factors can propel other divisions, pushing them to a higher level of job satisfaction and therefore increasing productivity. The factory initiative could be managed with the union as a pilot test in a small division of the company—dishwashers—and if it achieves its objectives, the change can be implemented throughout the company. The total cost is $1.5 million, and the addition has no impact on the project schedule.

#### 2. Train Workers in Technical Problem Solving

Implementation of this change will empower employees and rapidly increase product quality, process quality, and productivity. Training would have an immediate effect on worker involvement in, ownership of, and commitment to the success of the project. Like the factory initiative, it could have a snowball effect, prompting skilled workers to propose process improvements. This change would also increase the attractiveness of working in the plant, reinforcing the first change. Increased costs would be offset by the reduction of labor-related costs that would be incurred if the change were not implemented. Total cost would be $1.5 million. This change has no impact on the project's schedule.

### 3. Revise GE's Management Information and Support Systems

The IT change doesn't satisfy any of the three criteria, but it would ensure that the other changes are having an impact and goals are being met. However, this change is not essential for the success of Project C at this time and could be incorporated upon project completion, meaning no additional investment now, no additional complexity, and no extra workload for the team. The total cost is $2.8 million, and the change would extend the project schedule.

### 4. Add a Value Engineering Development Cycle

After PermaTuf A and B failed to meet the desired goals, one additional prototype cycle or iteration before market rollout seems to be a very sound measure. It will ensure high product quality and will also lower warranty and service costs. The most critical part of implementing this change is the project delay of three to four months. However, the value engineering cycle would increase product quality, lower costs, gain market share because of product improvements, and ensure that Project C does not run into the same problems as A and B. Although it is possible to delay this change for one or two years after the launch, by then it might be too late. The product's reputation could already be jeopardized, and it would be extremely difficult to convince both the sales force and customers that the product is the improved version they expected in the first place. In addition, senior management has been very clear: "Do it right the first time."

The total cost is $1.2 million. By year 3, the added cost of the proposals will be recovered through additional contribution from Project C. By year 7, Project C by itself will increase contribution 70 percent compared to total contribution in 1979. With each year after the launch of the new model, more and more of the increased revenue from the project will fall directly to the bottom line.

### 5. Drop (Postpone) Construction of the Integrated Computer Control Room

This option would release $1 million of approved budget for other implementations. Its main purpose was to prevent shop floor employees from losing power. On the other hand, it would be difficult to control a new automated plant without these systems. The control room would ensure that process quality and lower costs are actually being achieved. Taking this out of the project would put the rest of the project at risk and eliminate a way of tracking its success. The investment compared to the overall cost of the project is justifiable to ensure success factors are met and new systems are working according to plan.

## Recommendation

Options 1, 2, 4, and 5 should be pursued. The recommendation will require going back to senior management and the board of directors for approval of the additional investment of $4.2 million, 15 percent over the current budget but just 5 percent more than the cushion allowed any project. This option differs from the ones already agreed upon by the Project C team. However, leaving out one of the $1.5 million changes to avoid exceeding the 10 percent cushion is not consistent with a commitment to reach the critical success factors. Being world class means getting it right the first time. On the other hand, it's unlikely senior management and the board would approve the $6 or $7 million cost of the complete set of changes. The request could signal that the division isn't capable of good planning and cause senior executives to question the management of the project.

| Proposed action | Recommen-dation | Budget | Total additional budget |
|---|---|---|---|
| 1. Improving quality of the factory environment | Yes | $1.5 million | $1.5 million |
| 2. Skills training in technical problem solving | Yes | $1.5 million | $1.5 million |
| 3. Revisions in GE's management, information, and support systems | No | $2.8 million | 0 |
| 4. Adding a value engineering development cycle | Yes | $1.5 million | $1.2 million |
| 5. Drop (postpone) construction of the integrated computer control room | Yes | $1 million | 0 |
| | | Total | $4.2 million |

## Action Plan

Corcoran's team should persuade senior management to accept the recommendation, align stakeholders, and execute each proposal.

### Short Term (30 days)

- Tom Corcoran should prepare a convincing presentation of the proposal with help from people he trusts.

- Reach consensus on the recommendation and proposal.

- Designate team members to be in charge of each of the changes and make sure they are fully committed. Keep the union out of the loop prior to approval.

- Present the recommendation to senior management and the board. Don't hide anything. Make the additional cost, resource allocation, and risks completely transparent.

- Communicate outcome to all Project C managers and plan actual implementation.

- Communicate and negotiate changes with the union.

- Review and revise the implementation plan with everyone involved, including union members, and obtain commitment once the plan is finished.

### Medium Term (60–150 days)

- Start implementation of all changes.

- Track results and have a contingency team ready to intervene if serious problems arise.

- Communicate status on a monthly basis to senior management and board.

### Risks

- The main risk is not receiving approval for the additional budget.

- A second risk is longer-than-anticipated implementation time, which would begin to look like the division had not learned its lessons.

*Contingency Plan*

In the presentation, Corcoran should let management know that the team sees the additional investment as a small price to pay to avoid the mistakes of the past and push the division to a completely new level. He should draw their attention to the potential benefits throughout the company. If senior management won't approve new investment, Project C would then have to eliminate one of the $1.5 million changes to conform to the standard 10 percent cushion. Dropping the first proposal would probably have the least effect on the project.

The progress of all teams should be closely watched. A team should be on call during implementation to pitch in when a group falls behind schedule.

a. This essay is based on one written by Francisco "Paco" Demesa for a business school class and is used by permission.

## DECISION ESSAY 2

- *Case:* "Whistler Corporation (A)." Please read the case before reading the essay.

- *Writing task:* Recommend a decision to Stott, tell him why it's the best option, and draft an action plan.

Charles Stott must make a decision that will shape the future of Whistler Corporation. The company is losing $6 million a year and cannot sustain these losses and remain in business. Stott is considering three alternatives:

1. Reengineer domestic production.

2. Move all production offshore.

3. Transfer only low-end products offshore.

To make his decision, Stott should use two criteria:

1. The strategic importance of radar detectors to Whistler.

2. A manufacturing solution best suited to that importance.

## Partial Outsourcing

Stott should eliminate the third option. It sustains Whistler's flawed manufacturing process and therefore isn't the best solution under any circumstances.

The problems in Whistler's plants are the result of a long series of events. When the radar detector market exploded in the late 1980s, Whistler introduced many new products and increased production capacity quickly. It didn't consider the need to make changes in manufacturing as production increased and the number of products grew. Manufacturing was ill prepared for the market changes and suffered increasing work-in-progress and longer throughput times. Whistler's batch and kit process had worked fine in the early stages of the market when demand, the number of products, and volumes were low, and there was little pressure on costs. However, the process wasn't suitable for high demand combined with variable volumes and a growing number of SKUs. Additional factors compounded the drawbacks of the batch process. Increased process complexity pushed up inspection overhead and WIP costs. Volatility of demand in the mass market caused sudden schedule changes, longer TPT, and skyrocketing WIP costs. Whistler's habitual response to production problems has been to improvise capacity increases and accept the resulting cost increases.

In the end, Whistler's costs are 33 percent higher than those of offshore plants, a severe competitive disadvantage. Moving more of the volume to Korea would narrow the difference only slightly and leave the domestic manufacturing problems untouched.

## Process Reengineering

Stott has to decide between the two remaining options.

First, he needs to consider how important radar detectors are to Whistler. Demand, prices, and profitability are all declining. There is nothing to suggest that the decline isn't permanent. Competition is now based on price, which means the company with the lowest costs wins, and Whistler is clearly not winning. Most of Whistler's competitors have moved production offshore.

Reengineering the company's domestic manufacturing has numerous advantages. It would finally address the issues that have piled up over the years and could fix many of the most important ones. Breaking up production into steps and introducing a JIT system are likely to decrease WIP and TPT. Quality measures will ensure timely responses to production problems.

Reengineering should improve financial results as well. The exhibit shows that if MPL is implemented and the Fitchburg plant is closed, the company can expect a 26 percent reduction in unit cost. As the plant personnel gain experience in the revamped system, costs might well decline further. However, MPL results may not be scaleable across the entire company. Even with the benefits of the MPL, however, Whistler's domestic production cost per unit is still 11 percent higher than that of Asian vendors.

| Comparison of unit costs (USD) | | | |
|---|---|---|---|
| Cost | Current USD | MPL | Outsource |
| Material | $31.90 | $31.90 | $30.48 |
| Scrap | $3.83 | $.65 | $.92 |
| Direct labor | $9.00 | $3.64 | $1.88 |
| Variable overhead | $6.30 | $4.28 | $7.46 |
| Shipping | 0 | 0 | $.30 |
| Duty | 0 | 0 | $2.40 |
| Coordination | 0 | 0 | $1.00 |
| HQ overhead | $3.38 | $3.38 | $3.38 |
| Westford overhead | $9.28 | $9.28 | 0 |
| Fitchburg overhead | $8.14 | 0 | 0 |
| Total | $71.83 | $53.13 | $47.82 |

It is uncertain that the domestic plants will ever be able to compete on cost with offshore vendors. Therefore, reengineering isn't a good option for Whistler.

## Total Outsourcing

Whistler's long-term competitive advantage resides in design and engineering. The best decision will enable the company to concentrate on its core strengths and free up resources for expanded new product development. Whistler needs to follow the lead of its competitors and achieve the lowest possible unit cost through outsourcing. The second option is therefore the preferred decision because it satisfies both criteria.

## Disadvantages

The decision does have some disadvantages. Whistler will be entrusting an entire function to an outside organization. An unreliable partner could create a crisis worse than the one the company is experiencing now. The biggest disadvantage, though, is the closing of the domestic plants and the human cost that will inflict. The closings and layoffs are bound to be traumatic for the plant personnel and also for the remaining employees. The resulting decline in morale could hurt productivity and commitment when they are urgently needed.

The risk of the partnership can be minimized by thorough due diligence. The leading candidate could be Whistler's current outsourcing partner since they have a good relationship, and the vendor is already familiar with Whistler and its products. The negative effects of the plant closings can't be eliminated, but they can be contained. Laid-off workers should be provided with every transition resource the company can afford. One of the resources should be retraining workers for available jobs. The remaining Whistler employees should be thoroughly briefed on the reasons for the plant closures and assured that the painful actions offer the best chance for the company's long-term survival and the preservation of jobs.

## Action Plan

*Goal*: transfer production to an appropriate vendor as soon as possible, with a target of one year to begin transfers and two years to complete them.

### Short-Term Steps

- Establish a rock-solid consensus among senior executives and agree on transition dates and process. Form a multidisciplinary team to vet vendors and manage the transition.

- Develop as soon as possible a plan for assisting laid-off workers. It's critical to have this in place when the decision is announced. Communicate the decision to employees as soon as the assistance package is settled. The message should be honest, to the point, and sincere.

- Meet with the current partner and potential vendors and work up a short list of prospects. Start with the current Korean partner but take a serious look at other companies to avoid relying on one vendor. Selection should be based on high-quality production, on-time performance, and a history of being easy to work with.

- Select partner and agree on process details and schedules and run the first transfer as a test. Modify plans and schedules as needed.

### Medium-Term Steps

- Start outplacement services for the first round of layoffs. Make changes based on the learning from these early efforts.

- Finish the transfer. Establish a close technical and project coordination relationship with the partner.

### Long-Term Steps

- The supplier is a partner, not a vendor, and Whistler should commit to maintaining a healthy long-term relationship.

### Risks and Countermeasures

- The transfer process could break down and leave Whistler worse off than it is now. Whistler and the vendor can test the process and change it as necessary by making the initial transfers one product at a time. All but one of Whistler's competitors have moved manufacturing offshore, so there are precedents for smooth transfers.

- A second risk, opposition to the decision within the company and turmoil set off by the layoffs, is worse because it is difficult to prevent. Senior management should constantly repeat two messages: for employees who will be retained, they should highlight the necessity of outsourcing to survive and the bright prospects for competing on the company's real strengths; for employees who will be let go, they should stress that they sincerely regret having to lay off anyone and that Whistler will do everything it can to help them find new jobs.

## PLANNING TEMPLATES FOR A DECISION ESSAY[a]

These templates will help you build a decision essay. The first template uses the state-and-prove model. The second uses the prove-and-state model. (See the above explanation of the two models.) You don't have to follow the order of the templates. The important thing is to capture your ideas as they occur to you.

### State-and-Prove Model

*Proof*

*Position Statement: Recommended Decision.* State the decision you are recommending and summarize the reasons for it. Be brief! (Note: You can't start work on the position statement until you have a tentative recommendation and at least one reason for it. You can revise the statement as you work.)

| Decision: |
| --- |
|  |
|  |
| Reasons: |
|  |
|  |

*Decision Options.* List the decision options. They are usually stated in the case.

| Decision options: |
| --- |
|  |
|  |
|  |
|  |
|  |
|  |

*Decision Criteria.* State the decision criteria. They should be relevant, broad rather than narrow, and as few as possible. Specific ways to measure the criteria may be needed. Note them in the second column.

| Criteria | How to measure |
|---|---|
|  |  |
|  |  |
|  |  |

*Proof of Recommended Option.* List the criteria in the left column and the evidence they reveal that supports your recommendation. Focus on the strongest evidence you have.

| Criteria | Evidence |
|---|---|
|  |  |
|  |  |
|  |  |
|  |  |
|  |  |

*Critique of Options.* List the criteria in the left column and the evidence they reveal that shows why the other options should be rejected. Limit yourself to only the most compelling evidence against the options.

| Rejected option: | |
|---|---|
| *Criteria* | *Evidence* |
|  |  |
|  |  |
| **Rejected option:** | |
| *Criteria* | *Evidence* |
|  |  |
|  |  |

*Major Disadvantages of Recommendation.* List the one or two major disadvantages of your recommendation, any evidence that is needed to prove them, and how to mitigate them. (If you are writing an exam and running out of time, skip this!)

| Disadvantage | Evidence and mitigation |
|---|---|
|  |  |
|  |  |

## Action Plan

The general purpose of a decision action plan is to implement the decision as effectively as possible.

*Goal(s).* State the goal(s) of the plan—the major outcome(s) the steps are supposed to bring about.

| Goal(s) |
|---|
| 1. |
| 2. |
| 3. |

*Action Steps.* Write the steps of the plan without worrying too much about their order. When you finish, write numbers in the first column to indicate the final chronological order of the steps. The second column can help you think about steps as part of phases of the overall plan (e.g., consensus, communication, and improvement).

- Short term

| Order in essay | Phase | Step |
|---|---|---|
|  |  |  |
|  |  |  |
|  |  |  |
|  |  |  |
|  |  |  |
|  |  |  |

- Long term

| Order in essay | Phase | Step |
|---|---|---|
| | | |
| | | |
| | | |
| | | |
| | | |
| | | |

*Major Risks and Responses.* Identify the major risks that could undermine the plan. Propose responses that will eliminate or contain it.

| Risk | Response |
|---|---|
| | |
| | |
| | |

## Prove-and-State Model

### *Proof*

*Decision Options.* State the decision options. They are usually stated in the case.

| Decision options: |
|---|
| |
| |
| |

*Decision Criteria.* State the decision criteria. They should be relevant, broad rather than narrow, and as few as possible. Specific ways to measure the criteria may be needed. Note them in the second column.

| Criteria | How to measure |
|----------|----------------|
|          |                |
|          |                |
|          |                |
|          |                |
|          |                |

*Critique of Options.* List the criteria in the left column and the evidence they reveal that shows why the other options should be rejected. Limit yourself to only the most compelling evidence against the options.

| Rejected option: | |
|------------------|--|
| *Criteria* | *Evidence* |
|          |                |
|          |                |

| Rejected option: | |
|------------------|--|
| *Criteria* | *Evidence* |
|          |                |
|          |                |

*Proof of Recommended Option.* List the criteria in the left column and the evidence they reveal that supports your recommendation. Focus on the strongest evidence you have.

| Criteria | Evidence |
|----------|----------|
|          |          |
|          |          |
|          |          |

*Position Statement: Recommended Decision.* State the decision you are recommending and summarize the reasons for it. Be brief! (Note: You can't start work on the position statement until you have a tentative recommendation and at least one reason for it. You can revise the statement as you work.)

| Decision: |
| --- |
| |
| |
| **Reasons:** |
| |
| |

*Major Disadvantages of Recommendation.* List the one or two major disadvantages of your recommendation, any evidence that is needed to prove them, and how to mitigate them. (If you are writing an exam and running out of time, skip this!)

| Disadvantage | Evidence and mitigation |
| --- | --- |
| | |
| | |

### Action Plan

The general purpose of a decision action plan is to implement the decision as effectively as possible.

*Goal(s).* State the goal(s) of the plan—the major outcome(s) the steps are supposed to bring about.

| Goal(s) |
| --- |
| 1. |
| 2. |
| 3. |

*Action Steps.* Write the steps of the plan without worrying too much about their order. When you finish, write numbers in the first column to indicate the final chronological order of the steps. The second column can help you think about steps as part of phases of the overall plan (e.g., consensus, communication, and improvement).

- Short term

| Order in essay | Phase | Step |
|---|---|---|
| | | |
| | | |
| | | |
| | | |
| | | |
| | | |

- Long term

| Order in essay | Phase | Step |
|---|---|---|
| | | |
| | | |
| | | |
| | | |
| | | |
| | | |

*Major Risks and Responses.* Identify the major risks that could undermine the plan. Propose responses that will eliminate or contain them.

| Risk | Response |
|---|---|
| | |
| | |
| | |

a. Tehila Lieberman contributed substantially to the development of the essay planning templates.

# CHAPTER 12

# EVALUATION ESSAYS

Evaluations are judgments about the worth, value, or effectiveness of a performance, act, or outcome of some kind. An evaluation essay must look at both sides of the subject—factors supporting your bottom-line assessment, those opposing it, and any that fall in between. This chapter doesn't consider evaluations, like bank loan reviews, that are performed with and decided by formulas. It deals with evaluations in which the conclusion isn't determined by a formula but by judgment. (For more on evaluative situations in cases, see chapter 7.)

In this chapter's sample essay, the case references have been disguised. The original case is still taught, so a detailed discussion of it might lessen its usefulness, but the issues it raises are excellent for illustrating an evaluation. A summary of the disguised case, "The Bolivar Default Decision: Travesty or Turning Point?," is provided with the sample essay. Please read the case summary and the essay. You won't benefit from the chapter without reading both.

## HOW TO ORGANIZE AN EVALUATION ESSAY

An evaluation essay has five elements:

1. Bottom-line evaluation (position statement)

2. Evaluation criteria

3. Proof of the evaluation

4. Qualifications

5. Action plan

The structure of an evaluative essay differs substantially from problem and decision essays. The latter present arguments consisting almost entirely of content favorable to the position statement. A decision essay may talk about the recommendation's downside, but it is generally a small portion of the essay. An evaluation essay includes factors that don't support the position statement and the discussion of them can be extensive (as in the sample essay below). The subject accounts for the structure. Performances, acts, and outcomes inevitably have positive, negative, and ambiguous or uncertain facets. Think of a performance appraisal—the strengths and weaknesses it records reflect the fact that a performance is never perfect. In addition, an evaluation essay often has a section devoted to qualifications to the bottom-line judgment. In the sample essay, the writer attaches a major qualification to his support for a decision that has been made.

The essay outline above follows the state-and-prove model: you tell readers what you think and then show them why. The state-and-prove model encourages you to tell readers your recommendation first and then prove it. That structures the reader's task and gives you a sharply defined purpose, making it a good approach for written exams and other time-constrained situations.

An evaluation essay can also follow the prove-and-state model:

1. Evaluation criteria

2. Proof of the evaluation

3. Qualifications

4. Bottom-line evaluation (position statement)

5. Action plan

The model is *inductive* in the sense that it walks the reader through a process of determining a conclusion. If there is reason to believe that readers will resist a conclusion before it is proved, this model avoids that resistance. The approach can be persuasive because readers feel that the evaluation includes all the relevant factors, not just those favorable to the conclusion. One drawback is that you can spend so much time on the evaluation that you never get to the conclusion. You may also wander off point when you don't have an explicit statement of purpose at the beginning of the essay.

## BOTTOM-LINE EVALUATION

The most important sentence of the essay is the statement of your bottom-line judgment. On rare occasions, the conclusion of an evaluation might be restricted to a summary of pros and cons. In most instances, however, a conclusion about the evaluation has to be expressed. Without it, an evaluation isn't actionable and shifts the task of judgment to the reader.

Here's the first paragraph of the sample essay:

*Owing to the history of inconsistency and a string of political crises peculiar even for Bolivar, the national government faced the tough decision of whether to default on a large portion of its foreign debt. This was a situation in which all of the alternatives were unpalatable, and the decision was largely a negative one of choosing the least risky of high-risk alternatives.* All in all, President DiNardo's decision to default was harsh but right. I support his position—but only if the government defines and implements a long-term strategy that will institutionalize economic reform.

The non-italicized sentence is the position statement. It is the assertion that the essay must prove. As with any argument, a position statement at the beginning of the essay gives readers a purpose for reading.

### Evaluation Criteria

The results of an evaluation are extraordinarily sensitive to the criteria employed. Here's a simple example from economics. Let's say you're assessing the effectiveness of a nation's economic policies. One measure is GDP per capita. The numbers show a healthy increase over ten years, and so do other measures of national income. You could conclude that the policies are quite successful. When you measure income distribution, however, you find that most of the population remains poor. Wealth is concentrated in the hands of a few. Now the economic policies don't look as attractive for long-term stability.

From the standpoint of readers, an evaluation lacking defined and relevant criteria is arbitrary. The audience can't tell whether the judgment is reasonable. (The same rule is true for decision analysis.) The writer of the sample essay states his criteria clearly:

> *To evaluate the president's action, these criteria will be used:*
> * *The economic advantages and disadvantages of defaulting*
> * *The political advantages and disadvantages*
> * *The social advantages and disadvantages*

With evaluative or decision-making criteria, a crucial skill is knowing how to decide on the criteria. The two sources are the situation in the case and specialized methods. There are many business theories and frameworks that can be used for assessment. In an academic course, the professor may require or expect students to use a particular framework. The sample essay for this chapter employs three criteria derived from the frameworks used in an MBA course: macroeconomics, politics, and social dynamics. Relevance to the case situation will exclude frameworks or parts of them, so be careful not to use as many as possible under the assumption that more means better.

The second task related to criteria is deciding how to measure them. The case information guides your choice of measurements to use. The disguised case includes large amounts of economic data, some statistics on social welfare, and a small amount of information on politics. Therefore, the economic and social criteria can be measured quite well, but the application of the political criterion mostly relies on inference.

The three characteristics of criteria discussed in the decision essays chapter are worth repeating here:

- The number of criteria for an evaluation should be as small as possible. Proliferation of criteria leads to fragmented evaluations and unpersuasive arguments.

- Effective criteria tend to be broad, not narrow. There are usually an array of ways to measure broad criteria. The section of the sample essay on economic advantages and disadvantages illustrates this point very well; it includes macroeconomic indicators that help the writer clarify and assess a complex situation.

- Criteria are sometimes independent of one another and can be used in any order. Often, though, assessment criteria have a logical order of application. The criteria of the sample essay are intertwined because the underlying national dynamics are, but crisscrossing among them in an essay would leave readers with spinning heads. Since the act being evaluated is economic, its most direct and measurable effects will therefore be on the economy, which is therefore a logical place to start.

## PROOF OF EVALUATION

The proof of an evaluative essay has a two-tiered organization. The proof is organized by criteria, and the discussion of each criterion is organized by the terms of the assessment such as advantages and disadvantages, strengths and weaknesses, or effectiveness and ineffectiveness. Here is an outline of the sample essay's proof:

1. Economic factors
   - Advantages
   - Disadvantages

2. Political factors
   - Advantages
   - Disadvantages

3. Social factors
   - Advantages
   - Disadvantages

Advantages come first because the writer supports the decision being assessed. The purpose of an evaluative essay is to prove the bottom-line judgment. So under each criterion, you discuss the side of the evaluation that supports your position statement before taking up the other side. A writer who believed that the decision wasn't a good one would argue the disadvantages first.

The argument for advantages in the sample essay is worth paying attention to. It illustrates a well-constructed proof that uses evidence effectively. Walking through a part of the argument reveals some valuable points about the structure of an argument. The following paragraphs are a portion of the proof for the first economic advantage:

> After President Fernandez left office, a succession of weak presidents and disputed elections paralyzed economic policy. *Spending ran out of control, government revenues declined, and unemployment hit a new high of nearly 20 percent. The country then turned to foreign investors for $35 billion, but it wound up in the worst of both worlds, having too little revenue and too much debt, which rose to 110 percent of GDP in 1998. Emergency steps were taken, and they helped improve monetary policy problems but depressed wages to the point that well over half the country's population fell below the poverty level.*
>
> When DiNardo assumed office, he took measures that led to the beginning of an economic recovery. The measures were made possible by a suspension of interest payments on foreign debt. *Real GDP went from negative numbers to 4–5 percent growth in two years. Although still high, unemployment went down (from 20 percent to 14 percent) and wages rose; fixed investment started to recover along with the current account as exports grew and imports remained steady; and total debt as a percent of GDP fell below 100 percent.*
>
> Nevertheless, the cumulative problems of a badly managed economy threatened the recovery. *DiNardo could have blamed past presidents and proclaimed that he could not make good on all their mistakes. But he refused to take that route and was determined to sustain the modest recovery.* Maintaining the recovery was the chief economic strength of the decision. *A closely related positive was the signal it sent to the people that he was determined to put their needs before those of foreign investors, in particular to move as many of them as possible out of poverty.*

The non-italicized sentences are the backbone of the argument in these paragraphs. Paraphrasing the sentences and putting them in a list makes the logic of the argument easier to see:

1. A succession of weak presidents and disputed elections paralyzed economic policy.

2. President DiNardo was able to take some measures that started a small economic recovery.

3. A suspension of interest payments on foreign debt made the measures possible.

4. Nevertheless, the cumulative problems of a badly managed economy threatened the recovery.

5. Maintaining the recovery was the chief economic strength of the decision. (Implication of this sentence: the recovery can be maintained by funding from the unpaid debt.)

This outline brings out the movement of the argument. Four statements of fact show the economic logic of the president's decision and support the conclusion (statement 5). An effective case-based argument is built from logical units like this one. But, because none of the statements is self-evidently true, the writer must furnish evidence to show they are valid. Only then can the argument convince the reader.

An evaluative essay recognizes the factors opposed to the overall assessment. It portrays them honestly instead of ignoring, minimizing, or sugar-coating them. When readers are experts, they will readily detect these evasions, so it's foolish to try them. Nevertheless, the discussion of opposed factors should include mitigating circumstances or actions—if they exist. An example is the first economic disadvantage in the sample essay:

*The main economic weakness of the decision is the possible failure of the gamble. If the money saved isn't used wisely, the country could be worse off than it was before the decision.* The president can best defend against this outcome by ensuring that the government invests in long-term development.

The writer doesn't hide the disasters that would result if the decision doesn't pan out. At the same time, though, the non-italicized sentence notes that the disaster is avoidable. Factors on the opposite side of your position sometimes can only be managed, not eliminated. This is true of an economic disadvantage noted in the sample essay:

*Finally, some foreign debt holders have taken the country to court and many others might do the same. They have a case because the economic numbers in the two years before the decision were looking better, including a positive GDP. The country could counter that full repayment would have put the economy into a freefall, in which case investors would end up with less than they are going to receive under DiNardo's decision. Moreover, investors will receive something back.* Nevertheless, the country may suffer some adverse rulings.

## QUALIFICATIONS

Qualifications state factors not part of the evaluation that have a significant effect on it. The sample essay has a prominent qualification to the bottom-line judgment. The writer says the positive evaluation can be justified only if a long-term development strategy is put in place.

Do qualifications harm a conclusion by making it seem less decisive? Yes, when you pile them on and seem to be trying to avoid responsibility for a conclusion. When you confine yourself to a few with big impacts, the evaluation is strengthened. A substantial qualification makes an evaluation more congruent with the realities of a situation and therefore more convincing to readers.

## EVALUATION ACTION PLANS

The general purpose of an evaluation action plan varies according to the subject of the assessment. A plan for performance appraisals improves the individual's weaknesses and amplifies the strengths. A plan for the evaluation of an act such as a decision seeks to optimize the implementation of the decision in light of the findings of the assessment. (For more information on action plans, see chapter 9.)

The action plan of the sample essay is a map for implementing the president's decision. The plan has two goals, one for economic policy and another for explaining it to other nations. The evaluation informs the steps serving each goal. The sources of actionable content in the assessment are shown in exhibit 12-1. Creating an action plan begins with identifying actionable statements in the argument.

The order of steps conforms to the guidelines in chapter 9. Short-term steps are reserved for urgent or easy actions. In the sample action plan, the two short-term steps qualify as urgent. The decision has already been made, so it is imperative for the president (1) to begin to put the country on a

**EXHIBIT 12-1**

### Sources of action steps

| Action steps | Sources in essay |
|---|---|
| Policy | • Economic factors—one advantage, one disadvantage |
| | • Political factors—one advantage, one neutral factor |
| | • Qualifications |
| Informing other countries | • Economic factors—two disadvantages |
| | • Political factors—one disadvantage |

new development path and (2) through the country's diplomats, tell the country's side of the story to other governments and lending institutions.

An action plan for a performance evaluation is going to look more like a problem action plan. Problems call for solutions; evaluations call for improvements in the negative aspects of performance. Chapter 7 has an extended evaluation of Don Rogers' performance as a leader. Rogers' leadership report card (see exhibit 12-2) has a great deal of actionable content.

The goal of an action plan for Rogers would be to shore up his major weaknesses in leadership skills, ability to overcome obstacles, and change skills. Most of the plan would consist of steps for strengthening his performance in these three areas. Some of the steps, however, would have to deal with the external factors that affect his leadership. Corporate, for instance, has given him a promotion for which he is poorly qualified and seems to have a sink-or-swim attitude toward him. For the best interests of the company, they need to get involved and actively help him.

**EXHIBIT 12-2**

### Evaluation of Rogers' leadership

| Criteria | Evaluation |
|---|---|
| Leadership skills | Weak |
| Overcoming obstacles | Very weak |
| Change skills | Weak |
| Qualifications | External factors contributed to poor performance |

## EVALUATION ESSAY

"The Bolivar Default Decision: Travesty or Turning Point?" (disguised case):[a] The president of Bolivar, Alfredo DiNardo, has just decided to forgo repayment of a large portion of foreign debt. The decision was greeted by consternation in international financial markets, by anger (and litigation) from debt holders, and by applause from the people of the country. Bolivar has a history of turbulent politics and chronic economic instability. Political bargains often led to government decisions that sacrificed the long-term economic well-being of the nation. Some of these bargains involved economic favors to certain groups that retarded growth. The result was a cycle of slight recoveries and steep declines characterized by federal budget deficits, rising unemployment, high inflation, and social unrest.

At the time of the case, the new president, DiNardo, has been in negotiations with various foreign creditors. Meanwhile, defying expectations, Bolivar's economy has rebounded. Under DiNardo, the federal government narrowed the federal budget deficit through higher taxes and reduced expenditures, but he feared that these measures would not be enough to maintain economic improvement. He has decided to unilaterally cease payment on about 50% of Bolivar's external debt. The decision has sparked an international controversy, in part because, for creditors and foreign experts, the decision seems to mark a low point in Bolivar's management of its economy and reliability as a borrower. Some of them have issued dire warnings that Bolivar won't be able to borrow from foreign lenders for years and then only at very high interest rates. Inside the country, however, politicians and many individuals see the decision as a turning point in the economic health of the nation.

The real case provides an extensive economic history with a great deal of supporting data for recent years and a brief parallel narrative of domestic politics. It ends with twenty exhibits, most of them presenting statistics related to the economy and social conditions.

- *Writing task:* Evaluate the president's decision on the basis of its overall merits and specific advantages and disadvantages. Propose an action plan based on the evaluation.

Owing to the history of inconsistency and a string of political crises peculiar even for Bolivar, the national government faced the tough decision of whether to default on a large portion of its foreign debt. This was a situation in which all of the alternatives were unpalatable, and the decision was largely a negative one of choosing the least risky of high-risk alternatives. All in all, President DiNardo's decision to default was harsh but right. I support his position—but only if the government defines and implements a long-term strategy that will institutionalize economic reform.

To evaluate the president's action, these criteria will be used:

- The economic advantages and disadvantages of defaulting

- The political advantages and disadvantages

- The social advantages and disadvantages

### Economic Factors

*Advantages*

President DiNardo intends to finance continued recovery with the proceeds of repudiated debt. A history of poor economic management forced this strategy on him. It may fail, but the alternative would have been worse.

Historically, the revolving door of governments crippled the national economy. Over the ten years prior to DiNardo's term, inflation peaked at astounding levels as high as 900 percent, and deficits typically were 20 percent of GDP. Then-President Fernandez was elected on a platform of hope and initiated reforms to bring down inflation and deficits and promote growth. Specific steps were a fixed exchange rate tied to the U.S. dollar and a spike in government revenues owing to the sale of state-owned enterprises. The plan achieved some results—less inflation, budget surpluses, and GDP growth—but it increased unemployment (16 percent). The downside of the fixed exchange rate was a vulnerability to external financial problems. In one instance, Bolivar's central bank had to increase interest rates and take other steps to respond to a crisis in Mexico that reduced GDP and put more people out of work.

After President Fernandez left office, a succession of weak presidents and disputed elections paralyzed economic policy. Spending ran out of control, government revenues declined, and unemployment hit a new high of nearly 20 percent. The country then turned to foreign investors for $35 billion, and foreign debt rose to 110 percent of GDP in 1998. Emergency steps were taken, but wages fell, pushing half the country below the poverty level.

When DiNardo assumed office, he took measures that led to the beginning of an economic recovery. The measures were made possible by a suspension of interest payments on foreign debt. Real GDP went from negative numbers to 4–5 percent growth in two years. Although still high, unemployment went down (from 20 percent to 14 percent) and wages rose; fixed investment started to recover along with the current account as exports grew and imports remained steady; and total debt as a percent of GDP fell below 100 percent.

Nevertheless, the cumulative problems of a badly managed economy threatened the recovery. Maintaining the recovery was the chief economic strength of the decision. Also positive was the signal it sent to the people that he was determined to put their needs before those of foreign investors.

Another strength is the fact that many foreign investors are still going to make healthy profits from partial repayment of principal and interest. The securities had very high interest rates, and their value actually increased after the markets learned the president was not going to repudiate the entire debt. In addition, the international financial community was well aware of the country's history and the high risk involved.

### Disadvantages

The main economic weakness of the decision is the possible failure of the gamble. If the money saved isn't used wisely, the country could be worse off than it was before the decision. The president can best defend against this outcome by ensuring that the government invests the savings in long-term development.

A second disadvantage of the decision is the closing of foreign financial markets to the country with the exception of short-term debt at punitive interest rates. Paradoxically, if the partial default were to lead to a healthier economy, investors would be more likely to return. History shows, too, that greed often causes foreign investors to forget defaults. And some current investors can make handsome profits from partial repayment.

Finally, some foreign debt holders have taken the country to court and many others might do the same. They have a case because the economic numbers in the two years before the decision were looking better, including a positive GDP. The country could counter that full repayment would have put the economy into a freefall, in which case investors would end up with less than they are going to receive under DiNardo's decision. Moreover, investors will receive something back. Nevertheless, the country may suffer some adverse rulings.

## Political Factors

### Advantages

Bolivar's politics were a root cause of its economic woes. Charismatic politicians would declare themselves populists and take steps that did put money in the people's pockets (and their own). In the end, everyone, except the politicians, ended up poorer. By making the decision he did, DiNardo took away much of the leverage of these individuals in the opposition parties.

If DiNardo puts the money saved from debt payments into long-term assets such as infrastructure and education, he will move the paradigm from corruption and short-term consumption to buy political favor to long-term investment that builds a better standard of living.

### Neutral

The political dynamic can go one of two ways, but it is hard to predict the circumstances that will determine the direction. If the recovery continues, it could oblige parties vying for control of Congress and the presidency to toe a responsible line. On the other hand, rivals could pounce on the inevitable slow pace of recovery, promise better times, and make all the old mistakes.

## Social Stakes

### Advantages

Social conditions were starting to improve in the two years before the decision. In the prior years, poverty levels had more than doubled in the capital and increased more rapidly in the countryside. Crime rates surged, with the murder rate doubling over five years, and riots were commonplace in the cities. Literacy rates went down, as did access to health care. The decision was both substance and symbol.

Substantively, it frees up money to improve social conditions. Symbolically, the decision gives people some reason to hope.

*Neutral*

With no ability to borrow and a probable slowdown in foreign investment, the national recovery will be slower. The country will have to rely on itself more. The slow pace of recovery could translate into small gains in social conditions, which could lead to impatience and more violence. However, this weakness would also be true if the president had decided to pay in full. The money sucked out of the economy would depress economic and social progress.

## Qualifications

President DiNardo's decision is right if, and only if, he has a sensible plan for long-term development. Without one, the money saved from cutting loan payments will be squandered, angering foreign investors and lending institutions and closing international financial markets to the country for years. The plan should cover structural reforms, tax code changes, monetary and fiscal policy, import-export strategy, budgeting, and infrastructure investment.

## Action Plan

DiNardo should put in place the elements of a long-term plan and, through diplomacy, explain the reasons for his decision to the governments of important nations, particularly the United States and the European Union, and international institutions such as the IMF. The diplomatic team should assure all parties that the proceeds of the decision will be invested wisely.

*Short term*

- Rapidly install new economic policies: structural reforms such as tax breaks to encourage foreign direct investment and exports, a reduction in the paperwork needed to start a business, subsidies to strengthen industries with high potential, and better tax collection.

- Develop a single message to convince key nations and international institutions that the decision was a last resort and that the government will be as transparent as possible about the investment in the economy and social welfare.

*Medium term*

- To help restore government revenues, give provinces incentives they currently lack for tax collection: a bigger share of collections. In return, the president should require provinces to keep revenues from being soaked up by corruption.

- Approach leaders of Congress and convey a desire to work on policies for the long-term benefit of the country rather than short-term political advantage. If leaders rebuff him, he should take his case directly to the people and ask them to pressure members of Congress.

*Long term*

- Implement the full development strategy. Appoint a board of experts and prominent individuals with impeccable credentials to monitor the implementation and progress of the strategy. The board should have the power to make public statements and publish reports without needing the permission of the president or other executive branch officials.

a. This essay is based on one written by E. Ciprian Vatasescu for a business school class and is used by permission.

## PLANNING TEMPLATE FOR AN EVALUATION ESSAY

This template will help you build an evaluation essay. It follows the organization of an evaluation essay, but you don't have to use it in that order.[a] The important thing is to capture your ideas as they occur to you.

### Position Statement: Bottom-line Judgment

State your overall evaluation, the most significant positive and negative factors, and any qualifications. Be brief! The statement can be

revised as you work. (Note: You can't start work on the position statement until you have some confidence in your bottom-line judgment.)

| Overall evaluation: |
| --- |
| |
| |
| **Summary of major positive/negative factors:** |
| |
| |
| **Summary of any qualifications:** |
| |
| |

### Evaluation Criteria

State the evaluation criteria. They should be relevant, broad rather
than narrow, and as few as possible. Specific ways to measure the criteria may be needed. Note them in the second column.

| Criteria | How to measure them |
| --- | --- |
| | |
| | |
| | |
| | |

### Proof of the Evaluation

List positive and negative factors the criteria reveal and the evidence for them. The points can be revised and rearranged as you
work. If any criteria seem to have ambiguous results, note those. In
the essay, order positive and negative factors to support your position
statement. Also, note any ideas for action steps.

| Criterion 1 | | |
|---|---|---|
| | Evidence | Action plan ideas |
| Positive | | |
| Negative | | |

| Criterion 2 | | |
|---|---|---|
| | Evidence | Action plan ideas |
| Positive | | |
| Negative | | |

| Criterion 3 | | |
|---|---|---|
| | Evidence | Action plan ideas |
| Positive | | |
| Negative | | |

| Criterion 4 | | |
|---|---|---|
| | Evidence | Action plan ideas |
| Positive | | |
| Negative | | |

## Qualifications

Qualifications state factors not part of the evaluation that have a significant effect on it. A summary of the qualifications should be included in the position statement.

| Qualifications (if any): |
|---|
| |
| |
| |
| |
| |
| |

## Action Plan

The general purpose of an evaluation action plan is to improve the negative factors and enhance the positive. For the assessment of an act such as decision, the action plan can be an implementation plan that reflects the findings of the evaluation.

### Goal(s)

State the goal(s) of the plan—the major outcome(s) the steps are supposed to bring about.

| Goal(s) |
| --- |
| 1. |
| 2. |
| 3. |

### Action Steps

Write the steps of the plan without worrying too much about their order. When you finish, write numbers in the first column to indicate the final chronological order of the steps. The second column can help you think about steps as part of phases of the overall plan (e.g., consensus, communication, improvement).

### Short term

| Order in essay | Phase | Step |
| --- | --- | --- |
|  |  |  |
|  |  |  |
|  |  |  |
|  |  |  |
|  |  |  |
|  |  |  |

*Long term*

| Order in essay | Phase | Step |
|---|---|---|
| | | |
| | | |
| | | |
| | | |
| | | |
| | | |

### Major Risks and Responses

Identify the major risks that could undermine the plan. Propose responses that will eliminate or contain them.

| Risk | Response |
|---|---|
| | |
| | |
| | |

a. Tehila Lieberman contributed substantially to the development of the essay planning templates.

## PART IV

# CASES
# FOR ANALYSIS
# AND WRITING

# Allentown Materials Corporation:
# The Electronic Products Division (Abridged)

In July 1992, Don Rogers took a moment to reflect on the state of his organization. He had become the Vice President and General Manager of the Electronics Products Division (EPD) at Allentown Materials Corporation following his predecessor's untimely death two years before. The EPD faced a number of problems, and Rogers was not sure what he needed to do. He felt increasing pressure from headquarters. EPD was expected to continue to meet the corporation's 10% average annual growth rate and aggressive profit targets, despite increased competition in the electronic components industry. The division's performance had declined in 1991 and 1992 (See **Exhibit 1** for EPD's operating data) and most component manufacturers anticipated that they were competing for a shrinking total market. In addition, EPD's reputation for delivery and service had slipped, and their number of missed commitments was very high. Rogers commented:

> I have had some difficult times in my division over the past two years. Our business is becoming fiercely competitive and this has led to a decrease in sales. To deal with the downturn in business we have reduced the number of people and expenses sharply. This has been painful, but I think these actions have stemmed the tide. We are in control again, but the business continues to be very competitive. Morale is low; there is a lot of conflict between groups that we can not seem to resolve. There is a lack of mutual confidence and trust. The organization is just not pulling together and the lack of coordination is affecting our ability to develop new products. Most of my key people believe that we are having conflicts because business is bad. They say that if business would only get better we will stop crabbing at each other. Frankly, I am not sure if they are right. The conflicts might be due to the pressures we are under but more likely they indicate a more fundamental problem. I need to determine if the conflict between groups is serious, so I can decide what I should do about it.

## Allentown Materials Corporation

Allentown Materials Corporation, a leading manufacturer of specialty glass, was established in Allentown, Pennsylvania, in the late-1800s. The corporation's growth and reputation were based on its ability to invent and manufacture new glass products, and it had major businesses in a number of different glass and ceramic markets. In 1992, Allentown was in a strong financial and profit position. Its investment in R&D as a percent of sales was quite significant in comparison with that of other companies in industry. The company had established the first industrial research laboratory in the early 1900s, the Technical Staffs Division (R&D), which conducted basic research and product and process research

This case was prepared by Research Associate Jennifer M. Suesse (under the direction of Professor Michael Beer).

## CASE STUDY

### EDP sales and operating income, 1985–1992 ($ thousands)

|  | 1985 | 1986 | 1987 | 1988 | 1989 | 1990 | 1991 | 1992 |
|---|---|---|---|---|---|---|---|---|
| Sales | $54,518 | $93,177 | $93,852 | $85,854 | $108,496 | $113,780 | $102,206 | $102,986 |
| Operating income* | 12,902 | 23,349 | 24,964 | 12,846 | 21,746 | 17,868 | 6,680 | 6,745 |

*Income margin equals less manufacturing, administrative, and sales expenses.

*Source:* Company records.

in glass and related technologies. Strength in manufacturing contributed to Allentown's technological edge. Until now, Allentown had always been in the enviable position of growing profitably without substantial competitive pressures. Patents, technological know-how in manufacturing, and the requirement of substantial capital investment made it difficult for others to offer serious threats.

**Corporate organization**   Allentown's corporate organization reflected the close link between its growth and its technology. R&D was highly regarded by top management. Its vice president reported directly to the chairman of the board. Next to R&D, Allentown's strongest functional area was manufacturing. Many considered it to be the function through which one could rise to the top, as many of the company's top executives had been promoted from the ranks of manufacturing. To foster a strong manufacturing orientation, the company had developed a control system in which plants were viewed as profit centers. Financial results were reported every 28 days and were reviewed 13 times a year. These periodic reviews were conducted at all levels of the corporation.

For many years all of Allentown's operations were based in its headquarters, but as the company grew, plants and sales offices were established throughout the world. In 1992, all but two of the corporation's eight line divisions had their headquarters in Allentown. Thus, most divisions could discuss business problems on a face-to-face basis; the corporation operated like a relatively close-knit family. People saw each other frequently on Allentown's premises, on the streets of the town, and on social occasions. People at all levels and from diverse parts of the corporation interacted informally. It would not be uncommon for top-level corporate officers to meet divisional personnel in the main office building and to engage them in informal discussions about the state of their business—asking about orders, shipments, sales, and profits for the period.

## The EPD and Its History

The Electronic Products Division (EPD) manufactured high-quality electronic components (resistors and capacitors) for several markets. More than half of the EPD's 1992 sales were to original equipment manufacturers (OEMs) who bought resistors and capacitors in large volume for use in a variety of their products. The remainder of the division's sales were to distributors who resold the components in smaller quantities. Much like other Allentown businesses, the components business grew due to the EPD's unique technological capabilities. Many of their competitively unique new products were invented in response to needs from OEMs who wanted the EPD to apply its research and development strength to meet their stringent component specifications.

**The Component Market**    Through the mid-1980s, the space program and the military's reliance on missile defense systems created demand for highly reliable components, since failure threatened the integrity of very sophisticated and expensive equipment. The government was willing to pay premium prices for components that met its very strict specifications, and Allentown's knowledge base enabled it to serve this market well.

In the late 1980s, the nature of EPD's business began to shift. As the cold war began to ebb and the military market declined, the division concentrated more of its efforts in commercial markets. For example, the personal computer (PC) market was exploding. The growing market in telecommunications devices, such as cellular telephones, personal pagers (beepers), facsimile machines, and other consumer electronics products also provided new opportunities for the EPD components. Using its unique technological capabilities in product development and manufacturing, the EPD was able to enter these new markets and quickly establish a major position in them. In response to the high-volume demands of these markets, the EPD built a plant in Evans, Georgia in 1990.

By 1992, 60% of the EPD's sales were to the computer, telecommunications and consumer electronics markets. The EPD's management felt continual pressure to extend existing product lines as OEMs developed new end-use products for their growing markets. Responding to customers' unique needs with new product extensions was a competitive necessity because new products commanded higher prices in their early stages of development and thereby offered an opportunity for growth. At the same time that these commercial markets were growing, buyers were becoming more price sensitive. This prompted increased and often fierce price competition among component suppliers.

Competition hinged primarily on price but quality and service were also important. Customers were giving special consideration to manufacturers that could assure short delivery lead times (usually no more than four weeks), but efficiency in manufacturing operations demanded longer lead times. Stricter quality standards were also being demanded because poor quality often could shut down an OEM's production operation. As suppliers competed for large-volume contracts from major OEMs, prices fell sharply, putting pressure on costs. To Rogers and his managers, it appeared as if the EPD was becoming a commodity business.

The EPD's future in this dynamic and uncertain environment looked bleak indeed. It was the subject of much discussion and controversy in the division. Volume could always be increased by taking low-price business, but this reduced profitability. Most people within EPD looked to new products as a major source of both new volume and profits. Some managers wondered whether their division could meet Allentown's high expectations for profitability and growth, or even survive.

## CASE STUDY

**Management History: Joe Bennett's legacy**    Before 1990, Joe Bennett headed the EPD. An entrepreneur who sought to get his division into new businesses, Bennett had been in charge of the EPD since its infancy and nurtured it into a significant business for Allentown. Under Bennett's leadership, the EPD was one of the two Allentown divisions with headquarters outside Allentown, Pennsylvania. This was a source of some pride to Bennett. He fostered the desire to grow and a spirit of experimentation at the EPD. For example, Bennett seized one opportunity for growth by personally initiating research into a new technology that sought to bridge components and integrated circuits. Scott Allen, the division's controller until 1990, felt Bennett exemplified the division's strengths:

> We always tried new things. We always experimented. We set a fast pace. There was a feeling of urgency and commitment and dissatisfaction with the status quo. As an example, we were 14 steps ahead in computer applications. This stemmed from Bennett and the dynamic industry we were in.

Bennett, who was 48 years old when he died, was a big man with a quick and creative mind. He ran the division almost single-handedly. For example, both the Barnett (capacitors) and the Hopewell (resistors) plants had separate on-site market development and product development groups. The managers of all these groups reported to Bennett. Many of the key decisions were made by him and none were made without his knowledge and approval. People respected and also feared Bennett. A product development manager for capacitors described Bennett and his style:

> Joe was very authoritarian with me and others. As a result, the most successful people working for Bennett were political and manipulative. People did not extend themselves very much to disagree with him.

> Bennett had a significant impact on our organization; our managerial styles came to reflect his. We were all more authoritarian than we might otherwise have been. I was less willing to let my people make mistakes even though I thought it was important that people learn from their mistakes. The pressure and unrealistic standards were transmitted down to people throughout the organization. This resulted in our commitments often being unrealistic.

> There was little group activity and decision making by the top team except where there was a specific problem. It was not a natural group. We were never together except at formal managers' meetings. There was no cohesiveness in the group reporting to Bennett.

Bennett was a man of paradoxes. Although most people felt he was extremely directive in his management style, he was intensely interested in the field of organizational behavior and its applications to management. In 1989, Bennett initiated a division-wide management and organization development program. The program was to include several phases: an examination of individual management styles, group effectiveness, interfunctional coordination, and organization-wide problems. In all phases, action plans for improvement were to be developed.

## CASE STUDY

# Don Rogers Takes Charge

When Rogers took charge in June 1990, he inherited an organization which employed 900 people, 175 of whom were salaried managerial and professional employees. It had three plants and four sales districts and, with the exception of some R&D support from Allentown's Technical Staff Division, was a self-contained multifunction organization. Reporting to Don Rogers was a controller, a manufacturing manager, a marketing manager, a sales manager, and a product development manager. (**Exhibits 2** & **3** provide information about the EPD's organization.)

**Rogers' managerial background**    Prior to 1990, Rogers had been the director of electronic materials research in Allentown's Technical Staffs Division. His promotion to Vice President and General Manager was considered unusual because he lacked line experience. However, most of his colleagues realized that his knowledge and background were relevant to the EPD's business and he had a number of qualities that indicated his potential for a top management position. As electronic materials research director, Rogers had been responsible for all the research and development work going on in Technical Staffs. He was therefore knowledgeable about EPD's technology. He often sat in on the EPD's meetings and had a general knowledge of the electronics business.

---

**EXHIBIT 2**

## Background of EDP executives

**Don Rogers**—vice president and general manager, Electronic Products Division, 40 years old. He received a Ph.D. in chemistry from the University of Cincinnati, a master's in chemistry from St. Johns University, and a B.S. from Queens College in New York City. He joined Allentown in 1981 as a chemist in its Technical Staffs Division (R&D). In 1985 he became manager of electronic research and in 1988 director of electronic materials research in the same division. He was appointed the EPD's division manager in June 1990.

**Bill Lee**—marketing manager, 39 years old. He received a B.S. in chemical engineering from Rutgers. He joined Allentown Materials in 1974 as a staff engineer, and subsequently held several engineering and supervisory positions in glass plants. Following an assignment in corporate market planning, he became manager of marketing in the EPD in 1991.

**Ben Smith**—manufacturing manager, 43 years old. He received an engineering degree from Clarkson College. He became EPD's manufacturing manager in 1991 following numerous manufacturing positions in Allentown's Computer Products and Technical Products Divisions. He had started as a plant engineer and had also been a department supervisor, production superintendent, and plant manager in several glass plants in these divisions. Just before moving to the EPD he had been manufacturing manager in the Laboratory Glassware Division.

**Ted Moss**—product development manager, 45 years old. After receiving a degree in mechanical engineering from City College in New York City, he joined Allentown Materials Corporation as a staff engineer. After five years in other divisions he joined EPD in its early infancy. He served as a project engineer first and then held several managerial positions in product and process development. He became manager of product development for the EPD in 1992.

**Carolyn Green**—division controller, 31 years old. She joined Allentown Materials Corporation in 1986 after completing a B.S. in industrial administration at Yale, working in a major accounting firm, and completing an MBA at the Harvard Business School. Before joining the EPD as its division controller in 1991, she served in a variety of plant accounting positions in Allentown's Computer Products and Display Panel Products Divisions.

**Jack Simon**—sales manager, 34 years old. He went to St. Bonaventure University, where he received a degree in sociology. He joined Allentown in 1934 as a salesman. All of his experience with Allentown was with the EPD. He was a district sales manager when promoted to the division's sales manager in 1991.

CASE STUDY

**EXHIBIT 3**

**Electronic Products Division organizational chart**

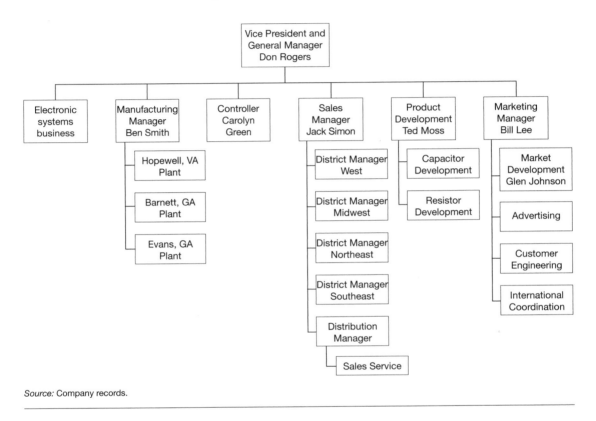

*Source:* Company records.

Rogers also had considerable personal assets. He was very bright, quick thinking, and could express himself extremely well in both small and large groups. EPD managers were impressed by his capacity to grasp a wide variety of complex problems ranging from technical to managerial. He was always very pleasant and friendly and could get people to be open with him, since he was also ready to share information and his own thoughts. In fact, people were often surprised by the things he was willing to reveal and discuss. He also involved people in problems and consulted them on decisions.

Despite these very positive attributes and managers' genuine liking and respect for Rogers, some aspects of his management style attracted criticism. His personality and his superior intellectual capabilities almost always assured that he was a dominant force in meetings. Some also had questions about how comfortable he was with conflict and how much leadership he took in difficult situations. Some of the EPD's managers described Rogers' style:

## CASE STUDY

Rogers does not listen too well. He interrupts, which prevents him from hearing others' opinions and makes it seem as if he really does not want criticism. What's more, he has been too soft on me. He should be holding me to my goals. I have not met some of these goals and he should be climbing all over me. Furthermore, you get the same record back from him regardless of what you say. It is safe to be open with him and tell him what's on your mind, but he does not always hear what you are saying.

He is not involved enough in the problems that arise from differences in the goals of functional departments. This may be because he spends too much time away on corporate assignments. But it doesn't change the fact that he is not involved enough.

Wave-makers are not wanted in the division and are being pushed out. People at the top do not create and confront conflict.

**Rogers' actions**    When Rogers became Vice President and General Manager of the EPD, he made a number of changes in the organization. At the urging of top management and believing that the EPD had to learn to relate more closely to the corporation, Rogers moved the headquarters from Barnett to Allentown. He also brought the market development groups back to Allentown. Furthermore, although the product development groups themselves remained at the plants, Rogers consolidated product development under Ted Moss, who was located in Allentown. Shortly after his promotion, Rogers also separated the marketing and sales functions. As he said later:

It seemed to me that marketing and sales had sufficiently different responsibilities to justify their separation. Sales, I felt, should be concerned with knocking on doors and getting the order while marketing should be concerned with strategies for pricing, new products, and identification of new opportunities for the future. Marketing is a strategic function, as opposed to a day-to-day function.

Another major change had to do with personnel. Rogers replaced all of his key managers with the exception of Ted Moss, the product development manager. Ben Smith, the new manufacturing manager, had held a similar job in Allentown's Laboratory Products Division. Bill Lee, the new marketing manager, had held positions in manufacturing in Allentown's other divisions and had recently been in charge of corporate market planning. Carolyn Green, the new controller, had worked in plants in Allentown's Computer Products Division. Of the new division staff only Jack Simon, the new sales manager, came from within the EPD.

Rogers also turned to improving the EPD's service. An information system was developed by the sales service function. In addition, the manufacturing manager held plant managers responsible for meeting specific goals for delivery commitments and shortening delivery lead times. Furthermore, Rogers requested a report on Bennett's organizational behavior program, which originally was designed to span a three-year period. Rogers learned that the program had made a positive impact on the division, but that the final phase, dealing with the improvement of interfunctional coordination, was not yet complete. In light of business difficulties and his relative newness to the division, Rogers decided to discontinue Bennett's program. He was not sure that the program was an effective way to tackle the problems he faced. He decided to review what he knew about each of the functional areas.

## Review of the Functional Departments in 1992

**Manufacturing**   Resistors and capacitors were manufactured in high volume at three plants—located in Evans, Georgia (resistors), Hopewell, Virginia (resistors), and Barnett, Georgia (capacitors). Each of these plants had a plant manager and a full complement of line and staff functions including production, engineering, quality control, purchasing, accounting and control, and personnel.

The plant managers, with one exception, had grown up in the EPD. As profit center managers, their performance was evaluated on the basis of gross margins and other manufacturing variances, including lead times and missed delivery commitments to customers. These plant managers felt that their reputations and therefore their promotability were dependent on plant growth and good gross margin performance. All saw their future advancement within the manufacturing hierarchy of the company leading to the possibility of promotion to general manager of a division. Since manufacturing was the dominant function, such an expectation was not unrealistic.

EPD's plant managers were extremely upset by the lack of growth in the division's business. In the last two years their volume had shrunk and, because of price cuts, their dollar volume had dropped substantially. Managers were thus under enormous pressure to reduce costs in order to maintain their gross margins. While they were able to reduce some costs, gross margins still declined. With some exceptions, EPD's plants had the smallest gross margins in the company. Plant managers expressed the following statements:

> We are experiencing price erosion in our product lines, and I do not see a large number of new products. We need something new and unique. I do not see growth potential in our existing products.

The frustration experienced by the manufacturing people was expressed most in their attitudes toward the sales and marketing functions. They felt sales focused exclusively on volume with no concern for gross margin. They blamed sales for getting low-gross-margin business and not fighting hard enough to get better price. Sales, in other words, was giving profits away at manufacturing's expense, and sales was not penalized for it.

Manufacturing was even more critical of the marketing function. They felt that marketing had failed in its responsibility to provide the division with a direction for profitable growth. They particularly blamed Bill Lee, the marketing manager, for lack of "strong leadership." They were upset by what they called the "disappearing carrot syndrome." As manufacturing saw it, marketing would come to the plant and project a market of several million dollars for a new resistor or capacitor (the carrot). On the basis of this projection, manufacturing would run samples and make other investments in preparation for the new product only to find out six months or a year later that marketing was now projecting much smaller sales and profits. Manufacturing concluded that marketing lacked the ability to forecast marketing trends accurately and was generally incompetent. Many felt that Bill Lee and some of his staff should be replaced.

Manufacturing was also unhappy with product development, which they felt had not always given them products that would run well on their production lines. They looked to product development to identify new low-cost components and saw nothing coming. When product development requested special runs on their manufacturing lines to develop new products, manufacturing wondered how they would be compensated for this sacrifice in efficiency.

**Marketing**    Marketing comprised several activities, including customer engineering, advertising, and its most important function, market development. Under Glen Johnson, market development was responsible for developing sales projections for the next year, market plans for the next three years, analyses of market share, and plans for improving market position. One of the primary means for increasing market share was the development of new types of resistors and capacitors (product extensions). It was market development's responsibility to identify these new opportunities and to assure the development of new products in coordination with other functions. Because the identification of new market opportunities was primarily their responsibility (with help from sales), as was the development of the new product plan, marketing felt the pressure for new product development fell on them.

The marketing function had many new people since it had been established as a separate function just a year earlier. Most of the people had transferred from the sales department. Johnson, for example, had been a district sales manager. The marketing specialists were generally recent technical or business graduates with one or two years of sales experience.

Overwhelmed by the tough job of forecasting, planning, and formulating strategy in a very turbulent marketplace, the marketing people felt that no one appreciated their difficulties. Some felt that Allentown had such high standards for profitability on new products that it was impossible to meet them in the components business. Johnson, the market development manager, said:

> While corporate financial people will admit that we need a different set of criteria, they informally convey to us that we are doing a lousy job, and it makes us run conservatively. The corporate environment is not a risk-taking one. We tend to want to bring a proprietary advantage to our business which we cannot do. This is slowing us down.

Marketing people were also critical of product development and its responsiveness to the divisions' needs. As marketing people saw it, product development's priorities were wrong and their projects were always late. According to Johnson, "Moss takes projects on without fully considering the resource implications. There are no procedures or criteria to establish priorities in development. Seventy percent of his time is in process rather than product development."

Marketing felt most resentful about the lack of cooperation and the continual sniping from manufacturing. They saw manufacturing as conservative and unwilling to take risks. This was particularly aggravating because many marketing people felt they were distracted from their primary responsibility by having to spend inordinate amounts of time dealing with manufacturing. Johnson indicated that he would not have taken the marketing job had he known that it would involve the many frustrations of getting manufacturing and others to do things.

**Sales**    EPD products were sold through a direct selling force of approximately 25 salespeople, organized into four sales districts. Each district was managed by a district sales manager who reported to the national sales manager, Jack Simon. Simon, like all the district sales managers, had come up through sales. The direct sales force visited manufacturers whose products incorporated electrical components, with the objective of learning about the customer's needs by talking to purchasing agents and design engineers, and then obtaining contracts for resistors or capacitors. The sales force consisted of both college graduates and older, more experienced salespeople who had worked in this industry for a long time.

The sales force was integrated, meaning that EPD salespeople sold capacitors and resistors to the same customers. Thus, the EPD sales force had to develop many relationships with purchasing agents and engineers, and relied on good relationships to obtain market intelligence and an opportunity to bid on contracts. But salespeople also had to negotiate with these same people to obtain the best possible price. Since their performance was evaluated on the basis of sales volume, they worked hard to beat their budgeted sales targets. However, the sales force was not paid on a commission basis; this was a subject of some discussion and discontent amongst them.

Simon reported mistrust, gamesmanship, maneuvering, and politicking between sales and marketing. He said, "We in sales do not believe that the information marketing gives us is the best." Major conflict arose in budget-setting sessions, partly because sales based its forecasts on customer canvassing while marketing used analytical tools to develop its projections. Simon said, "Conflicts are not resolved based on facts. Instead there are accusations. I don't trust them [marketing], and I do not trust that they have the capability to do their jobs." His view of manufacturing was somewhat more positive:

> Relations with manufacturing are personally good, but I have a number of concerns. I do not know and no one knows about actual cost reductions in the plant. I don't think manufacturing gets hit as hard for lack of cost reduction as sales takes it on the chin for price reductions. Another problem is Hopewell's service. It's putrid! There is constant gamesmanship in the Hopewell plant.

At lower levels of the organization, relationships between sales and manufacturing seemed even worse. There were shouting matches over the telephone between the Midwest district sales manager and the Evans plant manager. In one instance, sales had requested quick delivery to meet a major customer's needs, feeling that a slow response would damage the EPD's position with the customer. The plant said it could not provide delivery on such short notice without upsetting plant operations. The sales service

## CASE STUDY

manager commented, "The relationship with the Hopewell plant is bad. Measurement for plant managers has to change. They are not really measured on service. Things have improved somewhat, however, and they are a bit more concerned about service."

**Product Development**   Unlike the other Allentown divisions, the EPD had its own product development group. The EPD's product development group was responsible for developing extensions of the current product line, although they also relied on Technical Staffs for research and development support. (Most other divisions relied totally on the Technical Staffs Division for technical product development support and only had engineering groups for manufacturing staff support.) The product development department often became involved in manufacturing process development as well.

Usually, between 10 and 12 new product development projects were under way, often requiring significant technological development. The development group was divided into two parts: resistors (located in the Hopewell plant) and capacitors (located in Barnett). The manager of product development was based in Allentown, Pennsylvania, along with the rest of the divisional staff. The group was composed of technical people who had spent their careers in research and development work. While some of these people had come from the corporate R&D group, many had worked in the division for most of their careers or had held technical positions in other companies in the electronics industry. Ted Moss, manager of product development, described his relationship with other groups:

> In general, my department's relations with the plants are pretty good although some problems exist at Hopewell. My biggest concern is with marketing. I do not feel that marketing provides detailed product specification for new products. In addition, marketing people do not understand what is involved in specification changes. I think that writing specifications jointly with marketing would help this problem. Another problem is that marketing people have to look ahead more and predict the future better. They always need it yesterday. We need time!

> We also have problems with sales. We need comments from the sales group on our new products. I wanted to get the call reports they write and asked Simon for copies. He would not give them to me because, 'the marketing department has the responsibility for interpretation.' I finally had to go to Rogers to resolve the problem.

Moss was also critical of Allentown's Technical Staffs Division, which on occasion did product development work for the EPD:

> It is difficult to get a time schedule from them. Their direction is independent of ours since they report elsewhere. They will not wring their hands if they are behind schedule. They will more quickly try to relax requirements for the development if it is behind schedule. I need more influence on specifications when it comes to things they are working on. I often have to go upstairs [to speak with their bosses] to solve the problems that occur with this group.

# The New Product Development Process

As Rogers completed his review of the functional areas, he continued to ponder the EPD's new product development process. Two recent situations illustrated that the process was far from smooth.

**Two cases**    The situation with the W-1201 capacitor, a new product for the computer market, was one example. The W-1201 project had been killed and resurrected four times because different parts of the organization had differing knowledge of its status at given points in time. Marketing saw the W-1201 product as a clear opportunity and product development thought it was technically feasible. But sales questioned the product's ability to compete in the marketplace, because manufacturing's cost quotes were so high. As discussions progressed on needed product modifications to reduce costs, marketing's estimate of the potential market changed as did product development's assessment of technical feasibility. Because each function's management judged the viability of the product independently, the status of the project was never clear. At one point in time, salespeople were actually obtaining orders for samples of the W-1201 without knowing that manufacturing and marketing had decided that the product was unfeasible and had killed the idea.

In another case, severe conflict between marketing and plant personnel erupted over a potential new coating for resistors. Marketing had determined that a new, uniform coating was needed for competitive and efficiency reasons. They presented their views to the division's management and received what they thought was a commitment to change resistor coatings. But the plants were reluctant to convert their operations. They questioned whether product development had proved that the new coating would work and could be manufactured to meet product specifications at no additional cost. Moreover, the plants completely distrusted marketing's judgment of the need for this change. The marketing specialist in charge of the project would return from plant meetings angry and completely discouraged about his ability to influence plant people to advance the project.

**Product Development Meetings**    Two day-long meetings were held in Allentown, Pennsylvania, once each accounting period (28 days) to discuss, coordinate, and make decisions about new products. Separate meetings were held for capacitors and resistors. In all, approximately 20 people attended each meeting, including the division manager, his immediate staff, plant managers, and a few other key people in the other functions.

A continual stream of people flowed in and out of these meetings to obtain information from subordinates in their functional area. It was not uncommon for a plant manager to leave the meeting to call an engineer in his plant for details about a project's status. At one meeting Ted Young, a marketing specialist, was repeatedly cited as the person who knew the most about the project under discussion, yet he was not present. On other occasions marketing specialists (who were located in Allentown) were called in to share their information about a project. If necessary, plant people and product development people were also sometimes brought to Allentown for the meeting.

The meetings were chaired by Johnson, the market development manager, who typically sat at the head of the table. Johnson published an agenda ahead of time and usually directed the discussion as it moved from one project to another. For each project, progress was checked against goals agreed to by each function at the previous review. Each function described in some detail what had been done in its area to support the project (for example, what equipment changes had been made in a plant). If a function had not met its goals, as was often the case, new deadlines were set. While problems encountered were always described, the issue of slippage in goals and the underlying reasons for it were rarely discussed. Differences in opinion usually proved very hard to resolve. Often, these conflicts were ended only when people agreed to disagree and moved on to the next item on the agenda. While tempers flared occasionally, open hostility or aggression was rarely expressed in the meetings. Afterward, however, people often met in pairs or small groups in the hallways, over coffee, or in other offices to continue the debate.

In the past, the division manager had not attended product development meetings. In 1992 marketing asked Rogers to attend these meetings to help in moving decisions along. Rogers took a very active part in the meetings; he usually sat across the table from Johnson. He often became involved in the discussion of a new product, particularly its technical aspects. Frequently he explained technical points to others who did not understand them. His viewpoints were clearly heard and felt by others, and people thought that meetings had improved since he decided to sit in. Nevertheless, Johnson still dreaded the product development meetings:

> I never sleep well on the night before the meetings. I start thinking about the various projects and the problems I have in getting everyone to agree and be committed to a direction. We spend long hours in these meetings but people just don't seem to stick to their commitments to accomplish their objectives by a given date. Projects are slipping badly and we just can't seem to get them moving. In my opinion, we also have some projects that should be killed but we can't seem to be able to do that, either. Frankly, if I had it to do over again, I would not take this job. After all, how much marketing am I really doing? I seem to spend most of my time in meetings getting others to do things.

## The Outlook for 1993

Rogers knew that something needed to be done. As 1992 drew to a close, Rogers and his top management group were preparing for their second GLF (Great Leap Forward) meeting. This meeting had been instituted the year before as a forum for discussing major problem areas and developing commitment to division objectives for the coming year. Now it was time to look ahead to 1993.

# General Electric: Major Appliance
# Business Group (Abridged)

In December 1980, several key managers of General Electric's (GE's) dishwasher business (part of GE's Major Appliance Business Group, known as MABG) were excited about the progress that had been made on Project C, but concerned about the possible implications of some of the things they had learned over the past several months. In December 1979, following a full year of discussion, planning, analysis, and review, GE's board of directors had authorized an investment of $28 million in Project C. As stated in the formal proposal to the board, Project C had three primary objectives:

a. Achieve worldwide dishwasher industry leadership in product quality and profitability;

b. Achieve world class leadership in process quality, productivity, and quality of work life; and

c. Achieve increased job security through high quality, low cost products that gain increased market share.

The experience and discoveries of the past year had recently led to several heated discussions among managers on the project team regarding key elements of the project and possible modifications in some of the details already approved by corporate management and the board. Those most directly involved in managing the project, delivering on its objectives, and running the operations once the product was introduced in mid-1983 felt that some of these modifications might be appropriate and in GE's best interests. However, going back to senior management and the board for additional investment after approval had been received was highly unusual because it suggested inadequate up front planning and a lack of discipline in delivering on commitments. During 1980, a recession year with substantially lower volumes and profits than planned, MABG had experienced site-wide layoffs in Louisville of 17% (almost 2,000 employees) during the first eleven months of the year.

During the week of Thanksgiving 1980, Tom Corcoran, program manager for Project C, had organized a series of Project C team meetings to review progress-to-date, evaluate the potential modifications that had been identified, and discuss how the team should proceed. One major outcome was identification of five possible project modifications that warranted further analysis, four of which would increase, and one of which would decrease, total capital spending on the project.

While any combination of these five modifications might be feasible, those involved in the discussions tended to favor one of three combinations:

1. Not to pursue any changes now, but to wait until Project C was completed in mid-1983 and then, as part of a follow-on improvement effort, consider not only these modifications, but also any other improvements that might subsequently be discovered.

2. To go ahead now with some of the modifications, but to choose a combination that would increase capital investment by no more than $2.8 million (10% of the original approved amount). Although frowned upon, standard GE procedure allowed for investment overruns of up to 10% without formal board approval.

3. To go back to the board of directors within the next month for a substantial additional capital authorization sufficient to cover all of the modifications that the team concluded should be integrated into Project C before its completion.

As program manager for Project C, Corcoran was anxious to have the team agree on the appropriate action at this time so that they could concentrate all their energies on Project C and avoid unnecessary delays or subsequent surprises.

## MABG Background

During the 1970s, GE's MABG was the leading U.S. manufacturer of major kitchen appliances, including refrigerators, ranges, microwave ovens, and home laundry appliances, as well as dishwashers and disposal units. MABG was headquartered in Louisville, Kentucky, where it had primary manufacturing plants for each of its major appliance businesses, all located on a single site. MABG also operated a plastics components plant in Frankfort, Kentucky, and a dishwasher assembly plant in Milwaukee, Wisconsin, that produced GE's Hotpoint brand dishwashers with porcelain-coated metal interiors. With factory sales approaching $2 billion in 1979, MABG contributed approximately 10% of GE's corporate revenues and slightly more of its corporate earnings.

The MABG organization (see **Exhibit 1**) consisted of three major line functions: applied research and engineering, manufacturing, and marketing operations. A fourth division, product management, comprised a general manager for each of MABG's major product lines—refrigerators, dishwashers, ranges, and home laundry. MABG also maintained a group of staff support functions that reported directly to the senior vice president and group executive responsible for MABG. Within each of the three line functions there were four general managers, each responsible for one of the major product lines. These general managers reported in a matrix structure both to their functional vice president and to their respective general manager within the product management division, who had overall responsibility for his or her product line business results. The key players involved in the dishwasher business were Roger Schipke, general manager of dishwashers within the product management division, Roger Sundermeyer, head of dishwasher product improvement engineering in the applied research and engineering division, Gary Jones, responsible for dishwasher marketing in marketing operations, and Ray Rissler, responsible for dishwasher manufacturing in the manufacturing division.

## CASE STUDY

**EXHIBIT 1**

## MABG line operation (1980)

*Indicates key management team involved in Project C effort.
− − − Indicates matrix reporting relationship.

The four major MABG product lines were marketed under two brand names, General Electric and Hotpoint. (Hotpoint had been acquired by GE in the 1920s). During the 1970s, the two brands had been entirely integrated. Hotpoint was viewed as the company's "value" brand, while the GE brand served as the "quality line." Although price points overlapped, the Hotpoint line was more strongly represented at lower and middle price segments. Major feature innovations typically were introduced in the GE line a year or two before being introduced in the Hotpoint line. In 1979, 72% of MABG's dishwasher unit sales were GE brand and 27% were Hotpoint (with 1% private label). Their combined sales made GE number one in dishwasher market sales.

The dishwasher market consisted of several segments. Although some models were wheel-mounted portables designed to attach to kitchen faucets, the vast majority were designed to be built into kitchen cabinetry. About half of all built-in units were purchased by building contractors to be installed in newly constructed housing units. Contractors tended to be price-sensitive purchasers. The other half of built-in dishwashers were bought by remodeling contractors or by consumers themselves. In general, consumers tended to be more concerned about the long-term reliability, convenience, and cleaning performance of dishwashers than were contractors.

## The MABG Dishwasher Business in the 1970s

By the early 1970s, MABG management viewed its dishwasher business as a problem despite market shares exceeding 20+%, growing volumes, and generally strong financial performance overall (see **Exhibit 2**). Although GE was producing refrigerators and ranges of premium quality, management believed, and survey research with consumers and dealers had confirmed, that its dishwashers were viewed as merely adequate machines of medium quality.

The majority of GE's dishwashers incorporated a design that differed from most competitive models. Whereas most dishwasher tubs and door liners were constructed of a porcelain coated steel composite, the majority of GE's tubs and door liners were built of steel coated with a layer of soft vinyl known as Plastisol. Plastisol, unlike ceramic, was susceptible to scrapes and scratches from dropped cutlery, and surface lesions were aggravated by dishwasher detergents. Once scratched, the exposed steel tended to rust; rust was unsightly and shortened the life of the machine. Although porcelain coated tubs were not immune from rust problems, their incidence of rust was much lower. Another problem with GE's dishwashers was excessive noise. Finally, GE dishwashers were criticized as heavy water users, which translated into excessive energy use.

GE's dishwasher product managers had long been concerned about the quality of its products, and MABG's applied research and engineering division had begun in the early 1960s to investigate whether any of a number of new plastic compounds then being introduced could out-perform conventional liner materials in the harsh dishwasher operating environment—in which jets of 140° water filled with abra-

**EXHIBIT 2**

### MABG dishwasher performance data

|  | 1975 | 1976 | 1977 | 1978 | 1979 |
|---|---|---|---|---|---|
| Market share ($ basis) | 24% | 24% | 25% | 25% | 26% |
| Sales (000s) | $138,726 | $168,190 | $194,168 | $220,407 | $235,078 |
| Price index | 87.9 | 92.2 | 95.8 | 100.0 | 103.5 |
| Net income (000s) | $2,913 | $3,700 | $4,466 | $6,171 | $7,522 |
| Return on sales | 2.1% | 2.2% | 2.3% | 2.8% | 3.2% |
| Return on investment | 6.1% | 7.9% | 8.0% | 12.5% | 15.9% |

Note: 1974 was a recession year for major appliances, with 1975–1976 strong recovery years for the economy.
Source: Company records.

sive detergents were sprayed onto the liner for over 500 hours per year on average. After experimenting with commercially available materials such as nylon and polyester, GE's scientists invented and patented a glass-filled polypropylene composite material which performed well even under severe testing conditions.

GE named this material PermaTuf®, and gradually began introducing it into dishwashers—first as a detergent cap, then as the silverware basket, next as the pump housing. Each of these applications was progressively more demanding, yet GE experienced no warranty claims related to the PermaTuf material. By 1968 GE managers had developed enough confidence in the material to launch a development program for a new dishwasher with a PermaTuf tub and door liner. They saw in this program the potential to achieve what historically had been two mutually exclusive objectives in product design—create a lower-cost product with significantly improved performance. PermaTuf could not rust; would not dent; and was highly fracture-resistant. In addition, tests revealed that the plastic tub reduced operating noise by 15% relative to GE's Plastisol models. Costs would fall because GE's current tub was comprised of 15 parts, which needed to be individually machined, assembled, and then sealed. The PermaTuf tub would be a single molded piece.

Because of its lower cost, GE's marketers initially saw PermaTuf as a vehicle for strengthening the GE brand's share of the low-priced, contractor-oriented end of the market. In 1971, $17 million had been appropriated for this effort. Three years into the development, however, they decided to reverse this positioning decision. GE's market researchers had concluded that although PermaTuf tubs in fact outperformed porcelain-steel tubs on almost every dimension, plastic was still regarded by most consumers as a "cheap" material. They worried that using PermaTuf initially in a contractor-oriented low-end model would reinforce that image, and compromise GE's ability subsequently to pitch the PermaTuf tub as a premium feature to quality-conscious consumers at the high end of the market. Management therefore decided to deploy PermaTuf initially in a new high-end model (internally this was known as the PermaTuf A product); to follow that product two years later with a PermaTuf B model, positioned at the core of GE's line; and then to develop a truly low-cost version, the C model, targeted at the contractor end of the market. To reinforce PermaTuf's quality image, management also decided to offer a 10-year warranty against failure on the tub and door liner, compared to the industry's standard 5-year warranty.

This mid-program repositioning forced GE's design team into an intense 18 months of redesign, and the A model was introduced as the General Electric GSD 1050 in October 1976—over a year behind the original schedule. In its rush to get the model to market, management bypassed an in-home testing phase which it customarily relied upon as a final test of design quality. Unfortunately, after 28,000 models had been sold, GE was forced to withdraw the GSD 1050 from the market because of warranty claims unrelated to the PermaTuf material.

Once the source of the GSD 1050's problems was understood, management decided not to introduce a redesigned A model. Rather, they shifted the features and pricing of the B model somewhat up-market, and approved an additional $4 million for accelerated development and launch of that product. Three versions of this product, GSD 1200, GSD 1000, and GSD 900, were introduced in 1978. Sales were 30-40% below expectations, however, because neither GE salespeople nor dealers were eager to push new models using the same tub and door materials as had been used in the tainted A model.

## CASE STUDY

In 1979, despite problems with the A and B models, the performance of MABG's dishwasher business was still good; strong sales of the five mid- to low-priced models in GE's line had compensated for the problems at the high end. It was in this environment that marketing decided it was time to redesign the low-end products around a one-piece PermaTuf tub—to create Product C. Applied research and engineering had done preliminary work and felt prepared to support such an effort; the manufacturing division was ready to join the project as well.

Historically at MABG, funding of projects to redesign products was accompanied by additional funding to purchase tooling and manufacturing equipment for the new product. About 75% of the total appropriation for the A and B projects, for example, had been targeted toward manufacturing improvements. In formulating their proposal to fund development of Product C, therefore, a team with representatives from research, engineering, manufacturing, and marketing proposed to senior GE management an $18 million project—with $3 million targeted at product design and $15 million toward process improvement and new manufacturing equipment.

At the review for this proposal, the sector executive, Jack Welch, raised a number of critical questions. He was concerned that MABG was simply "fixing" the dishwasher business as opposed to making it a world class operation, second to none. Welch and others were especially concerned about two major shortcomings in the original redesign proposal. First was that the Louisville dishwasher plant had a poor reputation for quality, productivity, and flexibility. Second was that because of the strong union environment, GE traditionally had shied away from overinvesting in the dishwasher plant and the other factories located at the Louisville appliance site. Welch challenged the dishwasher management team to rethink its proposal to result in a world class product design *and* a world class factory—particularly with regard to automation and manufacturing competitiveness in quality and cost, but also addressing the workforce issues. Welch wanted a proposal to make the dishwasher facility a model for worker involvement and significantly improved worker attitudes and value-added. Welch made it clear that he was willing to consider an expanded project involving more capital if it would achieve world class status for GE's dishwasher efforts, be a model for the rest of major appliance and other GE businesses to emulate, and provide a strong financial return to the corporation and its stockholders. Thus it was back to the drawing boards for the dishwasher management.

# Project C

In response to Welch's challenge, a 13-member team was put together to architect and, once approved, implement a major step change in the product, process, and workforce aspects of GE's dishwasher business. The team included representatives from MABG's marketing, manufacturing, applied research and engineering, and finance functions as well as from many of the key support staff involved in the dishwasher business. Over the next several months, the team finalized a proposal calling for fundamental changes in the GE dishwasher product line made in Louisville and a new state-of-the-art, robot-equipped production process that would provide quality and productivity, with full participation and contribution from all parts of the workforce in the plant. Particularly important were the significant changes proposed in the manufacturing process.

## CASE STUDY

### Manufacturing Changes

Under the direction of Homer Moeller, Louisville dishwasher plant manager, and his manufacturing team, ideas were gathered from throughout GE and across firms considered leading worldwide manufacturers. The result was a proposal to totally redo major sections of the Louisville dishwasher plant so that they fully complemented and were integrated with the redesign of the product line to a PermaTuf tub and door. Automation was to be pursued aggressively—not just to reduce cost, but also to improve quality—and the product design was to be modified in accordance with the capabilities and constraints of the new process. In addition, more worker control and shorter factory throughput times were to be built into the process, and product testing was to be integrated more completely within manufacturing rather than being assigned to an entirely separate quality control organization.

In developing its part of the proposal, manufacturing adopted several principles it considered appropriate for achieving world class leadership in process quality, productivity, and quality of work life. First was the principle of focusing the Louisville dishwasher plant on the GE-branded PermaTuf C product line. By 1983, lower volume products would be moved to the Milwaukee facility (with union agreement) and a rational, integrated flow would be achieved in the Louisville plant layout. This principle also had implications for the number of parts going into the products made in the plant, and a goal was set to reduce them from 4,000 to 800.

Second, a cellular approach for each of the major stages of production was to be adopted. While cells were to be connected by conveyor lines with limited, closely controlled in-process inventories, a cellular approach would allow workers to be more of a team and would facilitate automation, process improvement, and testing of major subassemblies as well as of the final assembled dishwashers. A handful of primary cells were envisioned in the plant (see **Exhibit 3**).

### Workforce Changes

There were a number of significant workforce changes proposed as part of Project C. While union relations often had been strained at MABG's Louisville site, it was proposed on this project that employee attitudes—concerning their work, their environment, and their contribution to the success of GE's dishwasher business—become a major focus for improvement. This would require systematic data gathering regarding present attitudes, followed by periodic updates, to objectively measure the progress being made. As envisioned by the Project C management team, the union would be brought in early on project discussions to get their agreement and support. This was especially critical because to move the low volume part of GE's product line from Louisville to Milwaukee would require union agreement, something the union would normally be reluctant to grant.

A second need for union buy-in was that with the narrower plant focus and the automation and improved productivity of Project C, demand for hourly workers at the Louisville dishwasher plant would likely fall 15%-25% between 1979 and the first year of full production for the new product line. It was anticipated that increased market acceptance of the new product would add volume that, over the subsequent two to four years, would offset that decline; eventually, therefore, total employment at the dish-

## CASE STUDY

EXHIBIT 3

# Louisville dishwasher plant layout (Project C)

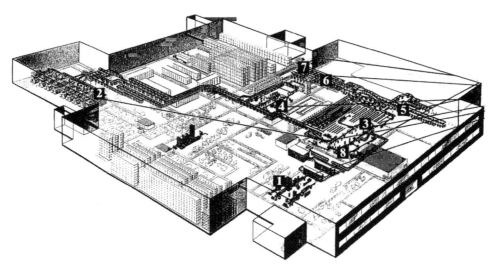

Dishwasher plant floor space is approximately 400' by 600'.

(1) *Parts Cell:* Parts would be fabricated for use in the inner door and tub assemblies. Production in this department would involve increased automation and process control and significant set-up reductions to ensure minimum work-in-process inventories.

(2) *PermaTuf Tub and Door Liner Cell:* Injection molding machines for door liners, each controlled by a GE programmable controller would allow for closed-loop feedback on several process variables and would ensure not only consistent tolerances but high productivity and short cycle times in this cell.

(3 and 4) *Tub Subassembly Cell and Door Subassembly Cell:* PermaTuf and metal components would be assembled in a largely automated fashion into subassemblies. Tubs and doors would not be unloaded or loaded by hand. Management felt that variations were introduced and costs were increased when product was manually handled. The plan called for a "make one—use one" philosophy for some parts, requiring that the parts machine be placed next to the subassembly workstation.

(5) *Final Assembly Cell:* Tub and door subassemblies would be joined with purchased parts that would be received just-In-time from a handful of outside suppliers. Operators would pull a unit off the moving conveyor line into their work space. Upon satisfactory completion of their tasks, they would return the unit to the moving conveyor line. This made workers directly responsible for the quality of their work.

(6) *Final Test Cell:* The test cell would conduct a rigorous 100% performance test of each unit. Repairs would be made immediately and repair information would be automatically sent back to the appropriate work station to ensure corrective action on a real-time basis.

(7) *Packaging and Shipment Cell*

(8) *Computer Control Center:* Perched 12'-15' above the factory floor, the center would monitor all manufacturing processes and work-in-process as well provide real-time management reports and visual monitoring of operations.

While each cell would be responsible for all of the activities performed within it and would have the necessary process controls and information to carry out its assignment, two features proposed as part of Project C linked the entire plant and integrated its operations. First was the physical conveyor system that connected every upstream work area to those downstream that depended on its output. Because there were a finite number of carrier positions on these conveyors, the conveyor system's design and layout established specific limits on the amount of in-process inventory. Second, a Kanban (card) system would be used to connect downstream department needs to upstream supply areas. Following the rules of JIT, a limited number of Kanbans would be in the system at any given moment and upstream departments could initiate production only when downstream departments issued those Kanbans.

washer plant would be as high as or possibly higher than it was in early 1979. Making sure the union understood and agreed to this pattern of workforce fluctuations was crucial to the project's success. (Management wanted to avoid any possible strike situation during new product rollout caused by union surprise or disagreement over staffing levels.)

Third, and perhaps even more important in the people dimension being proposed for Project C, was the shift from workers as interchangeable cogs in the production process to workers as a source of substantial value-added. This required a systematic employee involvement and training effort of the over 1,000 hourly workers anticipated as being on the dishwasher plant payroll in late 1983. That workforce would need to be transitioned from a point of awareness of Project C and its objectives to acceptance, involvement, commitment, and then ownership for its results. The goal of Project C's management team was to make the workers an integral part of the dishwasher business' success.

### Product Development Changes

Finally, the applied research and engineering division managers involved in the dishwasher business were asked to do a major rethink of their proposed product design effort. While they were already committed to the idea of PermaTuf tubs and door liners throughout the GE brand dishwasher product line, their thinking would need to undergo some revisions to incorporate additional manufacturability, product line and plant focus, and reduced part counts into their product design efforts. Engineering and design needed to focus increased attention on embedding in their designs higher quality and lower cost of ownership (determined by original purchase cost as well as warranty and service costs).

## Project C Approval

By late 1979, the Project C management team—with Corcoran's coordination and facilitation—had prepared a detailed development plan for product, manufacturing process, and people. It consisted of several key elements and was expected to provide significantly improved results along three dimensions: quality, productivity, and timeliness (see **Exhibit 4**). Perhaps even more important (given the way project approval and capital investment authorization worked at GE), it would provide significant improvement in market share, product positioning in the market place, and dishwasher business unit financial performance.

As proposed to the board of directors in December 1979, Project C called for fundamental changes to the GE build-in dishwasher line, a state-of-the-art robot-equipped production process, and a significantly improved working relationship with the Louisville plant workforce. As summarized in the authorization request, the plan was to use a PermaTuf-based design for GE brand dishwashers, with the following objectives:

1. To replace Plastisol tubs and doors with PermaTuf tubs and doors throughout the GE line, and to offer thereby a more durable product that would increase the actual and perceived quality of GE brand dishwashers.

## CASE STUDY

EXHIBIT 4

### Key elements of Project C

| Product | Manufacturing process | People |
|---|---|---|
| Higher quality, lower cost product | Rationalized, conveyor linked plant flow | Union involvement |
| PermaTuf® as tub/door material | JIT principles | Retraining for new process and TQM |
| Simpler product line (fewer products and parts) | Tighter tolerances (for GE and suppliers) | Cross-functional Project C management team |
| Product and process design integrated | Minimum inventory | Focus on business goals, not functional or union goals |
| | Less material handling | |
| | Automation | |
| | Rigorous final product test | |

**Projected areas of results**

| Quality | Productivity | Timeliness |
|---|---|---|
| Extended warranty | Less indirect labor | Less WIP |
| Fewer defects | Less direct labor | Faster throughput |
| Fewer final test failures | Added volume | Make one—Use one |
| Lower service call/ complaint rates | Increased inventory turns | Faster future new product development because of known process |
| | Increased up times for equipment | |

2. To implement a quality improvement program in concert with product line and manufacturing process changes. Improved quality would be derived primarily from gains in process uniformity obtained through automation, closer tolerances on both externally supplied and internally fabricated/assembled work, and enhanced concern for quality among management and workers.

3. To achieve significant cost reductions in three areas:

   a. Product costs—including materials, labor, scrap and rework—and more efficient use of invested capital (equipment and inventory). [Per unit savings over the existing Plastisol design = $8.52.]

   b. Outbound transportation costs due to finished units weighing 12 pounds less than the current Plastisol models. [Per unit savings over the Plastisol design = $0.91.]

   c. Service call costs due to lower service call rates during the first 90 days of ownership (since all units will have been thoroughly tested prior to shipment) and lower payments on warranty claims. [Per unit savings over the Plastisol design = $2.00.]

## CASE STUDY

These reductions, totaling $11.43, would be offset in part by the additional cost of providing a 10-year tub and door liner warranty on all PermaTuf models, leaving *$9.43 in net savings per unit.*

Under the proposal, production of lower-volume products—the PermaTuf B models and the portable dishwasher line—would be transferred to Milwaukee in 1982. Producing these models in Milwaukee would add an average of $7 cost per unit, but this was deemed worthwhile to sharpen the focus of the Louisville plant. The PermaTuf C models would be introduced in phases in Louisville in 1983. By 1985, the PermaTuf B models would be converted to the new design.

The required investment to implement Project C was estimated at *$28 million,* of which $1.9 million already had been spent on the development of prototype models and experimentation with advanced assembly techniques. Of the $28 million total, $5 million would be for product development, $4 million for process development, $3 million for relocating some existing products to the Milwaukee plant, $14.5 million for equipment, and $1.5 million for a minimum of two weeks of quality and job related training for each hourly employee. The Project C management team believed that the change to the full PermaTuf C product line would result in incremental retail market share for GE from 1983 on, because it would offer a better product (see **Exhibit 5** for proposed advertising copy and a product photo). The team projected a 1983 net increase in retail market share of 0.4%, rising to 2.0% by 1989. Because of the capacity limits of the proposed facility, projected at 1.02 million units in 1985, the incremental market share would be capped at 1.2% in 1986.

**EXHIBIT 5**

## Product mock-up for potential PermaTuf C advertising copy

## CASE STUDY

In forecasting industry sales, the team assumed incremental household penetration resulting in a 5% average annual unit growth from a normal year in the mid-1970s onward. The U.S. dishwasher market size was therefore projected to be 4.7 million units in 1986. The incremental contribution from the additional retail market share was calculated at $23.5 million through 1989, as indicated in **Exhibit 6**.

According to the teams' most likely scenario, the project promised product cost savings of $75 million by 1989. These figures were based on a detailed analysis of projected product costs savings (**Exhibit 7**) and a thorough analysis of income and cash flow projections (see **Exhibit 8**).

In order to be as thorough yet candid as possible, the Project C management team also had shared with senior management the areas in which it had concern. These included the following:

1. The challenge of convincing consumers that PermaTuf was a better material than porcelain coated tubs and doors, and thus that the entire product line was not only different than that of competitors, but higher quality.

2. By staking the entire GE brand line of dishwashers on PermaTuf, their reputation might be put at risk by a low-end competitor who might source offshore cheap plastic tubs and doors that would crack and leak in use.

3. Significant increases in petroleum prices of 100% above levels in 1979 would add $3 per unit to the projected PermaTuf costs.

4. Investing $28 million in incremental funds for a modern, computer-run plant at Louisville would give the labor union even more clout and leverage over the entire site.

**EXHIBIT 6**

### Projected market share impact—Project C

| Year | Relevant Retail Market Size in Units (000)* | Incremental Retail Market Share | Incremental GE Unit Volume (000) | Average GE Unit Contribution Margin Including Project C Manufacturing Cost Savings | Incremental Contribution ($000) |
|------|------|------|------|------|------|
| 1983 | 1,525 | 0.40% | 6.1 | $115.73 | $ 706 |
| 1984 | 1,650 | 0.80% | 13.2 | 131.82 | 1,740 |
| 1985 | 1,810 | 1.10% | 19.9 | 145.54 | 2,896 |
| 1986 | 2,000 | 1.20% | 24 | 161.37 | 3,873 |
| 1987 | 2,000 | 1.20% | 24 | 178.37 | 4,281 |
| 1988 | 2,000 | 1.20% | 24 | 198.01 | 4,752 |
| 1989 | 2,000 | 1.20% | 24 | 219.16 | 5,260 |
| Total | | | | | $23,508 |

*Only includes volume from segments served by PermaTuf C. (For example, does not include portables and certain other segments.)

*Source:* Company records.

## CASE STUDY

EXHIBIT 7

## Projected project cost savings—Project C

| | 1982 | 1983 | 1984 | 1985 | 1986 | 1987 | 1988 | 1989 | Total |
|---|---|---|---|---|---|---|---|---|---|
| **Volume (000s)** | | | | | | | | | |
| Plastisol to PermaTuf C | — | 300 | 690 | 761 | 866 | 866 | 866 | 866 | 5,215 |
| PermaTuf B to PermaTuf C | — | — | — | 80 | 173 | 173 | 173 | 173 | 772 |
| Portables to Milwaukee | 50 | 50 | 50 | 50 | 50 | 50 | 50 | 50 | 400 |
| **Cost Improvement per Unit: PermaTuf C vs. Plastisol** | | | | | | | | | |
| Material, Scrap, and Rework | — | $5.22 | $5.63 | $6.08 | $6.57 | $7.10 | $7.66 | $8.28 | |
| Labor, Other | — | 3.30 | 3.58 | 3.84 | 4.15 | 4.48 | 4.84 | 5.23 | |
| Outbound Transportation* | — | 0.91 | 0.98 | 1.06 | 1.14 | 1.23 | 1.33 | 1.44 | |
| 10-Year Tub and Door Warranty** | — | (2.00) | (2.00) | (2.00) | (2.00) | (2.00) | (2.00) | (2.00) | |
| Service Call Reduction, Concessions | — | 2.00 | 2.16 | 2.33 | 2.52 | 2.72 | 2.93 | 3.17 | |
| Total | — | 9.43 | 10.33 | 11.31 | 12.38 | 13.53 | 14.76 | 16.12 | |
| **Cost Improvement per Unit: PermaTuf C vs. PermaTuf B** | | | | | | | | | |
| Material, Scrap, and Rework | — | — | — | $5.30 | $5.73 | $6.19 | $6.68 | $7.22 | |
| Labor | — | — | — | 2.51 | 2.71 | 2.93 | 3.16 | 3.42 | |
| Overhead/Other | — | — | — | 1.31 | 1.42 | 1.53 | 1.65 | 1.78 | |
| Outbound Transportation* | — | — | — | 2.64 | 2.86 | 3.08 | 3.33 | 3.60 | |
| Total | — | — | — | 11.76 | 12.72 | 13.73 | 14.82 | 16.02 | |
| Portable Cost Penalty | ($7.00) | ($7.00) | ($7.00) | ($7.00) | ($7.00) | ($7.00) | ($7.00) | ($7.00) | |
| **Savings (000s)** | | | | | | | | | |
| Material, Scrap, and Rework | — | $1,566 | $3,885 | $5,051 | $6,681 | $7,219 | $7,789 | $8,420 | $40,611 |
| Labor, Other | — | 990 | 2,456 | 3,123 | 4,063 | 4,387 | 4,738 | 5,121 | $24,878 |
| Overhead/Other | — | — | — | 105 | 246 | 265 | 285 | 308 | $1,209 |
| Outbound Transportation | — | 273 | 676 | 1,018 | 1,482 | 1,598 | 1,728 | 1,870 | $8,645 |
| Warranty | — | (600) | (1,380) | (1,522) | (1,732) | (1,732) | (1,732) | (1,732) | ($10,430) |
| Service Call Reduction, Concessions | — | 600 | 1,490 | 1,773 | 2,182 | 2,356 | 2,537 | 2,745 | $13,683 |
| Portable Cost Penalty | (350) | (350) | (350) | (350) | (350) | (350) | (350) | (350) | ($2,800) |
| Total | ($350) | $2,479 | $6,777 | $9,198 | $12,572 | $13,743 | $14,995 | $16,382 | $75,796 |

*Note:* A factor of 8%/year has been used to escalate product cost savings/unit.

*PermaTuf C weighs 8 lbs. less than Plastisol unit and 20 pounds less than PermaTuf B.

**Represents same accrual now in effect on all PermaTuf B dishwashers.

*Source:* Company records.

CASE STUDY

---

**EXHIBIT 8**

## Projected income and cash flow—Project C ($000s)

| Incremental Net Income | 1979 | 1980 | 1981 | 1982 | 1983 | 1984 | 1985 | 1986 | 1987 | 1988 | 1989 | Total |
|---|---|---|---|---|---|---|---|---|---|---|---|---|
| Market Share Impact (Exhibit 6) | — | — | — | — | 706 | 1,740 | 2,896 | 3,873 | 4,281 | 4,752 | 5,260 | 23,508 |
| Product Cost Savings (Exhibit 7) | — | — | — | (350) | 2,479 | 6,777 | 9,198 | 12,572 | 13,743 | 14,995 | 16,382 | 75,796 |
| **Implementation Costs** | | | | | | | | | | | | |
| Investment Related Expense | (21) | (232) | (324) | (4,412) | (1,261) | (701) | (39) | — | — | — | — | (6,990) |
| Depreciation | — | (1) | (2) | (839) | (2,071) | (2,183) | (2,022) | (1,999) | (1,800) | (1,780) | (1,776) | (14,473) |
| Start-up | — | — | (10) | (170) | (490) | (330) | — | — | — | — | — | (1,000) |
| Maintenance Savings | — | — | — | — | 50 | 50 | 50 | 50 | 50 | 50 | 50 | 350 |
| Total | (21) | (233) | (336) | (5,421) | (3,772) | (3,164) | (2,011) | (1,949) | (1,750) | (1,730) | (1,726) | (22,113) |
| Income/(Loss) Before Tax | (21) | (233) | (336) | (5,771) | (587) | 5,353 | 10,083 | 14,496 | 16,274 | 18,017 | 19,916 | 77,191 |
| Federal Tax (46%) | 10 | 107 | 155 | 2,655 | 270 | (2,462) | (4,638) | (6,668) | (7,486) | (8,288) | (9,161) | (35,506) |
| Investment Credit (10%) | 1 | — | 16 | 1,972 | 195 | 36 | 0 | 0 | 0 | 0 | 0 | 2,220 |
| Net Income/(Loss) | ($10) | ($126) | ($165) | ($1,144) | ($122) | $2,927 | $5,445 | $7,828 | $8,788 | $9,729 | $10,755 | $43,905 |
| **Cash Flow–Current Year** | | | | | | | | | | | | |
| Net Income/(Loss) | ($10) | ($126) | ($165) | ($1,144) | ($122) | $2,927 | $5,445 | $7,828 | $8,788 | $9,729 | $10,755 | $43,905 |
| Depreciation | — | 1 | 2 | 839 | 2,071 | 2,183 | 2,022 | 1,999 | 1,800 | 1,780 | 1,776 | 14,473 |
| Capitalized Investment | (10) | (4) | (163) | (19,719) | (1,950) | (354) | — | — | — | — | – | (22,200) |
| Inventory Reductions | — | — | — | — | 60 | 750 | 190 | 50 | 50 | 50 | 50 | 1,200 |
| Warranty Reserve | — | — | — | — | 172 | 535 | 754 | 736 | 694 | 566 | 430 | 3,887 |
| Deferred Taxes on Reserve | — | — | — | — | (79) | (246) | (347) | (339) | (319) | (260) | (198) | (1,788) |
| Total | ($20) | ($129) | ($326) | ($20,024) | $152 | $5,795 | $8,064 | $10,274 | $11,013 | $11,865 | $12,813 | $39,477 |
| **Cumulative Cash Flow** | ($20) | ($149) | ($475) | ($20,499) | ($20,347) | ($14,552) | ($6,488) | $3,789 | $14,802 | $26,667 | $39,477 | |

*Source:* Company records.

---

5. The success of the overall program clearly hinged on getting union and workers to become fully committed and take ownership for product cost and quality in the dishwasher plant.

6. Some MABG managers believed that the dishwasher market was too small and its growth prospects too poor to justify a $28 million investment. They argued that GE would be better off spending these financial and managerial resources on something like MABG's Louisville refrigerator factory because it produced several times the amount of annual sales revenues and profits. This was generally countered by dishwasher managers arguing that the $28 million would give such a boost to the dishwasher business that no additional investment—other than possibly added capacity in the second half of the 1980s—would be required for the dishwasher business for another decade.

## CASE STUDY

Following a thorough and active discussion of the Project C proposal, its purposes, and anticipated results and risks, both senior management and the board of directors gave their authorization in December 1979. By late 1980, substantial headway had been made in implementing the product design portion, laying the groundwork for the union and workforce involvement portion, and preparing process plans and getting ready to let contracts for capital equipment and facilities engineering at the Louisville dishwasher plant.

## Possible Project C Modifications (November–December 1980)

Over the prior several months, the Project C management team had identified a handful of major modifications to the original proposal and now found themselves struggling with how to proceed. Debate had been heated and emotions were rising over the need to resolve the team's position on these issues. As program manager, Corcoran had tried to pull together the pros and cons that had been voiced regarding each of five modifications. In early December 1980, he summarized these as follows:

1. *Improving the quality of the factory environment.* This modification entailed additional capital spending of $1.5 million to install a hot food kitchen, renovate rest rooms, and add a multipurpose employee room in the dishwasher plant. There was strong support among the Project C team members, workers, the union, and others in the dishwasher business regarding the attractiveness of this investment: it was a positive response to employee suggestions, provided a quality environment consistent with the product and process quality efforts of Project C, and aligned management's actions with its rhetoric. The disadvantage was that other plants at the Louisville site would undoubtedly find themselves pressed by the union for similar facilities. Because those other plants represented 90% of the site's hourly workforce, such improvements might add substantially to MABG's fixed investment in Louisville.

2. *Skills training in technical problem solving.* This training would be for the top 20% of the hourly workforce and would cost $1.5 million to deliver. Its focus would be on teaching employees how to identify, solve, and eliminate technical problems so that during plant start-up and subsequently, these workers might become significant contributors to ongoing improvement efforts. This proposal had received mixed support, with dishwasher plant management, some union leaders, and some of the best workers very much in favor. The plant people saw it as insurance for a smoother product ramp-up in 1983 and beyond. The union supported the proposal in part because they anticipated negotiating as part of their labor contract a new, higher classification of job category with higher pay of $0.25 to $0.50 per hour for the roughly 200 employees receiving such training. Dishwasher plant management did not object to such an additional labor cost; they thought it would reduce "bumping" since when other MABG Louisville plants changed workforce levels, the affected people could bid only for jobs in their same or a lower job category.

    Three groups of people were opposed to this modification. First, support staff (maintenance, process engineering, materials planning, and quality control) within the dishwasher organization considered such training a vote of no confidence in their ability to start the plant up smoothly on PermaTuf C. They were joined, at least informally, by a majority of the workforce, who viewed such tasks as management's, not hourly's, responsibility. Finally, managers in the other GE plants on the Louisville site were very much opposed because it added a higher paid job category (that they would be pressured to add), and it hampered their ability to keep their best hourly workers from migrating to the dishwasher plant over time.

3. *Revisions in GE's management information and support systems.* This modification contemplated changes in existing GE systems for plant accounting, materials tracking, and quality reporting. It would ensure that the activities of Project C would be complemented, reinforced, and facilitated by GE's information support systems. While this would require a capital investment of $2.8 million and additional time commitments on the part of the Project C management team (since they would be architecting some of the system changes), it would ensure that such systems did not become road blocks that would slow subsequent factory improvements. By incorporating system changes during Project C, identified by those managers most knowledgeable about the project's goals, it would set the stage for subsequent, more extensive overhauls of these systems so they would become promoters of behaviors consistent with Project C.

   While the line managers viewed this as a critical long-term issue and feared that nothing would happen unless it were made an integral part of Project C, there was only weak support for adding it now: it was not essential to the success of Project C, because the team was not required to use GE's existing management systems during the implementation phase anyway, and it simply added to the complexity and work load of the team's assignment.

4. *Adding a value engineering development cycle.* This modification would entail adding one more prototype cycle (iteration) to the product and process development effort *before* final market roll-out of the PermaTuf C product line. The additional iteration would allow for further refinements, debugging, and integration of both the product and process designs. Direct costs of this value engineering cycle would be $1.2 million and the proposal would likely add 3 to 4 months to the project, delaying the introduction of the PermaTuf C line by that amount of time. The plant people were all in favor of this modification. They felt that the resulting product cost savings might be as much as $1 per unit and that the resulting quality improvements might provide additional market share gains of up to 0.5%. Over the prior several months, the operations people had discovered that they still had much to learn about "early manufacturing involvement" and effectively integrating product and process development. In addition, MABG's advanced development group favored the delay. They had come up with a number of ideas for improved features and performance which they felt they could incorporate into the line if given one more engineering cycle.

   Marketing opposed the delay; they did not want to risk being late to market with the new product. Finance was certain that the opportunity cost associated with any delay would wipe out any potential cost savings. Furthermore, both groups felt that if a sufficient number of improvement ideas were identified, a small improvement project could be undertaken in the 1984-1985 time period and achieve the same cost benefits (albeit requiring somewhat more resources), but without the penalty of a delayed market roll-out. They agreed that allowing the

## CASE STUDY

time line to slip, even for a good cause, would make Project C look like many past GE projects that had missed their target completion dates.

5. *Drop (postpone) construction of the integrated computer control room.* This modification would *save* $1.0 million of unspent, but approved, capital that could then be applied to other proposed modifications. Operations management had suggested this modification because they were increasingly skeptical of the control room's value and favored giving added responsibility and control to those on the shop floor rather than to a centralized staff group. They argued that even if a computer control room proved attractive later on, it would be better to add it then, when the specific requirements were better known, rather than trying to predict and build the "ideal control system" based on little or no experience. The negatives of postponing this part of the project, or dropping it completely, were that senior management and the marketing group already had publicized the control room as an integral part of GE dishwasher's "world class effort." In addition, the union already had accepted the concept following lengthy discussions, and the MIS and financial controller staffs saw it as the best way to ensure close coordination and control of the automated dishwasher plant.

As Corcoran saw it, the task now was to decide which, if any, of these modifications to incorporate into Project C. If those to be incorporated required more than 10% net additional investment ($2.8 million), the team would need to return to senior management and the board of directors for formal approval. While nobody liked the prospect, having spent a year trying to "do the right thing" and to respond consistently to Welch's injunction of "do it right the first time," Corcoran and the team wanted to make sure that the project and its outcomes were not compromised by their failure to act appropriately. To keep things on track, these issues needed to be resolved once and for all by the middle of the month so that resources and energies could be focused on successful pursuit of Project C.

# General Motors: Packard Electric Division

David Schramm, the chief engineer for Cable and Component Design (CCD), glanced at the RIM grommet in his hand and considered the risks and benefits (see the **Appendix** for a glossary of terms). Packard Electric had developed the RIM (Reaction Injection Molded) grommet as a new technology for passing the wires from the engine compartment through the fire wall to the passenger compartment of passenger automobiles.

The Product, Process, and Reliability (PPR) committee, which had the final responsibility for the new product development process, had asked Schramm for his analysis and recommendation as to whether Packard Electric should commit to the RIM grommet for a 1992 model year car. It was already March 1, 1990 and, because of the lead time on the equipment and tooling, the decision had to be made within the week (see **Exhibit 1** for the project schedule). While many of the product development people were very excited by the RIM grommet's possibilities, many of the manufacturing people were dead set against it.

## Packard Electric Background

The Packard brothers founded the Packard Company in the late 19th century to produce carbon filament lamps and transformers. In 1899, the company moved into the fledgling automobile industry and began to produce automobiles. Eventually the automobile business was sold, but Packard continued to be a supplier of ignition systems. General Motors bought the Packard Company in 1932, and it became the Packard Electric Division of GM.

The management of the Packard Electric division had remained fairly autonomous through the years. In the first 90 years of its existence, Packard had only seven general managers. Although the majority of its sales were to GM divisions, it did receive significant business from other automobile companies.

During the 1980s, GM experienced significant competition—particularly from Japanese imports. GM's share of the U.S. market had dropped from 45% in 1980 to about 34% in 1989. Despite its parent company's problems, Packard Electric's revenues and profitability grew steadily in the 1980s at a rate of 8-9% per year. This growth was attributed to two factors: increasing sales to other automobile manufacturers, and the growing electronic content of automobiles. By 1989, Packard had over $2 billion in sales, of which 25% was to non-GM customers.

This case was prepared by Geoffrey K. Gill (under the direction of Professor Steven C. Wheelwright).
Copyright © 1990 by the President and Fellows of Harvard College. Harvard Business School case 691-030.

## CASE STUDY

**EXHIBIT 1**

# RIM project schedule (3/1/90)[1]

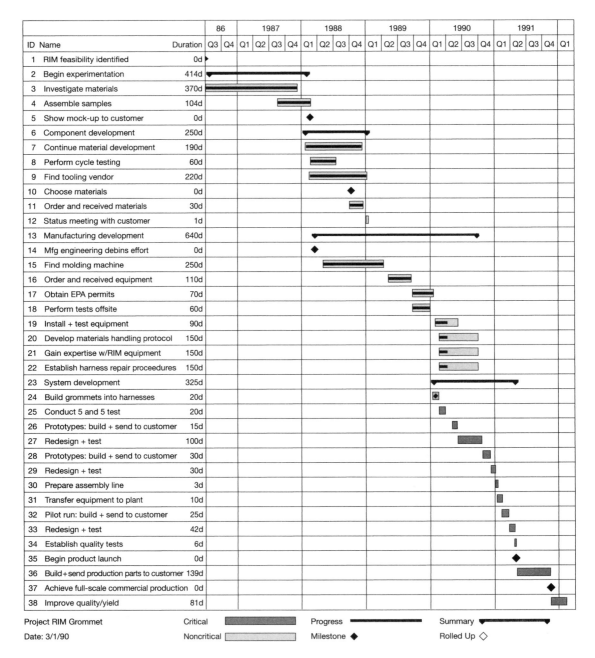

| ID | Name | Duration | 86 Q3 | Q4 | 1987 Q1 | Q2 | Q3 | Q4 | 1988 Q1 | Q2 | Q3 | Q4 | 1989 Q1 | Q2 | Q3 | Q4 | 1990 Q1 | Q2 | Q3 | Q4 | 1991 Q1 | Q2 | Q3 | Q4 | Q1 |
|----|------|----------|----|----|----|----|----|----|----|----|----|----|----|----|----|----|----|----|----|----|----|----|----|----|----|
| 1 | RIM feasibility identified | 0d | | | | | | | | | | | | | | | | | | | | | | | |
| 2 | Begin experimentation | 414d | | | | | | | | | | | | | | | | | | | | | | | |
| 3 | Investigate materials | 370d | | | | | | | | | | | | | | | | | | | | | | | |
| 4 | Assemble samples | 104d | | | | | | | | | | | | | | | | | | | | | | | |
| 5 | Show mock-up to customer | 0d | | | | | | | | | | | | | | | | | | | | | | | |
| 6 | Component development | 250d | | | | | | | | | | | | | | | | | | | | | | | |
| 7 | Continue material development | 190d | | | | | | | | | | | | | | | | | | | | | | | |
| 8 | Perform cycle testing | 60d | | | | | | | | | | | | | | | | | | | | | | | |
| 9 | Find tooling vendor | 220d | | | | | | | | | | | | | | | | | | | | | | | |
| 10 | Choose materials | 0d | | | | | | | | | | | | | | | | | | | | | | | |
| 11 | Order and received materials | 30d | | | | | | | | | | | | | | | | | | | | | | | |
| 12 | Status meeting with customer | 1d | | | | | | | | | | | | | | | | | | | | | | | |
| 13 | Manufacturing development | 640d | | | | | | | | | | | | | | | | | | | | | | | |
| 14 | Mfg engineering debins effort | 0d | | | | | | | | | | | | | | | | | | | | | | | |
| 15 | Find molding machine | 250d | | | | | | | | | | | | | | | | | | | | | | | |
| 16 | Order and received equipment | 110d | | | | | | | | | | | | | | | | | | | | | | | |
| 17 | Obtain EPA permits | 70d | | | | | | | | | | | | | | | | | | | | | | | |
| 18 | Perform tests offsite | 60d | | | | | | | | | | | | | | | | | | | | | | | |
| 19 | Install + test equipment | 90d | | | | | | | | | | | | | | | | | | | | | | | |
| 20 | Develop materials handling protocol | 150d | | | | | | | | | | | | | | | | | | | | | | | |
| 21 | Gain expertise w/RIM equipment | 150d | | | | | | | | | | | | | | | | | | | | | | | |
| 22 | Establish harness repair proceedures | 150d | | | | | | | | | | | | | | | | | | | | | | | |
| 23 | System development | 325d | | | | | | | | | | | | | | | | | | | | | | | |
| 24 | Build grommets into harnesses | 20d | | | | | | | | | | | | | | | | | | | | | | | |
| 25 | Conduct 5 and 5 test | 20d | | | | | | | | | | | | | | | | | | | | | | | |
| 26 | Prototypes: build + send to customer | 15d | | | | | | | | | | | | | | | | | | | | | | | |
| 27 | Redesign + test | 100d | | | | | | | | | | | | | | | | | | | | | | | |
| 28 | Prototypes: build + send to customer | 30d | | | | | | | | | | | | | | | | | | | | | | | |
| 29 | Redesign + test | 30d | | | | | | | | | | | | | | | | | | | | | | | |
| 30 | Prepare assembly line | 3d | | | | | | | | | | | | | | | | | | | | | | | |
| 31 | Transfer equipment to plant | 10d | | | | | | | | | | | | | | | | | | | | | | | |
| 32 | Pilot run: build + send to customer | 25d | | | | | | | | | | | | | | | | | | | | | | | |
| 33 | Redesign + test | 42d | | | | | | | | | | | | | | | | | | | | | | | |
| 34 | Establish quality tests | 6d | | | | | | | | | | | | | | | | | | | | | | | |
| 35 | Begin product launch | 0d | | | | | | | | | | | | | | | | | | | | | | | |
| 36 | Build+send production parts to customer | 139d | | | | | | | | | | | | | | | | | | | | | | | |
| 37 | Achieve full-scale commercial production | 0d | | | | | | | | | | | | | | | | | | | | | | | |
| 38 | Improve quality/yield | 81d | | | | | | | | | | | | | | | | | | | | | | | |

Project RIM Grommet          Critical ▬▬▬          Progress ▬▬▬▬          Summary ▼▬▬▬▬◄

Date: 3/1/90          Noncritical ▭▭▭          Milestone ◆          Rolled Up ◇

[1] Early in 1988 the RIM grommet became an official project targeted at a specific customer.

## CASE STUDY

### Packard Electric's Products

Packard Electric executives referred to Packard Electric's business as "power and signal distribution." Packard Electric sold all the electrical cabling and connectors required to interconnect the electrical devices in a vehicle (see **Exhibit 2**). The business was divided into two areas—components and assemblies. The components side involved the individual pieces that made up an automobile's electrical system. Components included cables, connectors, and conduits (sheaths for holding several cables together neatly). Packard Electric sold to the auto companies and GM divisions (such as Delco Electronics and Harrison Radiators) that integrated Packard Electric components into subsystems for automotive assembly plants, as well as to dealers in spare parts.

The assembly products were complete harnesses or subsystems that could be installed directly into an automobile. Typically, Packard Electric would sell the complete wiring system (called a harness) for an automobile which would then be installed by the automobile manufacturer on its final assembly line. Harnesses varied widely in complexity depending on the requirements of the automobile; a complex harness might have many hundred components and nearly a mile of wiring.

The design of harnesses was complicated by the fact that the engineers had to make sure that the harness could be installed in the assembly line as a single unit. Harnesses typically contained bundles of up to 150 wires. These bundles were very stiff and so the engineers had to determine a routing path that not only fit the car's design but also could be packaged neatly for shipment and installation.

The harness installation process was complicated because the cabling spanned the entire length and breadth of the car and connections had to be made at every step of the automobile's assembly process. This installation process consumed from 60 to 90 minutes of the 20 to 30 hours required to complete the final assembly of a typical automobile. As one Packard Electric engineer noted:

> The wiring people get to know everyone in an automotive company, from design through manufacturing. They get involved at every step of the process and must work out thousands of little details. The easiest thing you can change in a car is the wiring, so if there are any production problems, the wiring is the first thing to be changed. What's more, customers don't notice wiring unless there is a problem, and then it's a disaster. Most companies hate wiring because of all the details and the fact that you never get any positive feedback, but at Packard Electric this is what we do and we love it.

Because of the relative ease with which an automotive designer could change a harness, engineering change orders (ECOs) were a major effort at Packard Electric. A harness for even a mature car had an average of two major ECOs, as well as dozens of minor ones, each year. These ECOs ate up a tremendous amount of engineering time; Packard Electric estimated that approximately 50% of the time of its 500 engineers was spent on ECOs. The part proliferation caused by these constant changes was dramatic (see **Exhibit 3**). Because Packard Electric had to be able to fabricate spare parts for any component it had produced, drawings and tooling on over 45,000 parts needed to be maintained. While Schramm had never been able to get any good data on the cost of maintaining these parts, he felt sure that it was significant.

CASE STUDY

EXHIBIT 2

## Automobile power and signal distribution system

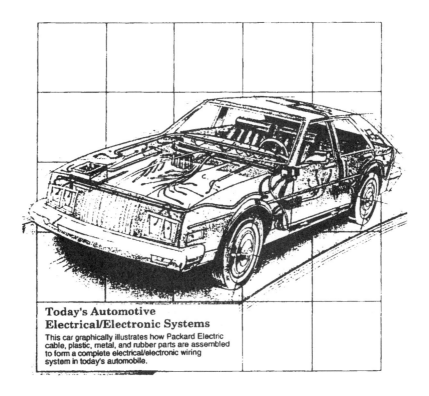

**Today's Automotive Electrical/Electronic Systems**

This car graphically illustrates how Packard Electric cable, plastic, metal, and rubber parts are assembled to form a complete electrical/electronic wiring system in today's automobile.

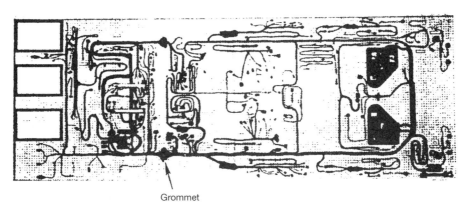

Grommet

**EXHIBIT 3**

## Statistics on part (SKU) proliferation and resources devoted to ECOs

| Statistics on Stock Keeping Units (SKUs)[1] | Application Engineering | Components Engineering |
|---|---|---|
| Number of Active SKUs | 2,800 | 45,000 |
| Number of SKUs Added Annually | 1,200 | 2,400 |
| Number of SKUs Deleted Annually | 1,100 | 300 |
| Life span of a Typical SKU | 2 years | 10 years |
| **Statistics on Engineering Effort** | | |
| Percent of Resources Developing New SKUs | 40% | 65% |
| Percent of Resources on Engineering Change Orders | 60% | 35% |

[1]For Application Engineering, a SKU was an assembled harness ready for installation. For Components Engineering, a SKU was an individual component.

Reducing the cost of the ECOs and part number maintenance were major goals at Packard Electric. In recent years, Packard Electric had become better at forcing change to occur earlier in the initial design process and reducing the subsequent changes per part. The total number of ECOs had remained fairly constant, however, because the complexity of the harnesses (as measured by total length of cable and the number of connectors) was increasing by 6-8% per year in concert with the increasing electrical content of automobiles.

## New Product Development Organization

Three functional groups were involved in new product development: *Product Engineering, Manufacturing Engineering*, and *Reliability* (see **Exhibit 4**). Product engineering did the product design and engineering; manufacturing engineering was responsible for developing the processes for manufacturing the components, cables, and harnesses. Reliability's mission was to oversee Packard Electric's commitment to quality and excellence in all phases of its business. *Cooperative Involvement Engineering* (CIE) reported to the director of reliability and was designed to provide a direct avenue for customer feedback into manufacturing operations, engineering, and Packard Electric upper management. Its role was that of a customer advocate and it examined any Packard Electric decision involving a customer.

Manufacturing Engineering was divided into several subgroups. Of these, the Manufacturing Process Engineering and Industrial Engineering departments were particularly important during the product development process. Manufacturing Process Engineering made a first pass at developing a manufacturing process to achieve a repeatable process, and then followed up with refinements and documentation. Industrial Engineering had responsibility for training the operators, fitting the process into the plant as a whole, and coordinating the ramp-up of the process.

CASE STUDY

EXHIBIT 4

## Partial Packard Electric product development organization

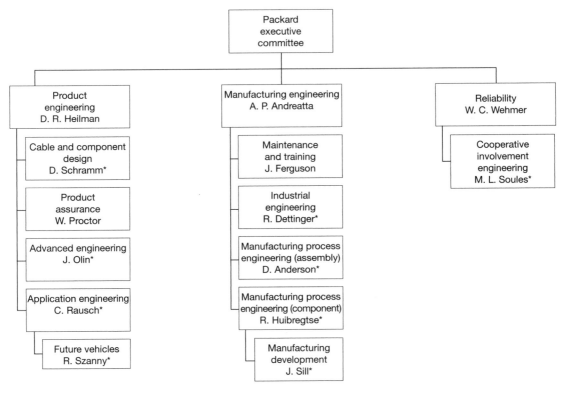

*Signifies member of the Product, Process, and Reliability (PPR) committee.

Four departments comprised the product engineering function. *Cable and Component Design* (CCD), as its name suggested, was responsible for the design of components (e.g., connectors and pass-through grommets) and cables. The design of cabling included determining the wire gauge required for the application, the number of wire strands to be wound together to make up the cable, and the type of insulation to be used. *Application Engineering* did the design of the harnesses as a whole—determining the number and length of cables, and the type of connectors and other components. Often Application Engineering would need a component that did not exist, which would have to be designed by CCD. The long term product development effort was done by the *Advanced Engineering* group. Finally, *Product Assurance* was responsible for making sure that all product designs met Packard Electric's quality standards.

Both CCD and Application Engineering had a "resident engineer program." Resident engineers were Packard Electric engineers who were assigned to one customer and who resided at the customer's plant or design center. Resident engineers from CCD interfaced primarily with the design group at the car company's internal or external electrical systems suppliers, while resident application engineers worked with the design group at the car company. The purpose of resident engineers was to help integrate Packard Electric's designs with customer needs. By taking responsibility for more and more of the electrical system design task, Packard Electric relieved the customer of the cost of doing the design and enabled Packard Electric to become more fully integrated into the design process.

The resident engineer program had been very successful, growing to almost 100 engineers. Customers were eager to reduce their engineering overhead. Some had been skeptical at the beginning, believing that resident engineers would make decisions based on what was good for Packard Electric rather than the customer. However, from the outset, Packard Electric had stressed that resident engineers' responsibility was to do what was right for the customer. Packard Electric benefited also because resident engineers were expected to make sure that Packard Electric knew exactly what the customer needed so that Packard Electric could provide the best solution.

The resident engineer program fit a trend whereby automotive assembly plant customers were transferring more and more of the design task to Packard Electric. Carl Rausch, the head of Application Engineering, described the trend:

> One way to think about it is to divide the types of customer design specifications you might get into three levels. Level 1 is a broad functional specification where the customer tells you what he or she wants to do, but you design the whole power and signal distribution system. Level 2 is a system specification, where the customer has done a system-wide design but left the choice of components to you. Level 3 is a detailed specification where all that is left to do is manufacture the components to spec and assemble them into the product. We used to get mainly level 3 designs from our customers, but we have pushed towards level 1 specs. Level 1 gives us more freedom and leverage—we can integrate our operations much better and develop standard ways to attack problems. This enables us to increase quality and reduce overall system costs.

To integrate the efforts of all these functional departments, the Product, Process, and Reliability (PPR) committee had been formed. This committee consisted of the managers of Cable and Component Design, Application Engineering, Advanced Engineering, Cooperative Involvement Engineering, Manufacturing Development, Manufacturing Process Engineering, and Industrial Engineering. Its purpose was to provide an overall strategy and process for the development effort, guide major technology decisions, and help coordinate activities between functional groups.

## The RIM Grommet

Much of the cabling in an automobile's harness needed to pass through the "front of dash" area between the engine compartment and the passenger compartment. A grommet (or housing) was used to pass the cables through the fire wall. It had three purposes: (1) to hold the cables in place so that they did not slip and possibly disconnect or wear off their insulation; (2) to dampen engine noise and keep the passenger compartment quiet; and (3) to prevent any water or vapors in the engine compartment from entering the passenger compartment.

Packard Electric's primary grommet, the injectable hardshell grommet or IHG (see **Exhibit 5**), had been developed in the late 1970s. The IHG grommet was essentially a hard plastic shell with a comb into which the cables were placed. The comb served to separate the cables; a plastic resin glue was injected into the comb area to seal it, preventing water from seeping through the grommet. Because the glue was quite viscous, however, it did not seal perfectly around all the wires. The resultant seal, although highly splash resistant, was not completely waterproof. It failed the most strenuous leak test— the static water test—which tested the seal with a column of five inches of water on one side of the seal for five minutes. (This test was commonly called the "five and five" test.)

Water in the passenger compartment had been a frequent assembly plant customer complaint in the 1980s, and Packard Electric engineers had searched to find a solution to the problem. In July 1986, Bob McFall, a process engineer at Packard Electric, came up with the idea of using reaction injection molding (RIM) technology to form a grommet around the cables. RIM was a type of injection molding technology that had been around for several years in large-sized applications like automobile door panels and fenders. The principle behind RIM was similar to that of epoxy—when two liquid materials were mixed, they set in less than a minute to form a rubbery solid (see **Exhibit 6**). Before the mixture set, it had a very low viscosity (about the same as that of water), which allowed it to seep between the cables to form an excellent seal.

## Development of the RIM Grommet

From July 1986 through the end of 1987, McFall worked on a RIM grommet as a side interest (about 10% of his time), experimenting with several different materials in the Packard Electric laboratory. By early 1988, he had developed several different configurations. During this period, McFall's principal activity had been helping design components for the electrical systems for a high-end automobile customer. He worked closely with Keith Turnbull, Packard's resident engineer, who was on-site full time at that customer's development center and worked with its team planning the 1992 launch of the new vehicle. Knowing that this customer was very concerned about any water leaking into the passenger compartment, McFall brought along one of his mock-ups of a RIM grommet on one of his frequent visits to Turnbull and the customer.

At the car company, both the electrical systems design and packaging team and the assembly process engineering team were excited about the RIM grommet. Turnbull had tracked complaints from the customers' assembly plants and knew that occasional breakage of the brittle IHG during assembly and leaks detected at the end of the line during the car's final assembly were perennial problems (see **Exhibit 7** for leak data). He had also heard talk of complaints from dealers' service mechanics through

## CASE STUDY

**EXHIBIT 5**

# Contrasting the options: IHG and RIM grommet

**IHG**

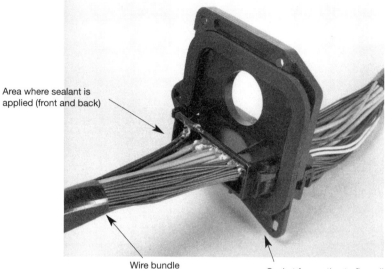

Area where sealant is applied (front and back)

Wire bundle

Gasket for seating to firewall

**RIM Grommet**

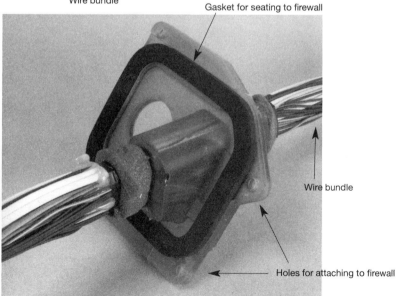

Wire bundle

Holes for attaching to firewall

## CASE STUDY

---

**EXHIBIT 6**

---

### Schematic of RIM machine

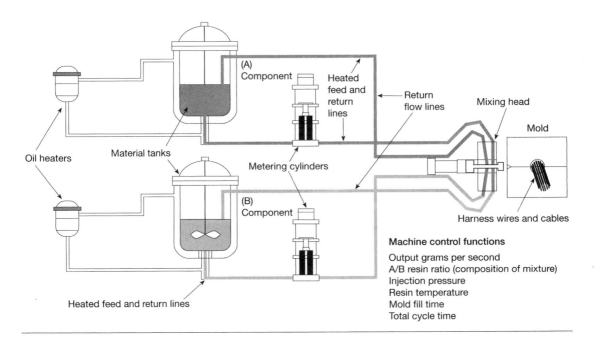

the warranty reporting system. Grommet repair after installation was a major undertaking, whether at the end of the vehicle assembly line (a minimum of two hours of labor at $45/hour) or in dealer repair shops (more than four hours of labor at a warranty cost of $35/hour).[1]

Hoping to eliminate these problems in future models, the customer (with Turnbull's urging) asked McFall if the grommet would be available for its high-end 1992 model. While McFall did not have the authority to agree to this time table, he felt that it was not unreasonable. Encouraged by the customer's reaction, McFall began to get other groups at Packard Electric involved in the effort. During the next year, CCD expanded its level of effort, and manufacturing engineering began to get involved with a low level of effort. Turnbull monitored the RIM's progress but spent most of his time on other projects until he perceived that "it definitely was a go."

During the next several months, McFall and others worked on several aspects of the RIM project. They worked on material development to find the RIM material that could best withstand the constant cycling between hot and cold without warping or becoming brittle. Eventually, they determined that the RIM grommet would need to be reinforced with an internal steel plate. They also began to look at

**EXHIBIT 7**

## Rayville auto assembly plant leak data

MEMORANDUM

To:      Bob McFall, Process Engineer

From:   Keith Turnbull, Resident Engineer, Application Engineering

Date:    12 February 1988

Our wiring harnesses that use the IHG grommet are still as good as any in the industry, but the water leak is a serious issue for Rayville. Your project can get us the inside track on future products if we solve the problem. My contacts working on the new car program continue to ask about progress on the RIM grommet.

The auto assembly plant people gave me some representative water leak data for their current vehicle, which uses our IHG. The harness for 1987 had many ECOs, so it was pretty much a new harness. Each vehicle is given a water spray test at the end of the assembly line; QC then takes leaky vehicles off-line to determine causes. The two tables below tell the story:

RAYVILLE AUTO ASSEMBLY: DAILY WATER LEAKS (1987)[1]

|  | Weeks Since Model Year Launch | | |
|---|---|---|---|
|  | Week 4 | Week 26 | Week 48 |
| Doors | 57 | 21 | 11 |
| Windows | 13 | 2 | 1 |
| Trunk | 7 | 3 | 1 |
| Under Dashboard |  |  |  |
| Heat/Air Ducts | 10 | 7 | 6 |
| Steering Column | 2 | 0 | 0 |
| Wire Harness | 30 | 11 | 3 |
| Foot Pedals | 3 | 1 | 0 |
| Total Build Rate/Day | 60 cars | 300 cars | 300 cars |

RAYVILLE ASSEMBLY PLANT: QC ASSIGNABLE CAUSES—UNDER DASH WATER LEAKS, WIRING HARNESS, IHG GROMMET (1987)[1]

|  | Weeks Since Model Year Launch | | |
|---|---|---|---|
|  | Week 4 | Week 26 | Week 48 |
| Misaligned Grommet | 14 | 2 | 0 |
| Bent Sheet Metal | 7 | 1 | 0 |
| Misaligned Screw Holes | 5 | 1 | 0 |
| Missing or Torn Gasket | 2 | 0 | 1 |
| Cracked Grommet | 7 | 3 | 2 |
| No Sealant in Combs | 5 | 1 | 0 |
| Insufficient Sealant in Combs | 8 | 1 | 0 |
| Other Leaks Through Wire Bundle | 4 | 7 | 1 |
| Missing Attachment Screws | 6 | 1 | 0 |
| Number of Vehicles with Leaks | 30 (of 60) | 11 (of 300) | 3 (of 300) |

[1]A single vehicle may have multiple defects; data is for a single day's production.

tooling. Progress was quite slow, however, because all the engineers were involved in other projects which took up most of their time.

In January 1989, the customer requested a status report on the RIM project. They were not pleased with what they heard. The project had not progressed very far, and it was not clear that it would be ready in time for the 1992 model year. Major RIM equipment producers had not yet developed a piece of equipment small enough to be practically used in this application. All known alternatives were expensive, labor intensive, and cumbersome. The customer made it very clear that they wanted the RIM grommet and were planning to use it for the 1992 vehicle to be produced at their Rayville plant. With this increased customer pressure, Packard Electric's level of effort on the RIM project was stepped up considerably, and Turnbull began working more closely with the Packard team.

For a while, it looked like the project would stall for lack of a molding machine that was an appropriate size for the grommet application. Most RIM machines were large and expensive because they were designed to make large, relatively high value, components. It was impossible to justify the cost of such a large machine for experimentation. The project was about to be canceled, when the chief engineer from Application Engineering ran across a small RIM machine at a trade show.

This RIM machine had been developed by an eight-person company. Its cost was only $80,000, and it was about the right size for Packard Electric's application. In June 1989 the machine was ordered; it arrived in October. Unfortunately, Packard Electric was unable to start testing the machine immediately because it was discovered that, due to the toxicity of the RIM materials, EPA permits were required to run the machine. The permits arrived and testing began on the machine in January 1990. During this time, product and process development continued using RIM equipment outside of Packard Electric.

## Current Status of the RIM Project

By the end of February 1990, several RIM grommets had been attached successfully to harnesses of the type required by the high-end customer. While the RIM grommet's leak performance was decidedly superior to the IHG, it was still not sufficient to pass the five and five test. Packard Electric engineers, however, were confident they could improve this performance and pass the test. The customer was also still very much in favor of using the RIM grommet—assuming that it could be produced reliably—despite the fact that the RIM unit cost was significantly more than the IHG (initially $7.00 compared to $4.40). **Exhibit 8** contains details of the differential costs.

There were a number of outstanding problems still to be solved with the RIM grommet process. Probably the most critical set involved materials handling. Keeping the two RIM materials separate was absolutely essential. For example, if the drum for "material A" was hooked up to the hose for "material B," the whole machine could be permanently solidified. This was not an idle worry; there had been incidents at other companies where a tanker truck had been filled from the wrong tank and the truck, hose, and tank had all been solidified into a block.

CASE STUDY

---

**EXHIBIT 8**

---

## Packard's operating cost differences between RIM and IHG (estimated January 1990)

| Recurring Additional RIM Cost per Vehicle | RIM Grommet vs. IHG | |
| --- | --- | --- |
| | 1992 | 1994 |
| Labor | ($.80) | ($.80) |
| Material | $.65 | $.65 |
| Overhead* | $2.75 | $.95 |
| Total Additional RIM Cost / Vehicle | $2.60 | $.80 |
| **Additional Investment Required for RIM:** | $350,000 | $450,000 |

*The overhead rate was based on non-direct charges such as salaries for management, engineering, and other non-direct labor, plant maintenance costs, taxes, and plant depreciation.

**Assumptions:**

1. 1992: 68,000 vehicles per year serviced by two final assembly lines, producing wiring for 300 vehicles per day.

2. 1994: 220,000 vehicles per year serviced by four final assembly lines producing wiring for 940 vehicles per day (assumes expansion to customer's other high-end models).

3. A full RIM or IHG setup required for each pair of harness assembly lines.

4. One redundant (back-up) molding system for each plant.

5. No tooling changes required.

---

An additional problem was that, prior to mixing, "material A" froze at 64° F (18° C); once frozen, it was ruined. It was therefore very important to keep the material well above 64° F. Finally, both materials were very toxic and would require special monitoring. Because of these properties, Packard Electric had to develop and adhere to a series of strict material handling procedures.

A second set of problems revolved around the risks of a failure in the production system. A failure in harness production could completely shut down the customer's assembly line—which was generally considered the worst thing that could possibly happen. Because all of Packard Electric's customers required just-in-time delivery and were moving toward shorter and shorter lead times, there was little margin for error. It was exceedingly important that the machine be able to run 16 hours a day without fail. Packard Electric's limited experience with the system made it difficult to guarantee, as yet, such failsafe operations.

The third set of problems involved repairing existing harnesses. The act of attaching the RIM grommet entailed some risk to the harness because the mold had to clamp down tightly on the harness to prevent the material from leaking out. If a cable were severed at this point or if the grommet were incompletely filled, the harness would have to be repaired because it was quite valuable (approximately $180) and could not just be discarded.

In addition to developing a repair process suitable for Packard Electric plants, there also was a need to establish a harness repair process for both auto assembly plants and retail dealers. Because the RIM grommet sealed tightly around the wires, once it had set there was no way to remove a defective cable. The solution would entail feeding an additional cable through a hole drilled in the grommet, but many details still needed to be worked out. Schramm estimated that four engineers would need to work approximately five months to address these issues specific to the RIM grommet.

## Views on the RIM Grommet

Schramm knew that the RIM grommet had become a very emotional issue for several people. Product development engineers were generally very positive about it. They felt that in addition to superior leak performance, the RIM grommet offered many other advantages, such as greatly reducing the complexity of the initial feed-through design. Because a comb was required to separate the wires in the IHG, upwards of 150 dimensions had to be specified, compared to only about 30 for the RIM grommet.

The RIM grommet also reduced the variety of feed-through options required to support a broad range of automobile models. Although there was some flexibility in the number of wires that could be fit into an IHG comb, it typically was redesigned every two or three years because of changes in the number of cables in the harness. These redesigns were almost as costly as the initial design and typically required approximately 600 hours of engineering (at about $50 per hour) and about $13,000 in retooling costs.

In contrast, the RIM grommet was simpler, so that the initial design of a RIM grommet took only about 100 engineering hours (and about $7000 in tooling costs). The RIM grommet was much more flexible because the number of wires it could pass through the fire wall was limited only by the available area. With the current design, Packard Electric could double the number of wires without redesigning the grommet. Furthermore, this greater flexibility meant that it might be possible to use the same grommet for different model cars—something unheard of with the IHG. While there would probably never be a single grommet for all models, sharing the same RIM grommet across three or four models was a distinct possibility.

An additional advantage lay in the fact that the RIM grommet saved space in the pass-through area. To achieve an acceptable seal, the IHG had to be lengthened every time the number of wires was increased. Currently, the IHG was 80 millimeters longer than the RIM grommet. In addition to taking up scarce space, the IHG became more susceptible to cracking (and leaking) at this length. With a trend towards increasing the number of wires in the harness, this problem was likely to get worse.

Another argument given by engineers favoring the RIM grommet was that it was a new technology. As Packard Electric became more experienced with the technology, it could expect costs to drop significantly. This would affect the RIM grommet and other future RIM projects as well.

## CASE STUDY

Manufacturing engineers generally felt very differently about RIM. They argued that the RIM process would not greatly decrease the leaks. Kitsa Airazas, a manufacturing process engineer, believed that the customer misunderstood the sources of leaks:

> The problem is that the [customer's] engineers do the "Dixie Cup" test, which consists of filling a paper Dixie cup with water and pouring it down along the wires. This is equivalent to a static water test but the thing is, you don't submerge your car in water. The grommet really only needs to pass a splash test at the end of the assembly line—which the IHG can do. I think the car company's engineers would understand this if it were explained properly, but they've formed an opinion of IHG capabilities that is difficult to change.

A component design engineer disputed Airazas's view:

> Here we go again! Engineering gets a great product and process idea, the customer loves it, and the manufacturing types want to sit on it. If we waited for them, we'd never introduce new technology.

The manufacturing engineers were quick to point out that any sensible engineer would see the obvious process reliability implications of the RIM grommet. The process control parameters were several times more complex than with IHG molding. Developing and implementing the strict materials handling procedures required would take a lot of effort and dramatically increase process complexity. Furthermore, even the act of putting the harness on the RIM machine entailed some risk because every time the harness was moved there was danger of damaging it.

The machine itself caused additional concerns. Considering the size of the vendor, it was likely that Packard Electric would be pretty much on its own. Although the IHG and RIM machines had approximately the same capacity (each could service approximately 70,000 harnesses per year), the RIM machine was much larger—requiring approximately 250 square feet compared with 100 for the IHG. At a cost of $25 per square foot per year, this differential translated to $3,750 per year per machine. Because the volume estimates for this particular 1992 model application were 50,000 to 70,000 cars per year, a single machine of either type would suffice.

The RIM machine also was much more difficult to move. Portability was quite important because the machine was likely to be moved between plants often. The RIM machine would be moved from the Warren, Ohio plant where process development was being done to Packard Electric's Mississippi plant where the initial manufacturing was expected to be done. From there, it was likely that eventually it would be moved to the final harness assembly location. Ron Szanny, an Application Engineering manager, pointed out an apparent conflict with Packard Electric's strategy:

> The RIM grommet is a good product, but I'm not sure how well it fits with Packard Electric's manufacturing strategy. Packard Electric's strategy has been to have high-tech

manufacturing of components in the U.S. and then to ship those components to Mexico where the assembly is done in a low-tech fashion. The RIM machine is a relatively high-tech machine, which eventually may be used in Mexico. The language problem and the distance would greatly exacerbate the control problems that are so important for the RIM technology.

Airazas spoke for many of the manufacturing process people when she said:

> The car companies and our own management have been stressing the need to reduce costs. We've had travel reductions, hiring freezes, and even layoffs. Now they're talking about spending almost twice as much for a component that complicates the process, increases risk, and may not improve performance. I don't deny that RIM is an important technology for some components, but this is the wrong application for it. Going with the RIM grommet would send a very bad message.

> I want to make it clear that I believe we can get the RIM grommet up and running if we want to, but it would require a lot of work, pain, and suffering. I don't think we want to do it because this cost issue will kill us. The car company's design engineers may be excited about it, but everyone knows the car company will eventually want the RIM grommet at the IHG price.

Schramm summed up the feelings of many of his subordinates, the product engineers:

> Look, if nothing else, the customer wants RIM and is willing to pay for it. They feel it is very important to maintain their technological leadership and RIM will help. The funny thing is that I was over at our Reinshagen subsidiary recently and saw them experimenting with a RIM grommet for a high-end German auto maker. They didn't ask what it cost, they just said, "if it improves performance, do it."

> Furthermore, there are cost savings that no one takes into account because they are difficult to calculate. For example, with the IHG, every worker along our wiring assembly line has to insert his or her wires and cables into the IHG's comb. With RIM that task is eliminated. I don't know how to calculate that improvement since it is a small amount of labor distributed among a number of workers, but there are some savings there (see **Exhibit 9** for the harness assembly process).

## Schramm's Options

The RIM grommet decision was a good example of the type of situation that Packard Electric wanted to avoid. A major decision had to be made in a hurry and there was still a deep division in the views of the concerned parties. No matter what decision was made, it was very likely that one group or another was going to be faced with a challenge—either to tell the customer "no," or to develop and implement a process in a compressed time frame. Turnbull's latest memo reconfirmed that the customer was counting on Packard to resolve problems that were as much its own doing as they were Packard Electric's (see **Exhibit 10**).

Schramm felt that there were essentially three options he could recommend. The first was to go exclusively with RIM for this customer's 1992 model. This was the riskiest option because if RIM failed in a major way and impacted the customer's production line, significant repercussions would be felt by all who bore any responsibility. One way to minimize that risk was to recommend the purchase of two RIM machines, one of which would be used as a backup, but Schramm did not like this one bit. In addition to the added expense, it removed some of the pressure from operations to perfect their processes.

A second option available was "parallel development." In this case, an IHG could be prepared in parallel with a RIM grommet for this customer's 1992 requirements. The drawbacks to this plan were

**EXHIBIT 9**

### Packard's wiring harness assembly process

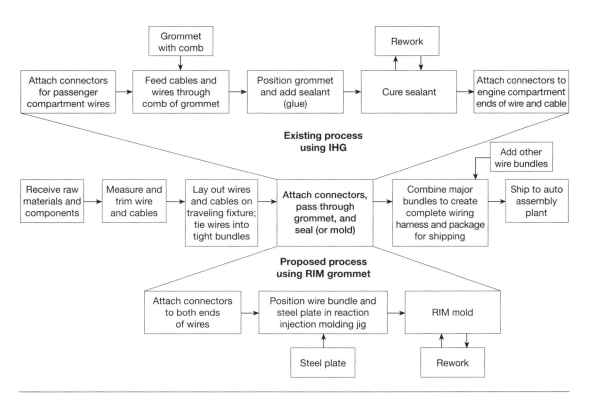

## CASE STUDY

**EXHIBIT 10**

## Packard grommet defects and car dealer data

MEMORANDUM

To:     David Schramm, Chief Engineer, CCD

From:   Keith Turnbull, Resident Engineer, Application Engineering

Re:     IHG Replacement

Date:   30 January 1990

I want to reconfirm our customer's plan to replace the IHG with the RIM grommet for their 1992 model car. Cobbled repairs to defective grommets on wiring harnesses are not a viable solution for its upscale car. The customer is looking to get rid of defects from all sources; water leaks are an unnecessary problem.

I checked with the QC manager at our Mexican plant, who believes his quality far exceeds other harness builders even with the IHG grommet. He thinks the Dixie Cup test is helpful when a new harness is launched, but it does not accurately reflect what actually occurs in use. He believes his harnesses do not have splash leaks. His data for the ships to the Rayville auto assembly plant this past year are summarized below. The story is easy to read—he can't make leak-free harnesses even after a year of trying.

Harnesses for Rayville Auto Assembly Plant (1989): Packard's Mexico Harness Assembly Plant Data—QC Assignable Causes, Inspection Prior to Harness Ship [IHG Grommet]

| | Weeks Since New Harness Launch* | | | |
|---|---|---|---|---|
| | Week 4 | Week 13 | Week 26 | Week 52 |
| Grommet location along bundle (out of tolerance ±1/4″) | 15 | 3 | 3 | 2 |
| Improper distribution of wires in combs | 14 | 7 | 3 | 3 |
| Need to replace wires and reseal | 3 | 0 | 0 | 1 |
| Excess sealant | 8 | 0 | 1 | 0 |
| Nonuniform distribution of sealant | 19 | 4 | 3 | 0 |
| Air bubbles in sealant | 7 | 4 | 4 | 3 |
| No sealant one side | 6 | 3 | 1 | 1 |
| No sealant both sides | 4 | 1 | 0 | 0 |
| Leaks through wire bundle (Dixie cup test) | 60 | 94 | 54 | 42 |
| Total harness build rate per day | 70 | 285 | 320 | 350 |

*Data for one representative day during the week indicated.

This controversy bothered me enough that I decided to visit two of the largest dealerships in the greater Detroit area to check if they saw wiring harness problems. Their files may not be complete but I did pull leak repair records. I tried to classify the defects according to handwritten comments on repair sheets for the final six months of the model year (weeks 27–52). The service managers don't like it when these under dash leak problems come in—they require hours to repair and the customers complain.

Dealer Repairs: Cause of Under Dash Leaks—IHG Wiring Harness

| | | | |
|---|---|---|---|
| Cracked grommet | 2 | Torn gasket | 1 |
| Leaks through wires | 1 | Missing attachment screws | 1 |

I estimate that this sample might represent anywhere from 1–2% of the 1989 model vehicles these dealers sold and now service. I hope that the RIM project will be a hit and allow us to get into several of the other new car programs.

many and obvious. Because Packard Electric had been caught up in the design of the RIM grommet, an IHG grommet would need to be designed quickly. Furthermore, it would become a logistical nightmare when the car went into production. Two sets of raw materials would have to be ordered and kept track of, and both the auto plant and Packard Electric's plant would have two different harnesses to deal with on the assembly line.

The final option was the simplest and least risky. Schramm could recommend that Packard Electric go with the IHG for all 1992 models. He did not like giving up on the new technology, since he personally felt it had many potential benefits. He feared that if RIM were not pursued actively at this point, it would lose momentum and not be applied in 1993 or beyond.

Schramm sighed. He had to present his recommendations to the PPR committee at the end of the week on the RIM grommet; he needed not only to be clear on the RIM versus IHG decision, but also to be prepared to tell them how to restructure the company's development process to avoid such problems in the future.

# Note

1. Depending on the cause, these charges would be billed to (or shared by) the car company or Packard Electric.

# Appendix

## Glossary of Terms

*CCD (Cable and Component Design)*—A product development department.

*CIE (Cooperative Involvement Engineering)*—Reporting to director of reliability, provides a direct avenue for customer feedback.

*Dash/Dashboard*—The console in front of the car driver and front seat passenger that houses the radio, air vents, and so forth.

*ECO (Engineering Change Order)*—The formal prescriptions for changing the specifications of a product or process.

*EPA (Environmental Protection Agency)*—The U.S. government agency that monitors and controls the use of toxic substances.

*Fire Wall*—The metal wall behind the dashboard that separates the passenger and engine compartments.

*Gasket*—The soft, pliable material between the grommet and fire wall which forms a seal between the metal and grommet.

*Grommet*—A plastic fixture that holds and supports electrical wires and cables as they pass through the fire wall of a vehicle. The grommet is attached to the metal wall (fire wall) that separates the engine compartment from the passenger compartment.

*Harness*—The bundle of wires and cables that carry electrical signals and power to and from the car's electronic and electrical components.

*IHG (Injectable Hardshell Grommet)*—A grommet made from injection molding of polymer pellets. The material is quite rigid and slightly brittle.

*Jig*—Fixture to hold wire cable bundle and steel plate in the mold while resins are injection molded around them.

*PPR (Product, Process, and Reliability Committee)*—Manages Packard Electric's new product development processes.

*RIM (Reaction Injection Molding)*—The injection into a mold of two very fluid resins (polymeric chemicals) that react to form a solid plastic with the consistency of hard rubber.

*Sealant*—Resins and glues used to join materials and make them impervious to water.

*SKU (Stock Keeping Unit)*—Each component, subassembly, or assembly that has a unique identification number and identity in Packard Electric's production system.

# Malaysia in the 1990s (A)

In the early autumn of 1991, Mahathir bin Mohamad, the Malaysian prime minister, was preparing to visit New York City, where he was to address the United Nations General Assembly and to meet with American business people interested in investing in Malaysia. During the three decades since its independence, Malaysia had enjoyed rapid economic growth and relative political stability. The prime minister was determined to maintain that stability, in part by realizing even more ambitious economic objectives in the future.

Malaysia's international reputation could be tarnished by reports that the Malaysian government was insufficiently respectful of environmental values. The Western press was especially critical of what it saw as rampant deforestation in the East Malaysian state of Sarawak, in the northern part of the island of Borneo (see **Exhibits 1** and **2**). According to one British environmental group, the rain forest in Sarawak was "being cut down so fast that it will be logged out within eight years."[1] Western environmental groups were lobbying their governments to ban imports of Malaysian timber products and were trying to change Malaysian forestry policy by appealing to international bodies like the International Tropical Timber Organization.

This environmental activism further complicated an already intricate set of economic and political problems surrounding natural resource development in Malaysia. Exports of timber and other natural resources were an important source of foreign exchange. Downstream vertical integration, from the production of natural resource commodities through the manufacture of finished goods, was part of Malaysia's economic growth strategy. Concern over environmental values in Europe and the United States could shrink the demand for Malaysian products and interfere with the government's economic plans. In his address to the UN, as in the formulation of his policies, Prime Minister Mahathir had to consider the connections among his government's ambitious economic strategy, the use of natural resources like forests, and his country's relations with environmentalists and other groups outside Malaysia.

## Malaysia

During the eighteenth century, the British took control of the colony of Malaya, south of Thailand on the Malay Peninsula; the area had previously been controlled by the Portuguese and then by the Dutch. The British later assumed control of the northern parts of the island of Borneo, four hundred miles east of Malaya across the South China Sea.

During the colonial period, the British brought laborers from India to Malaya to work in the new rubber plantations. And while ethnic Chinese had lived in the region for centuries, immigrants from

Professor Forest Reinhardt prepared this case. It is adapted from "Forest Policy in Malaysia" (HBS case No. 792-099).

## CASE STUDY

---

**EXHIBIT 1**

---

## Southeast Asia

---

China came in large numbers during the period of British hegemony to work in the mines and plantations. The Indians and Chinese joined a population that already exhibited considerable ethnic heterogeneity: Islamic Malays inhabited the peninsula, while northern Borneo was populated by numerous indigenous ethnic groups.

The entire region, including Malaya, Singapore, Borneo, Sumatra, and Java, fell into Japanese hands during the Second World War. Malaya became independent of British rule in 1957, and in 1963 was joined by Singapore in the new federation called Malaysia. The states of Sarawak and Sabah in northern Borneo also joined the federation. Singapore remained in the federation for only two years, withdrawing in 1965. (The former colony of Malaya is now called "peninsular Malaysia" or "West Malaysia"; Sabah and Sarawak together are called "East Malaysia.")

CASE STUDY

EXHIBIT 2

## Area and population

|  | Total Malaysia | Peninsula | Sarawak | Sabah |
|---|---|---|---|---|
| Area in thousand square miles | 127 | 50 | 48 | 29 |
| Population in millions: |  |  |  |  |
| 1980 | 13.7 | 11.4 | 1.3 | 1.0 |
| 1990 | 18.0 | 14.7 | 1.7 | 1.5 |
| Population density (people per square mile), 1990 | 142 | 294 | 36 | 49 |
| Population growth rate per year, 1980–1990 | 2.8% | 2.6% | 2.5% | 3.9% |

Note: Numbers may not add to totals because of rounding.

Sources: The Economist Intelligence Unit, "Malaysia, Brunei Country Profile" (September 1991); Government of Malaysia, "Sixth Malaysia Plan 1991–1995" (Kuala Lumpur, 1991).

## Economic Strategy

The new nation of Malaysia was well situated for the production of rubber and was richly endowed with natural resources, particularly timber and tin. Nearly half of Malaysia's export revenues came from rubber as of 1960, but this figure subsequently fell as the export economy diversified. Tin contributed substantially to export earnings throughout the 1960s and 1970s; after the 1973 oil shock, petroleum and natural gas became important export earners as well. By 1980, fuels accounted for one-fourth of export earnings, and contributions from Petronas, the government-owned oil company, accounted for a similar fraction of total federal government revenue.[2]

Like many other developing nations, Malaysia pursued a strategy of import substitution during the late 1950s and 1960s, in part at the urging of the World Bank.[3] Starting in the late 1960s, the government shifted its focus to the promotion of exports, although the restrictions on imports and the incentives for firms to invest for production to serve the domestic market did not entirely disappear. The Malaysian government used a variety of policy instruments to encourage export-oriented growth. These included the establishment of a dozen free trade zones, to which components and raw materials could be imported duty-free; tax holidays and other investment incentives; and lenient technology-sharing requirements.

Low wages and the relatively widespread use of English complemented these policy initiatives in creating an attractive environment for foreign direct investment. Intel, National Semiconductor, and other high-technology firms built assembly plants in West Malaysia during the 1970s and 1980s, and Malaysia's semiconductor industry grew by 20% a year between 1975 and 1985.[4]

At the same time, Malaysia sought to diversify its natural resource portfolio further. Timber production and exports increased steadily during the 1960s and 1970s.[5] Malaysians also planted vast quantities of oil palm, a tree whose seeds are crushed to produce edible oil; by the late 1980s, palm oil was producing more export revenues than rubber. Both rubber and oil palm trees were grown on plantations after the original forest was cleared away.

In addition to this commodity diversification, Malaysia encouraged its natural resource industries to integrate downstream to escape exposure to commodity price fluctuations. Through tax holidays, other tax incentives, and restrictions on the exports of raw materials, the government encouraged the domestic manufacture of lumber, plywood, wooden moldings, furniture, tires, latex gloves, and similar products to replace the exportation of raw timber and natural rubber. In the late 1980s, however, over half of Malaysia's forest products were still exported in the form of logs, and most of the rubber was exported in raw form rather than in finished products.[6]

Malaysian officials were critical of alternative models of economic development, including not only import substitution but also the model, which they attributed to the World Bank and the International Monetary Fund, that pushed raw material commodity exports as a way of earning foreign currency with which to buy consumer and capital goods from industrialized nations. In Prime Minister Mahathir's view, such a program would lead to overproduction of agricultural and resource commodities and a fall in developing nations' terms of trade. "We are today looking at the ruins of this model in many parts of the world, especially in Africa," he said.[7]

Instead, the Malaysian government planned for continuously increasing exports of manufactured goods, while natural resource commodities gradually declined in relative importance. The government's plans called for a fourfold increase in manufactured exports during the 1990s; during the same period, revenues from export of fuels and tin were expected to fall slightly, and revenues from the export of logs and lumber were projected to drop by 50%.[8] (**Exhibits 3** through **7** show economic data for Malaysia during the 1980s, including national income, balance of payments, composition of exports, and income distribution; **Exhibit 8** shows comparative economic data for Malaysia and other nations.)

Malaysia's ambitious agenda included the promotion of Proton Saga automobiles, the first of which were produced in 1985. A joint venture between Mitsubishi Motors and a Malaysian government-owned company designed and made the vehicles, which accounted for the majority of cars sold in Malaysia. Mitsubishi provided much of the engineering and management expertise; it took over management of the Proton plant in 1988, and in the following year Proton recorded its first profit. Pride in the joint venture's technological accomplishments and optimism about the car's market prospects abroad were tempered by doubts about whether automobile manufacture was an appropriate endeavor for Malaysia. These doubts were fueled, in part, by the continued presence of high tariffs on automobile imports. Malaysia, like many other Asian nations, protected a wide range of manufacturing industries as part of its economic development strategy.[9]

Malaysia belonged to the Association of Southeast Asian Nations (ASEAN), whose other members were Brunei, Indonesia, the Philippines, Singapore, and Thailand. ASEAN was established in 1967 as a consultative forum for foreign and security affairs, but turned its attention to economic cooperation after the end of the Vietnam War. For example, as of the early 1990s, Malaysia and its neighbors were beginning to discuss the creation of an ASEAN free trade area, within which trade would be subject to

CASE STUDY

**EXHIBIT 3**

## Gross Domestic Product (figures in billions of 1978 Malaysian ringgits)

|  | 1980 | 1981 | 1982 | 1983 | 1984 | 1985 | 1986 | 1987 | 1988 | 1989 | 1990 |
|---|---|---|---|---|---|---|---|---|---|---|---|
| GDP | 44.5 | 47.6 | 50.4 | 53.6 | 57.7 | 57.1 | 57.8 | 60.9 | 66.3 | 72.1 | 78.9 |
| Private consumption | 24.4 | 25.7 | 26.5 | 27.4 | 29.1 | 29.2 | 26.3 | 26.9 | 31.2 | 35.6 | 39.4 |
| Government consumption | 7.8 | 8.8 | 9.6 | 10.0 | 9.5 | 9.4 | 9.5 | 9.7 | 10.1 | 10.9 | 11.6 |
| Investment | 13.9 | 16.5 | 17.8 | 19.2 | 19.8 | 17.9 | 14.6 | 14.0 | 16.1 | 21.2 | 25.4 |
| Inventory changes | –0.3 | –0.5 | 0.5 | 0.4 | 1.0 | –1.3 | –0.2 | 0.1 | 1.2 | –0.1 | –0.5 |
| Exports | 22.6 | 22.4 | 24.8 | 27.9 | 31.7 | 31.9 | 35.6 | 40.8 | 45.6 | 53.9 | 62.2 |
| Imports | 23.9 | 25.3 | 28.7 | 31.3 | 33.3 | 30.1 | 28.1 | 30.5 | 38.0 | 49.4 | 59.2 |
| **Fractions of GDP:** | | | | | | | | | | | |
| Private consumption | 55% | 54% | 53% | 51% | 50% | 51% | 46% | 44% | 47% | 49% | 50% |
| Government consumption | 17 | 18 | 19 | 19 | 16 | 16 | 17 | 16 | 15 | 15 | 15 |
| Investment | 31 | 35 | 35 | 36 | 34 | 31 | 25 | 23 | 24 | 29 | 32 |
| Inventory changes | –1 | –1 | 1 | 1 | 2 | –2 | 0 | 0 | 2 | 0 | –1 |
| Exports | 51 | 47 | 49 | 52 | 55 | 56 | 62 | 67 | 69 | 75 | 79 |
| Imports | 54 | 53 | 57 | 58 | 58 | 53 | 49 | 50 | 57 | 69 | 75 |
| Agriculture, forestry, fisheries | 23% | | | | | 21% | | | | | 19% |
| Mining and quarrying | 10 | | | | | 11 | | | | | 10 |
| Manufacturing | 20 | | | | | 20 | | | | | 27 |
| Construction | 5 | | | | | 5 | | | | | 4 |
| Electricity, gas, and water | 1 | | | | | 2 | | | | | 2 |
| Services | 41 | | | | | 43 | | | | | 39 |

*Note:* Numbers may not add to totals because of rounding.

*Sources:* Asian Development Bank, "Key indicators of Developing Asian and Pacific Countries," Volume XXII (1991); The Economist Intelligence Unit, "Malaysia, Brunei Country Profile" (1991).

very low tariffs and minimal other restrictions. Some observers thought, however, that an ASEAN free trade area would be unhelpful and possibly counterproductive. "ASEAN countries have stronger economic ties with the rest of the Pacific [e.g., with the US and Japan] than among themselves. . . . ASEAN economies by and large are competitive and not complementary. Under these circumstances, any attempt to increase intra-regional trade through discriminatory tariff reductions would probably result in substantial trade diversion, shifting the sources of imports from low-cost third countries to high-cost partners."[10] (In 1988, US$5.1 billion of Malaysian merchandise exports went to ASEAN, but $4.1 billion of this total went to Singapore. The same year, Malaysia sent merchandise exports worth $4.2 billion to Japan, and $3.7 billion to the United States.[11])

CASE STUDY

EXHIBIT 4

## Balance of payments (figures in billions of US$)

|  | 1980 | 1981 | 1982 | 1983 | 1984 | 1985 | 1986 | 1987 | 1988 | 1989 | 1990 |
|---|---|---|---|---|---|---|---|---|---|---|---|
| Merchandise exports | $12.9 | $11.7 | $12.0 | $13.7 | $16.4 | $15.1 | $13.5 | $17.8 | $20.9 | $24.8 | $29.0 |
| Merchandise imports | −10.5 | −11.8 | −12.7 | −13.3 | −13.4 | −11.6 | −10.3 | −11.9 | −15.3 | −20.9 | −26.5 |
| Trade balance | 2.4 | −0.1 | −0.8 | 0.4 | 3.0 | 3.6 | 3.2 | 5.8 | 5.5 | 3.9 | 2.5 |
| Other goods, services, and income[a] | −2.7 | −2.3 | −2.8 | −3.9 | −4.6 | −4.2 | −3.4 | −3.3 | −3.9 | −4.2 | −3.8 |
| Unrequited transfers | 0.0 | 0.0 | 0.0 | 0.0 | 0.0 | 0.0 | 0.0 | 0.1 | 0.2 | 0.1 | 0.1 |
| Current balance | −0.3 | −2.4 | −3.6 | −3.5 | −1.7 | −0.6 | −0.1 | 2.6 | 1.8 | −0.2 | −1.2 |
| Direct investment | 0.9 | 1.3 | 1.4 | 1.3 | 0.8 | 0.7 | 0.5 | 0.4 | 0.7 | 1.8 | 3.1 |
| Portfolio investment | 0.0 | 1.1 | 1.8 | 1.4 | 1.0 | 0.3 | 0.6 | −0.9 | −1.0 | −0.2 | [b] |
| Other long-term capital | 0.1 | 0.2 | 0.4 | 1.3 | 1.0 | 0.7 | 0.2 | 0.0 | −1.0 | −0.8 | −0.9 |
| Other short-term capital | 0.4 | 0.0 | 0.1 | −0.1 | −0.1 | 0.4 | 0.0 | −1.0 | −1.1 | 0.3 | 0.4 |
| Errors and omissions | −0.7 | −0.6 | −0.4 | −0.4 | −0.9 | −0.1 | 0.5 | 0.1 | 0.1 | 0.2 | 0.2 |
| Overall balance | 0.5 | −0.5 | −0.3 | 0.0 | 0.1 | 1.3 | 1.7 | 1.1 | −0.4 | 1.2 | 1.6 |

[a]Of the totals shown, net investment income was −0.6 billion in 1980, −2.2 billion in 1984 and in 1985, and −1.8 billion in 1990 (*Source:* IMF Balance of Payments Statistics, various years).

[b]Portfolio investment for 1990 is included in other long-term capital.

*Source:* Asian Development Bank.

EXHIBIT 5

## Composition of exports

| As a Fraction of Total | 1980 | 1981 | 1982 | 1983 | 1984 | 1985 | 1986 | 1987 | 1988 | 1989 | 1990 |
|---|---|---|---|---|---|---|---|---|---|---|---|
| Rubber | 16% | 14% | 9% | 11% | 10% | 8% | 9% | 9% | 10% | 6% | 4% |
| Tin | 9 | 8 | 5 | 5 | 3 | 4 | 2 | 2 | 2 | 2 | 1 |
| Logs and timber | 14 | 13 | 16 | 13 | 10 | 10 | 11 | 13 | 11 | 11 | 9 |
| Palm oil | 9 | 10 | 10 | 9 | 12 | 10 | 9 | 7 | 8 | 7 | 6 |
| Petroleum | 24 | 26 | 27 | 24 | 23 | 23 | 15 | 14 | 11 | 12 | 13 |
| All other[a] | 28 | 29 | 32 | 38 | 43 | 45 | 54 | 55 | 59 | 63 | 67 |

[a]"All other" consists primarily of manufactured goods. It also includes small quantities of food and beverage products.

*Source:* Asian Development Bank.

CASE STUDY

## EXHIBIT 6

## Economic indicators and government finance

| | 1980 | 1981 | 1982 | 1983 | 1984 | 1985 | 1986 | 1987 | 1988 | 1989 | 1990 |
|---|---|---|---|---|---|---|---|---|---|---|---|
| Unemployment rate | 5.6% | 4.7% | 4.6% | 5.2% | 5.8% | 6.9% | 8.3% | 8.2% | 8.1% | 7.1% | 6.3% |
| Exchange rate (M$/US$) | 2.22 | 2.24 | 2.32 | 2.34 | 2.43 | 2.43 | 2.60 | 2.49 | 2.72 | 2.70 | 2.70 |
| Change in Consumer Price Index | 6.8% | 9.7% | 5.7% | 3.7% | 3.6% | 0.4% | 0.6% | 0.8% | 2.5% | 2.8% | 3.1% |
| Change in M1 | 15.0% | 12.8% | 13.3% | 7.7% | −0.6% | 1.7% | 2.8% | 13.0% | 14.6% | 17.6% | 14.0% |
| **Federal government finance (in billions of M$):** | | | | | | | | | | | |
| Revenue | $13.9 | $15.8 | $16.7 | $18.6 | $20.8 | $21.1 | $19.5 | $18.1 | $22.0 | $25.3 | $27.2 |
| Current expenditure | 13.7 | 15.7 | 16.7 | 18.4 | 19.8 | 20.1 | 20.1 | 20.2 | 21.8 | 24.8 | 26.0 |
| Current surplus | 0.2 | 0.1 | 0.0 | 0.2 | 1.0 | 1.0 | −0.6 | −2.0 | 0.2 | 0.4 | 1.2 |
| Capital expenditure | 7.3 | 11.1 | 11.2 | 9.4 | 8.1 | 6.8 | 7.0 | 4.1 | 4.0 | 5.7 | 8.0 |
| Overall surplus | −7.1 | −11.0 | −11.2 | −9.2 | −7.1 | −5.7 | −7.5 | −6.2 | −3.9 | −5.3 | −6.8 |
| Net domestic borrowing | 2.3 | 4.1 | 6.0 | 4.5 | 3.2 | 3.6 | 5.0 | 8.7 | 7.9 | 2.5 | 3.8 |
| Net foreign borrowing | 0.3 | 3.4 | 4.9 | 4.6 | 3.1 | 1.0 | 1.3 | −2.4 | −3.1 | −1.0 | −0.8 |
| Other[a] | 4.5 | 3.5 | 0.2 | 0.1 | 0.8 | 1.2 | 1.2 | −0.1 | −0.9 | 3.8 | 3.8 |
| Gross domestic product | 53.3 | 57.6 | 62.6 | 70.4 | 79.6 | 77.5 | 71.6 | 79.6 | 90.6 | 101.5 | 115.0 |
| **Government financial flows as fraction of GDP** | | | | | | | | | | | |
| Current surplus | 0.4% | 0.2% | 0.0% | 0.3% | 1.3% | 1.4% | −0.8% | −2.6% | 0.2% | 0.4% | 1.1% |
| Overall surplus | −13.3 | −19.1 | −17.8 | −13.0 | −8.9 | −7.4 | −10.5 | −7.7 | −4.3 | −5.2 | −5.9 |
| Net foreign borrowing | 0.6 | 5.9 | 7.8 | 6.5 | 3.9 | 1.2 | 1.9 | −3.1 | −3.4 | −1.0 | −0.7 |

[a]Includes special receipts, use of cash balances, and asset sales.

*Source:* Asian Development Bank.

## Social Conditions

Malaysian leaders saw rapid economic growth as a precondition for political stability. Many Malaysians and foreign observers regarded ethnic and religious tension as the central problem for Malaysian politicians and, indeed, the central fact of Malaysian life. For example, *The Economist* wrote in 1987 that "Malaysia remains an uneasy racial mix, in which the tensions have perhaps been kept in check only because there has been high employment and more money in the pay packet each year."[12]

The Malays, along with members of the numerous indigenous ethnic groups of northern Borneo, were classified by the government as *Bumiputras*, literally "sons of the soil." Together, these groups made up just over half of the Malaysian population in 1990. The Chinese accounted for about a third of the Malaysian population, and Indians for most of the rest.

CASE STUDY

EXHIBIT 7

**Average monthly household income by area and ethnic group, 1976 and 1990 (figures in 1990 Malaysian ringgits)**

| | | 1976 Value | 1976 Percent of National Average | 1990 Value | 1990 Percent of National Average | CAGR 1976–1990 |
|---|---|---|---|---|---|---|
| **All Malaysia** | Overall | 850 | 100% | 1,167 | 100% | 2.3% |
| | Bumiputra | 571 | 67 | 829 | 71 | 2.7 |
| | Chinese | 1,340 | 158 | 1,631 | 140 | 1.4 |
| | Indians | 904 | 106 | 1,201 | 103 | 2.0 |
| | Other | 1,677 | 197 | 3,292 | 282 | 4.9 |
| **Sarawak** | Overall | 719 | 85 | 1,208 | 104 | 3.8 |
| | Bumiputra | 485 | 57 | 932 | 80 | 4.8 |
| | Chinese | 1,192 | 140 | 1,754 | 150 | 2.8 |
| | Other | 4,905 | 577 | 4,235 | 363 | −1.0 |
| **Sabah** | Overall | 864 | 102 | 1,148 | 98 | 2.1 |
| | Bumiputra | 579 | 68 | 895 | 77 | 3.2 |
| | Chinese | 2,005 | 236 | 2,242 | 192 | 0.8 |
| | Other | 2,382 | 280 | 2,262 | 194 | −0.4 |

*Sources:* Government of Malaysia, "The Second Outline Perspective Plan, 1991–2000" (1991); World Bank, "World Tables 1991"; Asian Development Bank.

The Chinese in Malaysia formed the nucleus of the modern business community under British rule and continued to dominate Malaysian economic activity after independence.[13] "Malays continued to lag behind in everything from education to commercial enterprises, and their resentment finally erupted into riots in 1969, when the Chinese opposition parties more than doubled their parliamentary seats, threatening Malay political primacy."[14] Hundreds died during the rioting.

In response, the government instituted its New Economic Policy (NEP), described by the government as "an exercise in social engineering designed to reduce the socio-economic imbalances among ethnic groups and across regions."[15] The NEP included ethnic quotas "in education, employment, and ownership, as well as a variety of subsidies, licenses, and credit schemes."[16] The plan called for Malays to increase their share of corporate equity ownership from 1.5% in 1971 to 30% by 1990. "New universities and technical institutions for Malay students were established, and Malay became the official language of university instruction. The Chinese were denied the right to have their own Chinese university. Quotas were established for university admissions, and in the higher civil and diplomatic services a 4 to 1 ratio of Malays to non-Malays was required."[17]

CASE STUDY

**EXHIBIT 8**

## Comparative economic and social indicators

| | Malaysia | South Korea | Taiwan | Indonesia | Thailand | Philippines | Japan | United States |
|---|---|---|---|---|---|---|---|---|
| Area (in square miles) | 128,400 | 38,031 | 12,456 | 782,659 | 198,772 | 116,000 | 143,750 | 3,618,769 |
| Population (millions, 1990) | 17.5 | 43.0 | 20.5 | 190.1 | 55.1 | 66.1 | 123.6 | 250.4 |
| Population density (persons per square mile) | 136 | 1,132 | 1,650 | 243 | 277 | 570 | 860 | 69 |
| Gross national product (in billions of US$): | | | | | | | | |
| 1980 | $22.8 | $83.3 | $65.1 | $54.4 | $47.4 | $37.0 | $2,080.0 | $3,865.0 |
| 1988 | 32.3 | 168.9 | 119.4 | 76.2 | 58.0 | 40.4 | 2,856.0 | 4,881.0 |
| Per capita GNP (in 1988 US$): | | | | | | | | |
| 1980 | $1,659 | $2,184 | $3,659 | $351 | $1,012 | $727 | $17,810 | $16,970 |
| 1988 | 1,972 | 3,950 | 5,968 | 414 | 1,063 | 639 | 23,290 | 19,840 |
| Compound annual growth rates, 1980-1988: | | | | | | | | |
| GNP | 4.5% | 9.2% | 7.9% | 4.3% | 2.6% | 1.1% | 4.0% | 3.0% |
| Per capita GNP | 2.2% | 7.7% | 6.3% | 2.1% | 0.6% | −1.6% | 3.4% | 2.0% |
| Life expectancy at birth, 1990 | 67.8 | 69.6 | 74.1 | 60.3 | 66.8 | 65.9 | 79.3 | 75.6 |
| Telephones per 100 people (mid-1980s) | 9.1 | 25.5 | 35.9 | 0.5 | 1.9 | 1.5 | 55.5 | 76.0 |
| Military expenditures (1988): | | | | | | | | |
| In US$ millions | $908 | $7,202 | $6,156 | $1,400 | $1,718 | $680 | $28,870 | $307,700 |
| As percent of GNP | 2.8% | 4.3% | 5.2% | 1.8% | 3.1% | 1.7% | 1.0% | 6.3% |

*Source: Statistical Abstract of the United States.*

Under the NEP, the disparities among incomes of various ethnic groups had shrunk; the average income of richer Chinese households rose, but that of *Bumiputra* households rose faster. (See **Exhibit 7**.) The NEP did not eradicate income differentials among ethnic groups, and also failed to meet some of its numerical targets, like the 30% equity ownership figure. Still, in 1991 the government declared the NEP an overall success: "Malaysia is . . . one of the very few countries which has, in a span of 20 years, succeeded remarkably well not only in achieving growth but also in addressing more effectively the problems of poverty and economic imbalances." The government concluded the NEP and instituted the National Development Policy (NDP), which included many of the same objectives but did not contain explicit numerical targets.[18]

Under these plans, Chinese-managed companies needed Malay partners to satisfy the corporate ownership requirements. These and related regulations arguably led to new forms of rent-seeking and inefficiency. One Malay entrepreneur said, "My partners are all Chinese; they put up the capital and I demand 51% share. I make sure my investors are with the right faction in politics. I go see government officials, politicians to make sure we get all the licenses and approvals we need. They get to do what they want to do, and I make a lot of money."[19]

Defenders of the NEP claimed that the policy's critics failed to understand or appreciate the need to redistribute wealth among ethnic groups in order to enhance political stability. "We are sitting on dynamite, and there are plenty of fools who want to shorten the fuse," said a Cabinet minister in 1991. "Our job is to keep them from becoming important actors." The prime minister constantly stressed the importance of eliminating poverty and redistributing wealth so that each citizen would see himself or herself as having a stake in the Malaysian economy. By investing heavily in education, further modernizing the country's infrastructure, continuing to attract foreign direct investment, and integrating downstream from natural resources, Malaysia planned to become a "fully developed country" by 2020.

## Political Structure

Since its founding, Malaysia's parliamentary government had been dominated by a coalition of political parties, collectively called the Barisan Nasional (BN). The dominant party within the BN was the United Malays National Organization, or UMNO, whose members were Malay. The BN included several other parties, among them the Malaysian Chinese Association, the Malaysian Indian Congress, and the Gerakan party. In Sarawak, the BN was represented by the Sarawak National Party, the Parti Pesaka Bumiputra Bersatu, the Sarawak United People's Party, and the Parti Bangsa Dayak Sarawak. For the most part, each of the constituent parties of the BN included members of a single ethnic group.

According to *The Economist*, "Malaysia is not a democracy in the exact sense of that word. Every adult has a vote. The elections are conducted almost fairly. . . . The UMNO coalition may win easily, or not so easily, but it will always win. The opposition can never expect to form a government, although if an opposition party does well it may be invited to join the coalition and take part in the decision making and share the perks of office."[20] The Malaysian style of government, with a broad coalition allocating seats in the legislature and cabinet among its constituent parties, and consistently winning elections, was seen by some as similar to that of Japan.

## Economic Performance

Even while its leaders concentrated much of their efforts on income distribution and political stability, Malaysia's economy grew at 7.6% per year in the 1970s.[21] The economy stumbled in the mid-1980s, when world prices of petroleum, tin, rubber, and palm oil plummeted simultaneously, but Malaysia ended the decade with three years of real GNP growth averaging 9%. Over the 1980s, the real growth rate was 5.9%. These impressive numbers seemed to support Prime Minister Mahathir's conviction that Malaysia could become a fully developed country in 30 years, increasing per capita GNP tenfold from its 1990 level of US$2,300. Other observers, however, worried that Malaysia remained dependent on foreign investors who would seek even lower-cost labor in Thailand, Indonesia, China, or Vietnam as Malaysian wages rose. They also pointed out that the richest fifth of the Malaysian population still had 16 times the income of the poorest fifth, making Malaysia's income distribution less equal than that of Korea, Taiwan, Singapore, or Indonesia.[22]

# The Forest Products Industry in Malaysia

In 1991, timber generated more foreign exchange for Malaysia than tin and rubber combined (see **Exhibit 5**). The forest products industry received considerable attention from Malaysian government officials, who saw it as an ideal setting for resource-based industrialization. It also received attention from Western journalists and environmentalists, who saw an ecological horror story involving waste, overharvesting, and destruction of traditional cultures.

Like most other governments in the world, Malaysia's intervened heavily in the forest products industry. Most Malaysian forest land was owned by the states. Although the states of peninsular Malaysia had effectively transferred much of the authority over forestry policy to the federal government, the East Malaysian states of Sabah and Sarawak retained direct control over the exploitation of forest resources within their boundaries.

## Timberland Classification and Forestry Planning

Government agencies set harvest levels for timber from their lands through a complicated scheme of land classification and planning. Government officials designated each forested area according to the uses to which it seemed best suited. Most of the government-owned forests were classified as Permanent Forest Estate (PFE). The government forest agencies were required to manage the PFE "with the objective of maximising social, economic and environmental benefits for the Nation and its people in accordance with the principles of sound forest management."[23] Other lands were designated as wildlife preserves or national parks, and timber production there was forbidden. The rest of the government-owned lands were called stateland forests, and were slated either for forestry or for conversion to agricultural use. (**Exhibit 9** shows the acreage in each category in peninsular Malaysia, Sarawak, and Sabah.)

If an area of stateland forest was slated for agricultural use or for plantations of rubber or oil palm trees, then timber harvesting there resulted in the removal of all of the original forest cover (a process called clearcutting). By contrast, statelands not suitable for agriculture were supposed to be harvested in a way that would ensure the ability to reharvest later. So were all of the lands in the PFE. According to Malaysian foresters, natural stands of rain forest in the PFE were harvested selectively. Only three or four trees per acre were harvested. Over the subsequent 25 to 30 years, the largest of the remaining trees would attain the size of the trees that had been harvested. Government planners assumed that after that time had elapsed, the area could be reharvested, again selectively, and the cycle repeated indefinitely.

## CASE STUDY

**EXHIBIT 9**

### Land use and timber harvests

|  | Peninsula | Sarawak | Sabah | Total |
|---|---|---|---|---|
| **Land Use (1988; in millions of acres)** | | | | |
| Natural forest: | 15.2 | 23.3 | 11.0 | 49.4 |
| logged | 7.5 | 7.9 | 7.3 | 22.6 |
| undisturbed | 7.7 | 15.4 | 3.7 | 26.8 |
| Tree crops | 8.4 | 0.7 | 1.3 | 10.4 |
| Plantation forests | 0.1 | 0.0 | 0.1 | 0.2 |
| All other | 8.8 | 6.5 | 5.9 | 21.2 |
| TOTAL | 32.5 | 30.5 | 18.2 | 81.2 |
| **Administrative Status of Government-owned Lands (in millions of acres)** | | | | |
| Permanent forest estate: | 11.7 | 11.0 | 8.3 | 31.0 |
| logged | 4.6 | 4.1 | 4.9 | 13.6 |
| undisturbed | 7.1 | 6.9 | 3.5 | 17.6 |
| Other state-owned lands: | 3.6 | 9.4 | 2.3 | 15.3 |
| logged | 3.2 | 6.1 | 2.2 | 11.4 |
| undisturbed | 0.4 | 3.4 | 0.1 | 3.9 |
| "Totally protected areas" (national parks and wildlife preserves) | 1.5 | 0.7 | 1.2 | 3.4 |
| TOTAL | 16.8 | 21.2 | 11.8 | 49.7 |
| Percentage undisturbed | 53.6% | 52.1% | 40.9% | 50.1% |
| **Harvests** | **Peninsula** | **Sarawak** | **Sabah** | |
| Years | 1981–87 | 1983–90 | 1984–87 | |
| Annual average area logged (thousands of acres) | 578 | 546 | 436 | |
| Annual average harvest volume (million cubic meters) | 9.35 | 11.76 | N/A | |
| Average annual acreage logged/total forest acreage | 3.8% | 2.3% | 4.0% | |

*Note:* Numbers may not add to totals due to rounding.

*Sources:* Malaysian Ministry of Primary Industries, "Forestry in Malaysia" (n.d.); Sarawak Forest Department, "Forestry in Sarawak Malaysia" (1991).

## The Concession System

The government agencies that controlled Malaysian timberland granted logging concessions to private parties. A concession from the forest agency gave the holder the right, contingent on payment of fees and royalties, to harvest a certain amount of timber from a specified tract of timberland over some period of time. Concession holders commonly contracted the actual logging to other firms.

## CASE STUDY

Concessionaires could sell their logs to independent mills or process the timber from the concession lands themselves. In 1990, over 1,000 sawmills and 80 mills producing veneer and plywood competed for raw timber in Malaysia. (In addition, some 650 other timber-processing mills made furniture, parquet flooring, chipboard, fiberboard, wooden molding, matches, pencils, and other wood products.[24]) Alternatively, concessionaires in Sabah and Sarawak could still sell their logs into export markets.

In the hill forests that comprised most of Sarawak's commercial timberland, government foresters regarded harvesting cycles of about 25 to 30 years as appropriate. Licenses on the PFE in Sarawak had lifetimes of 10 to 15 years, but could be renewed on expiration with the approval of the state forest department. Each concession in the PFE covered an area ranging from 50,000 to 250,000 acres. (By contrast, Rhode Island's area is 776,000 acres.)

The license holders paid royalties to the government based on harvest volumes. Royalties typically ranged from 15% to 30% of the price of the logs, depending on the species; timber royalties accounted for 40% to 45% of the Sarawak state government's total revenues. In addition to the royalties and permits, concessionaires paid relatively small premiums to the government which were earmarked for medical and educational services provided to inhabitants of the rain forest.[25]

Some Western observers were offended at the manner in which the logging concessions were allocated and operated, charging that it contributed to rapid deforestation. Concessionaires were typically corporate entities whose only substantial asset was the concession itself, and the identities of the people who controlled these concessions were not normally made public. *The Economist* wrote in 1990 that "Sarawak's chief minister hands out logging licenses at his discretion," that the chief minister before 1987 had granted concessions covering over 3 million acres to members of his own family, and that the chief minister's replacement, himself a relative of his predecessor, had allocated another 4 million acres to his family members. The state's tourism and environment minister "exercises no restraint—but then he owns three large concessions himself," *The Economist* wrote.[26]

Illegal logging by some concessionaires, their contractors, or other parties was held to be a significant problem. With only about 1,600 employees in total, the Sarawak Forest Department policed a rugged, undeveloped, largely roadless area the size of the state of New York. Harvest targets were difficult to enforce. A single log of meranti, the most widely harvested hardwood tree in Sarawak, might contain wood worth two and a half months' income for the average Malaysian.

Malaysian government officials argued that the existing system, however imperfect, was better than any imaginable alternative. "If the actual harvests are 10% to 20% greater than the amounts in the Forest Management Plan, that is an acceptable price to pay for political stability," said one senior minister.

### Encouragement of Downstream Industries

The governments of Malaysia, Sarawak, and Sabah all used subsidies and tax breaks to encourage the local production of lumber, veneer, furniture, and other wood products. At the same time, they restricted entry into wood processing industries: firms required government licenses in order to build

## CASE STUDY

new factories. Despite the incentives, the export of logs from Sabah and Sarawak remained the most valuable operation in the Malaysian forest products sector in the early 1990s (see **Exhibit 10**).

In 1985, the Malaysian government banned the export of unprocessed logs from peninsular Malaysia to encourage the domestic processing of wood. By 1991, officials were thinking of raising export duties on lumber and plywood to encourage even further vertical integration. For similar reasons, the Malaysian federal government encouraged the restrictions of log exports from Sabah and Sarawak, but log exports from East Malaysia continued in the early 1990s.

### EXHIBIT 10

### Wood production and exports

| A. Wood products production and exports (includes lumber, plywood, and veneer) | W. Malaysia | Sarawak | Sabah | Total |
| --- | --- | --- | --- | --- |
| Production, 1980 (thousands of cubic meters) | 6,112 | 380 | 646 | 7,138 |
| Production, 1990 (thousands of cubic meters) | 7,529 | 781 | 2,375 | 10,685 |
| Exports, 1990 (thousands of cubic meters) | 3,642 | 544 | 2,391 | 6,577 |
| Exports/production, 1990 | 48% | 70% | 101% | 62% |
| Annual growth rate in production, 1980–1990 | 2.1% | 7.5% | 3.9% | 4.1% |

| B. Log production and exports | W. Malaysia | Sarawak | Sabah | Total |
| --- | --- | --- | --- | --- |
| Production, 1980 (thousands of cubic meters) | 10,453 | 8,399 | 9,063 | 27,915 |
| Production, 1990 (thousands of cubic meters) | 10,620 | 18,838 | 8,445 | 37,903 |
| Exports, 1990 (thousands of cubic meters) | | 15,898 | 4,564 | 20,462 |
| Exports/production, 1990 | 0% | 84% | 54% | 54% |
| Annual growth rate in production, 1980–1990 | 0.2% | 8.4% | –0.7% | 3.1% |

| C. Destination and value of Malaysian log exports | Japan | Korea | Taiwan | Thailand | All Other | Total |
| --- | --- | --- | --- | --- | --- | --- |
| Volume, 1980 (thousands of cubic meters) | 8,825 | 1,689 | 2,847 | — | 1,725 | 15,087 |
| Volume, 1990 (thousands of cubic meters) | 10,439 | 3,118 | 3,137 | 765 | 2,857 | 20,316 |
| Average value, 1980 (M$/cubic meter) | 200 | 180 | 123 | NA | 114 | 173 |
| Average value, 1990 (M$/cubic meter) | 222 | 194 | 149 | 208 | 171 | 199 |

*Note:* Total export figure for 1990 differs slightly between parts B and C of this exhibit due to inconsistencies in original data.

*Sources:* Malaysian Ministry of Primary Industries, "Statistics on Commodities," pp. 150ff.; Sarawak Forest Department, "Forestry in Sarawak," p. 35.

Downstream integration into lumber, plywood, or furniture would free Malaysia from the alleged collusion of the Japanese trading firms who purchased most of the logs, as well as from the usual tyranny of volatile commodity prices. Downstream integration would increase employment in the forest products sector; it arguably would reduce the pressure on the forests at the same time, since the same amount of timber would produce more jobs and export revenues. (In Sarawak, timber and related industries were said to employ about 75,000 people, or close to a tenth of the market labor force.)

The Sarawak state government rebated 80% of the royalties on logs if the logs were processed within the state boundaries. In addition, the federal Malaysian government offered generous tax breaks for companies investing in wood processing factories. Companies with "pioneer status," which included most forest products companies in Sarawak, received five-year exemptions from income tax, and investment tax credits further reduced the federal tax burden for new wood processing firms.[27]

## Environmental Concerns

According to a widely cited report by the World Commission on Environment and Development (WCED), about 2.25 billion acres of tropical rain forest still existed worldwide in the 1980s. By that time, however, human activity had destroyed the forest cover on another 1.5 billion to 1.75 billion acres. Each year, more than 25 million acres of tropical rain forest were eliminated, and another 25 million acres were seriously disrupted.[28]

For several reasons, this loss of tropical rain forest was deeply disturbing to environmentalists. At the local level, loss of forest cover could increase erosion, soil loss, and the chance of catastrophic floods. Tropical deforestation also accelerated the extinction of plant and animal species. Although they covered only 6% of Earth's land area, tropical rain forests contained at least half, and possibly up to 90%, of the world's species of plants and animals. Many biologists believed that the human-caused rate of species extinction was hundreds or thousands of times higher than the background rate.[29]

Loss of these species, most of which had been poorly studied and many of which probably were never identified, meant that any potential they might have for human development went untapped. Many wild species had already proven useful in producing medicines, in creating new strains of agricultural crops, or in contributing "gums, oils, resins, dyes, tannins, vegetable fats and waxes, insecticides, and many other compounds."[30] Unknown numbers of other species might prove similarly useful.

Loss of forest cover was also thought to contribute to increases in global average temperature caused by the buildup of carbon dioxide and other gases in the earth's atmosphere. Different studies suggested that between 5% and 15% of global climate change might be due to deforestation.[31]

Although Malaysia contained no more than 2% to 3% of the world's tropical forests, the thick forests—rich in biological resources—that covered the hills of northern Borneo received particular attention from environmental groups and the Western press, and were the center of especially heated controversy.

Reliable data on timber harvesting and forest loss were difficult to obtain in Malaysia and in most other tropical countries. It appeared, though, that logging in Malaysia had affected between 2% and 4% of the country's forested area annually during the 1980s (see **Exhibit 9**). Western environmental groups argued that the amounts of timber harvested exceeded the growth of the remaining timber, so that the forests were being "mined." This raised questions about economic welfare in the long run as timber harvests declined.[32]

Malaysian forestry officials disagreed. First, they argued that the environmentalists failed to realize that logging an acre of rain forest did not mean destroying it; trees would be left standing on the site, and the same acre could be logged again 25 or 30 years later. Second, while acknowledging that timber harvests from Malaysia as a whole were greater than the sustainable level, the officials thought it made no sense to include forests slated for conversion to agricultural use in calculating the sustainable yield.

Further, Malaysian government officials felt that small-scale, temporary conversion to agriculture was a bigger problem than commercial logging. Rural people would clear and burn small patches of jungle and plant crops, moving on to clear and burn other areas a few years later. According to the Sarawak forest department, a state agency, shifting cultivation was responsible for much of the forest loss in Sarawak.[33]

Some Western groups also argued that logging violated the rights of self-determination of indigenous people in the Borneo jungle. Attention centered on the Penans, nomadic forest dwellers whose way of life was threatened by logging; their number was estimated at 9,000 by the Singaporean and Malaysian British Society (SIMBA), although Malaysian government officials said that only 300 still pursued a traditional nomadic way of life. When indigenous people tried to stop the logging by burning bridges or blocking roads, they were prosecuted and jailed.[34]

## Possible Changes in Forest Management

### The ITTO Report and Its Recommendations

In 1989 and 1990, the governments of Sarwak and Malaysia invited the International Tropical Timber Organization (ITTO) to send a group of observers to Sarawak to visit the timberlands, assess forestry practices, and present some recommendations. The ITTO, whose member governments were exporters and consumers of tropical forest products, worked with both environmental groups and trade associations. Its purpose was "to strike a balance between utilization and conservation of tropical forest resources through enhanced benefits to promote sustainable management of such forests."[35]

The mission released its report to the ITTO in May 1990. Its central recommendation was that the timber harvest in Sarawak be reduced to 9.2 million cubic meters per year: 6.3 million cubic meters per year from the PFE, and another 2.9 million from the statelands that apparently were not needed for conversion to agriculture or plantations.[36] The mission based this recommendation on its own calculation of

## CASE STUDY

the sustainable annual yield from the PFE and the stateland forests in Sarawak, after excluding the parts of the forest that it thought were too steep to be logged in an environmentally acceptable manner. According to foresters in the Sarawak government, harvests in the state in 1990 totaled about 18 million cubic meters, or nearly twice the total that the ITTO recommended. About one-third of this total came from land clearing on the statelands, and the rest from the PFE. The Sarawak government stated formally that it "accepts in principle the recommendations in the ITTO Mission Report and will implement the recommendations based on available resources and with the assistance and cooperation of the international community."[37]

Controversy persisted after the ITTO report was released. One of the mission's main recommendations was that "the staff of the Forest Department must be comprehensively strengthened."[38] A year and a half after the mission's completion, however, practically no new foresters had been hired. The Sarawak government needed permission from the federal government to increase its employment; officials in the Forest Department said they were anxious to hire at least 400 people, but that officials in Kuala Lumpur were sitting on the necessary paperwork. Federal officials countered that responsibility for the hiring really rested in the Sarawak capital of Kuching. Meanwhile, harvests continued at a rate well above the ITTO recommendations.

### Other Measures

Many observers, including the ITTO mission, suggested that the Sarawak and Malaysia governments increase the size of their Totally Protected Areas (national parks and wildlife preserves). Sarawak had agreed to quadruple the acreage of those areas. This meant management headaches in the short run, as people were displaced from areas where they had traditionally used the forest, and could also mean forgone revenues in the long term. In response, some westerners suggested that, since the Sarawak rain forests were in effect a globally valuable asset, the inhabitants of Borneo should somehow be compensated for maintaining them in a pristine state.

### A Western Timber Ban?

Less-patient environmentalists suggested that Western nations ban imports of forest products from Malaysia until the government reformed its forest policies.[39] In response, Malaysians pointed out that most of the furniture they exported to the United States and Europe originated in West Malaysia, while all of the log exports came from East Malaysia. Further, Malaysia's biggest log customers were in the Far East. It seemed unlikely that they would join any sort of boycott of Malaysian wood.

Many Malaysians saw behind the proposed timber trade restrictions the sinister hand of the Western softwood timber producers. Government officials and industry leaders alike spoke of alliances between the Western environmental groups and the companies that produce lumber and plywood in North America and Scandinavia. "They are worried that they will lose market share to tropical timber, so they fund the environmental groups to engage in anti-tropical hardwood campaigns," said one official. And Prime Minister Mahathir's own speechwriters had written in the draft of the address he was to give before the United Nations in September 1991 that "the idea that the tropical forests can be saved only by boycotting tropical timber smacks more of economic arm-twisting than a real desire to save the forests. . . . This is a ploy to keep us poor."[40]

# Notes

1. London Rainforest Movement and Singaporean and Malaysian British Association, "Sarawak: The Disposable Forest" (London, 1991).

2. Fong Chan Onn, *The Malaysian Economic Challenge in the 1990s* (Singapore: Longman, 1989), pp. 98, 159, 203, 177–178.

3. Mohamed Ariff, *The Malaysian Economy: Pacific Connections* (Singapore: Oxford University Press, 1991), p. 10.

4. Keith Colquhoun, "Malaysia: The Struggle for Survival," *The Economist*, January 31, 1987, Survey, p. 9.

5. Raj Kumar, *The Forest Resources of Malaysia* (Singapore: Oxford University Press, 1986), pp. 38–39.

6. Ministry of Primary Industries Malaysia, "Profile: Malaysia's Primary Commodities" (Kuala Lumpur, 1990), pp. 117–119, 223ff.; Bank Negara Malaysia, "Annual Report 1990" (Kuala Lumpur), pp. 211-212.

7. Ai Leng Choo and Nayan Chandra, "Prime Minister of Malaysia Criticizes Western Model for Economic Growth," *The Wall Street Journal*, September 30, 1991, p. A5B.

8. Government of Malaysia, "The Second Outline Perspective Plan" (Kuala Lumpur, 1990), p. 80.

9. World Bank, *The East Asian Miracle: Economic Growth and Public Policy* (New York: Oxford University Press, 1993), Chapter 6.

10. Ariff, pp. 164–165.

11. Ariff, p. 16.

12. Colquhoun, p. 13.

13. Ian Buruma, *God's Dust* (London: Vintage, 1991), pp. 113–114.

14. Margaret Scott, "Where the Quota Is King," *The New York Times*, November 17, 1991, VI, p. 63.

15. Malaysia, "The Second Outline Perspective Plan," p. 8.

16. Lucian Pye, *Asian Power and Politics: The Cultural Dimensions of Authority* (Cambridge: Belknap Press of Harvard, 1985), p. 262.

17. Pye, p. 262.

18. Malaysia, "Second Outline Perspective Plan," pp. 45, 7–21.

19. Quoted by Scott, p. 67.

20. Colquhoun, p. 8.

21. Ariff, p.8.

22. Andrew Cowley, "Asia's Emerging Economies," *The Economist*, November 16, 1991, Survey p. 17.

23. Ministry of Primary Industries Malaysia, "Forestry in Malaysia" (n.d.), p. 6.

24. Ministry of Primary Industries Malaysia, "Statistics on Commodities" (1991), pp. 156–157.

25. In "The dwindling forest beyond Long San," *The Economist* (August 18, 1990, pp. 23ff.) reported that royalties in Sarawak were just 2% of the timber's value. In 1990, the Sarawak government took in 520 million Malaysian ringgits (M$) in timber tax revenues, according to government budget documents; that year, log exports

## CASE STUDY

from the state were worth about M$2,800 million. Various premiums totalled M$52 million in 1990.

26. "The dwindling forest beyond Long San," *The Economist* (August 18, 1990), p. 23.

27. Ministry of Primary Industries Malaysia, "Profile: Malaysia's Primary Commodities," p. 1.

28. World Commission on Environment and Development, *Our Common Future* [also known as "the Brundtland report"; hereinafter cited as "WCED"] (Oxford: Oxford U.P., 1987), p. 151.

29. WCED, p. 150.

30. WCED, p. 156.

31. See "Global Climate Change" and Supplements (HBS Case Nos. 391-180 through 391-188).

32. See "Sarawak: The Disposable Forest."

33. Sarawak Forest Department, "Forestry in Sarawak" (Kuching, 1991), p. 8; see also Ministry of Primary Industries Malaysia, "Profile: Malaysia's Primary Commodities," p. 138.

34. Singaporean and Malaysian British Association, "Attempts to Protect Land End in Severe Jail Terms," Press release, 1991.

35. International Tropical Timber Organization, Report submitted to the International Tropical Timber Council by Mission Established Pursuant to Resolution I (VI), "The Promotion of Sustainable Forest Management: A Case Study in Sarawak, Malaysia" (May 1990) [hereinafter "ITTO Mission Report."], p. 1.

36. ITTO Mission Report, pp. 34, 71.

37. "Statements by the State Government of Sarawak Malaysia on the ITTO Mission Report" (n.d.).

38. ITTO Mission Report, p. 71.

39. ITTO Mission Report, pp. 5-6. The ITTO Mission did not support these proposals.

40. Malaysia Embassy to the United Nations, "Statement by H.E. Data' Seri Dr. Mahathir Mohamad, United Nations General Assembly, New York, 24 September 1991."

# Whistler Corporation (A)[1]

In the summer of 1987, Charles Stott, the recently appointed President of the Whistler Corporation, realized that the company had reached a critical juncture—the once profitable maker of radar detectors was losing $500,000 per month. Stott had been brought in by Whistler's corporate parent, the Dynatech Corporation, to return the company to profitability. Within the next few weeks, Stott was to present a decision to Dynatech regarding the future of Whistler's manufacturing operations.

Stott was considering radically restructuring Whistler's domestic manufacturing operations in an attempt to become cost competitive with off-shore manufacturers. A pilot "just-in-time" (JIT) synchronized production line that had been in operation for less than three months would be the model for the new manufacturing system. If the synchronized production system could be successfully scaled up, Whistler could expect significant cost savings from reduced work-in-process inventory, better quality, higher labor productivity, and more efficient utilization of floor space. Major savings in fixed costs would also come from being able to close the company's plant in Fitchburg, Massachusetts.

A second option being contemplated was instead to expand the company's long standing and successful relationship with a Korean consumer electronics company. This company was already supplying complete "low-end"[2] radar detectors to Whistler at very attractive prices. Turning over additional low-end products to this Korean supplier would allow Whistler to be more cost competitive in this segment of the market. It would also alleviate some of the capacity problems the company was experiencing in its two domestic plants (in Westford and Fitchburg, Massachusetts). A third, and more extreme option was also being given serious consideration: Move all production off-shore and shut down the company's two domestic plants. This route had been taken by all but one of Whistler's competitors in the radar-detection market.

## Background

Radar detectors, known in the vernacular as "Fuzz-busters"™[3], are small electronic devices which alert drivers to the presence of police band radar used to track vehicle speeds (**Exhibit 1**). The device contains three basic functional (internal) parts. The *microwave assembly* is an antenna which picks up microwave signals (emitted by police "radar guns") and converts them into lower frequency radio signals. These signals are then processed and interpreted by the *radio frequency assembly*. If police band radar signals are detected, the *control assembly* alerts the driver through flashing lights, a beep, or some combination of visual and audio cues.

The first radar detectors were introduced in 1972. Truck drivers were then the overwhelmingly dominant users of radar detectors. In the late 1970's, the use of radar detectors began to spread to automobile

This case was prepared by Professor Gary Pisano.

CASE STUDY

EXHIBIT 1

## Representative products of Whistler Corporation

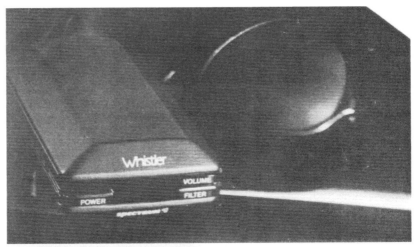

"enthusiasts", salespeople, and others who frequently drove long distances on highways. It was still a small, specialized niche market when the Whistler Corporation decided to enter the business in 1978.

Whistler was founded by Dodge Morgan in the early 1970's. In its earliest days, the company designed and manufactured electronic specialty products (voice scramblers, marine radars, and gas leak detectors) in the founder's garage. As revenues began to grow, the company relocated first to an old mill and then to a larger, more modern facility in Westford, Massachusetts.

Because of the company's strong design and engineering capabilities, it quickly became a dominant and profitable player in the small, but growing market for radar detectors. Its first radar detector, designed in 1978, became a leading seller. In 1982, Whistler introduced two more models. In 1983, Whistler was one of six companies competing in what was still a rather specialized, but profitable, niche market. In this same year, Whistler was acquired by Dynatech, a Burlington, Massachusetts company whose strategy was to purchase small to medium sized companies with dominant positions in niche markets.

## Explosive Growth: 1983–1987

Shortly after Dynatech acquired Whistler, a number of interrelated changes occurred in the market for radar detection devices. As indicated in Exhibit 2, unit aggregate demand exploded. Between 1982 and 1987, the total number of radar detectors sold in the United States increased by more than 450%. Annual rates of market growth during this period averaged 35.6%.

This growth was associated with a fundamental change in the composition of demand. "Mass" consumers became the dominant buyer segment. The market became segmented according to price, quality, performance, and purchasing convenience. Distribution expanded from specialty auto and truck shops to a variety of general retail outlets (electronics shops, mass merchandisers, and mail-order catalogues). To serve as many segments of the rapidly growing consumer market as possible, Whistler introduced nine new models between 1982-1987.

As could be expected, demand growth attracted new competition. By 1987, Whistler had 19 competitors. While many of these were American companies, virtually all of them sold radar detectors which were manufactured under subcontracting arrangements with Asian suppliers. The majority sourced exclusively from Asia. In the wake of intense competition and access to low-cost off-shore producers, the average price of radar detectors declined steadily (**Exhibit 2**).

It was during this period of rapid growth that Whistler experienced severe problems in its manufacturing operations.

## Manufacturing Operations

Manufacturing at Whistler was divided into two sets of operations: subassembly production and final assembly. Before 1985, both subassembly and final assembly operations were done in Whistler's

CASE STUDY

EXHIBIT 2

## U.S. market for radar detectors (units)

| Year | Number of units | % Increase | Average retail price |
|------|-----------------|------------|----------------------|
| 1980 | 473,000 | | |
| 1981 | 583,000 | 23 | |
| 1982 | 618,000 | 6 | |
| 1983 | 985,000 | 59 | $150 |
| 1984 | 1,458,000 | 48 | 136 |
| 1985 | 1,910,000 | 31 | 125 |
| 1986 | 2,505,000 | 31 | 115 |
| 1987 | 2,840,000 | 13 | 95 |
| 1988* | 2,982,000 | 5 | 90 |
| 1989* | 2,684,000 | −10 | 88 |
| 1990* | 2,415,000 | −10 | 85 |
| 1991* | 2,295,000 | −5 | 80 |

*Projected

40,000 square foot plant in Westford. In 1985, Whistler moved final assembly operations to a new 20,000 square foot plant in Fitchburg, Massachusetts (approximately 25 miles from its Westford plant).

## Subassembly

As indicated earlier, radar detectors consist of three internal major subassemblies: 1) a microwave subassembly, 2) a radio frequency (RF) subassembly, and 3) a control subassembly. Whistler designed and built all three of these subassemblies in-house. Both the RF and control subassemblies consisted of printed circuit boards containing through-hole soldered, as well as surface mounted, electronic components. The RF and control boards were assembled from electronic components and bare printed circuit boards purchased from outside vendors. The microwave subassembly was manufactured using zinc die castings supplied by an outside vendor. Normally, these subassemblies were produced in batch sizes large enough to meet the requirements of one month of final assembly.

Circuit board production required a number of steps. First, all of the components required to produce a batch of a particular circuit board were brought from the stockroom to the circuit board production area. Then, electronic components were automatically mounted onto the surface of the bare panels. After this "surface mounting", the batch was inspected to ensure that all of the appropriate components were correctly placed. The entire batch then moved to the "hand stuffing" work area where components that could not be automatically mounted were manually inserted into the board. These "hand-stuffed" components were then soldered into place on an automated wave solderer.

The entire batch of boards was then tested; boards which failed the test were marked. All panels were then sent to the "waterknife" which used a high-pressure stream of water to cut the panel into individual circuit boards, a process known as "depalletization". After depalletization, any defective boards were sent to the printed circuit board re-work area. The boards which had passed the first step were sent to a another work station for RF tuning and functional testing. Boards which failed this second test were also sent to the re-work area. Finally, the entire batch went through a final quality control audit to ensure that only good boards would be sent to the board inventory in the stockroom[4] and ultimately on to final assembly.

Microwave assemblies were assembled in a separate part of the factory. Like the RF and control boards, the microwave assemblies were produced in batches large enough to meet one month's final assembly requirements.

### Final Assembly

Final assembly consisted of six steps. First, the three major internal subassemblies were wired together. Second, a "quick test" of the integrated electronic system was done. Defective units were sent to a final assembly rework area. Third, the now-integrated electronic systems were attached to the bottom half of the unit's plastic molded shell. Fourth, the top half of the exterior shell was fastened onto the bottom half (now containing the electronic system). Fifth, the entire unit was tested (defective units were sent to the re-work area). Finally, the unit was packaged with instructions and sent to the finished goods storage area.

## Production Control

The flow of materials was controlled by what is commonly referred to as a "batch-and-kit" method. In a batch-and-kit operation, all subassemblies and final assemblies are produced in batches—at Whistler, normally monthly batches. For example, if 5000 Spectrum 1 radar detectors were scheduled for production in a month, all 5000 would be assembled in one batch.

Before the final assembly of a batch could begin, all requisite subassemblies and parts had to be ready. Several weeks before final assembly of a batch of Spectrum 1s was scheduled to begin, the subassembly area produced 5000 of the appropriate RF boards, 5000 of the appropriate control boards, and 5000 of the appropriate microwave assemblies. The finished batches were then sent to the stockroom. Just prior to the time at which final assembly was scheduled, all the required subassemblies were picked from the stockroom and organized into a "kit"—all those parts required for the final assembly of one batch of finished product of that model. The kit was then sent to final assembly.

Most of the small electronic components used by Whistler were supplied by vendors located in Asia. For these components, the lead time from order to delivery was about ten weeks. Due to these long lead times, and because of the relatively low cost of these components, Whistler generally stocked enough raw materials to satisfy the next two months of scheduled production.

## Strains in Manufacturing

As production volume began to increase rapidly after 1983, manufacturing operations experienced a number of problems. When Whistler had been producing four models in relatively low volumes, the number and size of production batches were manageable. However, increases in both total production volume and the number of models meant an increase in the number and size of batches. With a total of 13 models in production, the factory often found itself with several batches of in-process units lined up and waiting between work areas. With available stockroom space full, the floor of the Westford factory quickly became cluttered with work-in-process.

Floor space was not the only constraint in the Westford plant. There were many electronics companies in the Westford-Lowell area. Because of defense spending and a general expansion in the economy, these companies were experiencing a boom in business. Demand for semiskilled assembly workers was extremely high. Whistler, competing for labor with such companies as Digital Equipment Corporation (DEC) and Wang, found it difficult to staff its production operations at the wages it could pay.

A decision was made to lease a factory in Fitchburg, Massachusetts where both labor and space were more economically available. Management viewed the Fitchburg plant as a way to quickly add capacity and capture some of the business Whistler had been losing. In 1985, the Fitchburg plant was opened. All final assembly and test operations were moved to Fitchburg. Subassembly operations and packaging remained in Westford. Thus, the process flow was altered as follows: RF boards, control boards, and microwave subassemblies were produced and tested in Westford. These subassemblies and all the other parts required to make a batch of a particular model were "kitted" and then trucked to Fitchburg. In Fitchburg, the kits were assembled into final products and tested. The entire batch (or multiple batches) were then trucked back to Westford where finished product was packaged and stored.

During this time period, Whistler began to experience quality problems in the subassembly of RF and control boards. Some of these problems were due to defects in components sourced from outside vendors. However, a major part of the problem was caused by the new surface mount technology (SMT). Components which are surface mounted take up less space on the circuit board than those that must be inserted and soldered into holes. As a result, surface mounting allows more components to be packed onto a smaller circuit board. The trend toward smaller radar detectors made this technology desirable. When automated, the surface mounting process reduced cycle time dramatically. Given the need to increase production volume to keep up with demand as well as the increased demand for smaller detectors, SMT was a natural technology to adopt, even though it was a far more complex process than traditional methods.

The first SMT equipment was installed in 1986. The yields on the SMT process were quite low while operators, designers, and process engineers learned about and adjusted to the subtleties of the new process. By early 1987, the first-pass yield (the percentage of "good" output the first time through, before rework) had climbed to 75%. Through diligent inspection and extensive rework[5], the quality of products reaching customers remained extremely high. However, ensuring that reliability in the field was quite costly. For example, at the end of 1986, 100 of the company's 250 production workers were deployed to fix defective boards. About 30% of the Westford plant's floor space was taken up with in-process rework. Rework accounted for approximately $600,000 of the company's $2 million of work-in-process inventories.

Defective boards also hampered smooth material flow. A strict batch-oriented material flow discipline requires that an adequate number of subassemblies of each type be available to complete a kit. High rates of defective subassemblies created problems in matching subassemblies to create final assembly kits. In final assembly, incomplete kits could sit for weeks waiting for defective subassemblies to be reworked. The pressure to ship products was so great that common parts from other batches in process would sometimes be used as replacements. Unfortunately, this "borrowing" of components often went unrecorded. As a result, the missing parts were not available when the other batch was ready for final assembly. High defect rates became so normal that they were built into the production schedule. For example, as a matter of policy, the Production and Control Department ordered 20% more subassemblies than the final assembly production schedule called for.

Work-in-process piled up because of frequent unexpected schedule changes. When Whistler had been producing only four models for a rather narrow market, the schedule could be set well in advance. The "mass" market, however, was far more volatile. As one production scheduler put it:

> Out of the blue we could get an order for 5000 Spectrum 2's from a big retailer running a weekend promotion. If we had the products to ship, we had the order. If not, we lost it. This was something we just weren't used to. Truckers don't go out and buy a radar detector just because it's George Washington's birthday.

Production schedule changes often meant stopping work on one batch of products to free up resources to start another. In early 1987, work-in-process inventory had reached $2 million. A production controller who had worked on the production line described the scene: "The place was a total zoo. Boards and half-assembled units were piled up from floor to ceiling. We even had to rent three trailers to handle the overflow."

Work-in-process had also become a materials-handling nightmare. The longer kits remained on the factory floor and the more they were reshuffled (to make room for other work-in-process), the greater the likelihood of damage to delicate electronic parts and further problems in final assembly. In 1987, by the time a unit had completed final assembly, it had spent an average of 23 days in process, although actual production time was only eight hours.

## Performance

Until late 1986, manufacturing was of little concern to the Whistler management. Innovative design and good marketing were, as one executive put it, "the name of the game". Sales had been growing

## CASE STUDY

rapidly and manufacturing, despite its internal problems, had managed to keep up. In 1985, profits before taxes were 20% of sales; the company had a pretax return on assets of 40%. In that year, the company was the market share leader with 21% of the domestic radar detector market (units). The "build as many as you can, any way you can" strategy seemed to be working.

In 1986, however, financial performance deteriorated rapidly. High manufacturing costs were making it difficult to compete with off-shore manufacturers. The manufacturing costs of Asian subcontractors were substantially lower than those of Whistler (**Exhibit 3**). A marketing analysis suggested that, due to their performance, quality, reputation, and brand image, Whistler's products could support a 10% price premium, but not much more. By the end of l986, Whistler's market share had fallen to 12%. By the end of the summer of 1986, the company began to lose money for the first time in its history, at the rate of almost $500,000 per month. The problems in manufacturing began to draw notice.

According to Jack Turner, Vice President of design and engineering, who headed manufacturing at the time: "We knew manufacturing was sick. We knew something had to be done. We just didn't know what it was."

In September 1986, a consulting firm was hired to study Whistler's manufacturing process and to make suggestions for change.

**EXHIBIT 3**

### Off-shore sourcing alternatives: U.S vs. far east manufacturing (spectrum 1)

|                          | United States Current (1/87)[1] | Far East (in $ U.S.) |
|--------------------------|:-------------------------------:|:--------------------:|
| Material                 | $31.90                          | $30.48               |
| Scrap                    | 3.83                            | 0.92                 |
| Direct labor             | 9.00                            | 1.88                 |
| Variable overhead        | 6.30                            | 7.46[2]              |
| Shipping                 | —                               | 0.30                 |
| Duty                     | —                               | 2.40                 |
| U.S. coordination costs  | —                               | 1.00                 |
| Fixed overhead           |                                 |                      |
| Westford (HQ)            | 3.38                            | 3.38                 |
| Westford plant           | 9.28                            | —                    |
| Fitchburg plant          | 8.14                            | —                    |
|                          | $20.80                          | $3.38                |
| Total                    | $71.83                          | $47.82               |

[1]Data for traditional manufacturing system; does not include estimated results from MPL.

[2]Includes the subcontractor's fixed overhead, variable overhead, and profit margin.

## CASE STUDY

# The RACE-ME Program

The consulting firm suggested a comprehensive program to reform manufacturing operations. The program was dubbed RACE-ME (Restoring A Competitive Edge Through Manufacturing Excellence). Its goal was to make Whistler's manufacturing as efficient as its Far Eastern competitors within 24 months.

The RACE-ME program included reforms in materials handling practices, operator training, process lay-out, inspection and quality control, tooling, and production flow. A model (pilot) production line (MPL) was set up in a corner of the Westford plant to implement, evaluate, and demonstrate various reforms. The line consisted of a series of connected work benches. For symbolism, the benches were a different style and different color than those found in the main manufacturing operations. The relatively high-volume Spectrum 1 was chosen to be produced on the MPL.

The MPL was designed to change the flow of materials and work-in-process. Rather than a batch flow, the MPL would operate as a "repetitive" or a synchronous line-flow manufacturing process with only very small buffer stocks between adjacent stages of production. In the traditional system, a work station received large batches of components and subassemblies as scheduled, whether or not it was ready to start working on them. On the MPL, a work station would receive materials or work-in-process only when it requested them. The second major change was in the production schedule. The MPL was scheduled to produce the same quantity of detectors day after day.

After some trial-and-error, the MPL process evolved as follows: RF boards, control boards, and microwave subassemblies were produced with the same equipment and through the same process as before. However, separate inspection points were eliminated. Each work station was made responsible for identifying and correcting its own quality problems.

Batch sizes and production flow were dramatically different. Rather than produce boards in one-month batches, the SMT operation ran only enough boards to supply one day of final assembly. The batch sizes were only 2 hours in the board assembly operations after SMT (hand stuffing, wave soldering, and depalletization).

The production flow was controlled by "kanban"[6] racks between each work station. Workers at any particular work station were instructed to work on a particular batch of boards only when an empty tray appeared in the rack between it and the next work station. When a specific work station needed more of a certain type of board, a worker would place an empty tray (with a production control card indicating the type and number of boards required) in the rack. This would signal a worker in the preceding work station to begin making a batch of those boards. The worker receiving the "produce" signal first checked the inventory in the rack between it and the station preceding it. If the appropriate work-in-process or components were there, the worker could begin processing immediately. If not, he or she would order them from the preceding station by putting an empty tray with the appropriate production control card on the rack. Through this kanban chain, materials and work-in-process were pulled as needed by downstream stations.

The flow of materials through subassembly was similarly controlled by the final assembly line. When required, final assembly would pull small lots of boards (a 15 to 30 minute supply) from the kanban rack located after the depalletization area. The small lot would then be tested. Boards that failed were sent to a rework area assigned especially for the MPL. A limit had been set on the maximum number of boards permitted in the board rework station. Once the limit was reached, the board subassembly operation would be shut down until the cause of the quality problem could be identified and corrected. It was hoped that this line shut-down procedure would help keep the process under control by drawing attention to defects and by forcing shop management to deal with their causes.

The boards were then passed along to the unit integration station where the three major subassemblies were joined. The MPL operated as a worker-paced assembly line. After completing a particular assembly step, the operator would pass the work piece a few feet down the bench to the next station's incoming work tray. These trays could hold a maximum of six work pieces. Once the tray was filled to capacity, the operator at the preceding station was instructed to stop working. He or she could resume assembly only when the tray contained fewer than six in-process work pieces. At the end of the MPL, an enclosed work station[7] performed the final test. Any unit failing this final test was sent to another rework station. The entire production line would be shut down if one day of inventory accumulated in this rework area.

Each worker on the MPL received 15 hours of training in work methods, quality inspection, and statistical process control.

## MPL Results: April–June 1987

The MPL began producing Spectrum 1's on April 7, 1987. By late June, a study of the pilot line was completed. The data (summarized in **Exhibit 4**) suggested that it might be possible for Whistler to achieve substantial improvements in the productivity of people, equipment, and space if the manufacturing methods used on the MPL were used to produce all of Whistler's radar detectors. In addition, the MPL enabled Whistler to produce a Spectrum 1 from start to finish in 1.5 days, as compared to the 23 days required in the traditional system.

One option was to implement MPL concepts throughout the Westford plant. The expected gains in productivity were expected to allow Whistler to close the Fitchburg plant and reduce its total labor force. However, several questions remained.

Some managers in the company wondered whether the results of the pilot project could be replicated on a plant-wide basis. Which product lines might be best suited to the repetitive manufacturing process? Ed Johnson, the Director of Marketing, argued:

> This is extremely risky. You're talking about changing the entire manufacturing system and maybe shutting down one of our plants. Frankly, the possibilities scare me to death. Any kind of major disruption in output could really hurt us. I know things aren't very good now,

CASE STUDY

**EXHIBIT 4**

## Pilot results of RACE-ME (two months of operation)

| Category | January 1987* | June 1987 |
|---|---|---|
| Output (units) per direct employee | 100 | 237 |
| Output (units) per sq. ft. | 100 | 146 |
| Work-in-process (units) | 100 | 46 |
| RF board: 1st pass yield | 100 | 114 |
| Variable Overhead[†] | 100 | 68 |
| Scrap | 100 | 17 |

*Note: 100 = index for each category

[†]Indirect labor (materials handlers, stockroom employees) accounted for virtually all of variable overhead.

but, at least we are getting product out the door. I think we should make changes in manu-facturing, but let's phase them in more slowly.

Larry Santos, the plant manager at the Fitchburg plant, was also concerned:

I know this sounds like I am just looking after my own job, but I have to say I am not sure closing Fitchburg is the best decision. First, the plant has only been open for two years. The people there have been showing some real commitment. In fact, most of the quality and scheduling problems have originated in Westford.

The Director of Operations Planning, Sharon Katz was also concerned about closing Fitchburg:

I'd have to agree with Larry about closing Fitchburg, but for a different reason. If we plan to grow, we're eventually going to need the extra capacity Fitchburg gives us. It's going to very expensive to start up a new plant in a few years.

The Executive Vice President of Finance, Margaret Curry, had a more extreme viewpoint:

I am very impressed by the results of the MPL experiment, but I just don't think the cost savings will be enough. I just don't believe we can compete by manufacturing our prod-ucts domestically.

The offshore option buys us tremendous sourcing flexibility. We can shop around for the best suppliers in cost, quality, and delivery. If one isn't working out, there are plenty of other potential suppliers throughout Asia we can go to. We can take care of the foreign exchange risks with appropriate hedging positions, so that needn't cloud our analysis.

## CASE STUDY

Some within the company believed that despite the success of the MPL pilot project, manufacturing was not what Whistler should be worrying about. One executive, who had been with the company eight years, argued:

> I agree with Margaret. We should be focusing on what we do best, perhaps better than any of our competitors—design and engineering. Our competitive edge is high performance in a small package. But, Cobra, Bel, and other competitors are really putting the heat on our technological lead. If we try to do everything, we'll lose our edge in technology. Manufacturing, while obviously an important part of the value chain, can be efficiently handled by our Korean partner or other overseas suppliers, if necessary. Every dollar we save by manufacturing offshore is another dollar we can invest in product development.

Ed Johnson added: "Or it's another dollar for advertising and market research!"

Richard Packer, a member of the outside consulting team, raised another issue: "I think there's a benefit of MPL that's been overlooked. By shrinking the throughput time from 23 to 1.5 days, the new system gives you the flexibility to respond quickly to changes in the market."

Charles Stott was worried about larger issues. Growth in the market for radar detectors had essentially stopped. In addition, two states had recently banned radar detectors; several more states had such legislation under consideration. The domestic market could evaporate quickly; expanding overseas sales into Europe, the next biggest potential market, was not a realistic option because most European countries had legislation already banning detectors. In Stott's view, diversifying out of radar detectors might soon be a strategic imperative. The marketing group was already looking at potential product lines which could be sold through the same channels of distribution under the Whistler brand name. The design engineering group had commenced early development projects in several new product areas—CB radios, battery chargers, anti-theft devices, FM antenna boosters, emergency lights, breath analyzers, collision avoidance radar, scanners, and marine UHF radios. In view of these changes in Whistler's business, Stott contemplated the role that manufacturing would play in its future.

## Notes

1. Some proprietary data have been disguised.

2. In the radar detector market, "low-end" indicates a product with basic features, relatively low engineering costs, and modest performance specifications.

3. "Fuzz-buster" is a registered trademark of Electrolert, one of Whistler's major U.S. competitors.

4. It was not unusual for there to be no room in the stockroom for finished boards. In these instances, finished boards were stored on the factory floor until the batch was needed in final assembly.

5. Defective boards were reworked because they were too valuable to scrap.

6. "Kanban" is a Japanese word meaning "sign." It refers to the cards or signs attached to the containers holding work-in-process in some Japanese factories using the just-in-time approach.

7. This testing station was enclosed to prevent stray microwave interference from invalidating the test.

# ACKNOWLEDGMENTS

MBA students are virtual coauthors of this book. I wish I could acknowledge all of them, particularly the students I have been lucky enough to work with in the PreMBA program at Harvard Business School. Here I can only thank students who contributed directly to this book: Oscar Zagrean, Chuljoong Jurng, Jorge Novis, Yosef Hojchman, Vvivi Rongrong Hu, Emily Mei Dong, Chris Cagne, Rastislav "Rasto" Kulich, E. Ciprian "Cip" Vatasescu, and Agam Sharma. Cip and Francisco "Paco" Demesa allowed me to use their essays as the basis for the samples in chapters 11 and 12. Yusuke Watanabe not only contributed to the case discussion chapter but also gave me invaluable assistance in gathering comments from other students.

I can't acknowledge everything I have gained from Maureen Walker, associate director of MBA Support Services at HBS, because the list is too long. Her knowledge is reflected throughout the book, and she was a principal source for the chapter on case discussion. Pat Light, director of MBA Support Services at HBS, has for years supported writing assistance for MBA students, providing me many opportunities to help and learn from them.

The writing group I am fortunate to belong to—Tehila Lieberman, Bob Dall, Kari Bodnarchuk, Cathy Armer, Lucy McCauley, Laurie Covens, and Sara Fraser—consists of fiction and literary nonfiction writers. Yet, these patient, perceptive individuals listened to drafts of a manuscript on case method study and improved it—and they supported me all the way to this point. Tehila has become a collaborator in developing concepts about analyzing cases and writing case-based essays. Among her contributions are the original versions of the essay planning templates at the end of chapters 10, 11, and 12.

Andrea Oseas and Joelle Andre have tried out my ideas, helping me understand which ones work and which ones need work. Shelley Fishman was my first collaborator on case-based writing. Besides expertise on writing instruction, she shared the belief that we could give students more than generic advice about case-based essays.

Jeff Kehoe, acquisitions editor at Harvard Business School Press, saw the potential in this book and acted quickly on that belief. I appreciate the opportunity he and his colleagues at the Press have given me. My agent,

Charles B. Everitt, has been a reliable guide throughout the publishing process. Erin Scheffler, Manager of MBA Course Distribution at HBS, generously provided assistance in researching cases for this book. The book was ushered through production by Dino Malvone and Marcy Barnes-Henrie of the Press. They belied the sluggish stereotype of book publishing. Monica Jainschigg meticulously copyedited the manuscript.

I owe much to the anonymous reviewers recruited by Harvard Business School Press. Diligent and undogmatic, they read the manuscript closely and made many suggestions that have enhanced it. Charles Bambach came down from the heights of Heidegger to read portions of the manuscript and talk through its methodological underpinnings. His most valuable offering, though, was friendship. Although we have never met, James W. Harris, a practitioner and professor, accepted my request to read a pivotal chapter; his comments led to a substantial revision of it.

Finally, my wife Jane took up the household slack all too often when I needed to work. My son Will tolerated my distraction amazingly well, considering I have been working on this book for half of his life. (He's seven years old.) Their support and understanding have been crucial every step of the way.

To you all, I am more grateful than I can fully express.

William Ellet
November 2006

# INDEX

# ABOUT THE AUTHOR

**William Ellet** has worked with MBA students for over fifteen years. He teaches a second-year course, "Persuading Business Audiences," at Harvard Business School, as well as the writing portion of the school's PreMBA program, and gives presentations to first-year students on analyzing and writing about cases. He is principal and editor of *Training Media Review*, a review of business training content and technology for both live and online training.